JOURNAL FOR THE STUDY OF THE OLD TESTAMENT
SUPPLEMENT SERIES
382

*Editors*
David J.A. Clines
Philip R. Davies

*Executive Editor*
Andrew Mein

*Editorial Board*
Richard J. Coggins, Alan Cooper, J. Cheryl Exum,
John Goldingay, Robert P. Gordon, Norman K. Gottwald,
John Jarick, Andrew D.H. Mayes, Carol Meyers,
Patrick D. Miller

# Redirected Travel

Alternative Journeys and Places in Biblical Studies

edited by

Roland Boer & Edgar W. Conrad

T & T CLARK INTERNATIONAL
*A Continuum imprint*
LONDON • NEW YORK

Copyright © 2003 T&T Clark International
*A Continuum imprint*

Published by T&T Clark International
The Tower Building, 11 York Road, London SE1 7NX
15 East 26th Street, Suite 1703, New York, NY 10010

www.tandtclark.com

All rights reserved. No part of this publication may be reproduced or transmitted in any form or by any means, electronic or mechanical, including photocopying, recording or any information storage or retrieval system, without permission in writing from the publishers.

British Library Cataloguing-in-Publication Data
A catalogue record for this book is available from the British Library

Library of Congress Cataloging-in-Publication Data
A catalogue record for this book is available from the Library of Congress

Typeset by CA Typesetting, Sheffield
Printed on acid-free paper in Great Britain by MPG Books Ltd, Bodmin, Cornwall

ISBN 0-8264-6766-0

CONTENTS

List of Contributors     vii

INTRODUCTION: THE BIBLE AND CRITICAL THEORY
   Roland Boer and Edgar W. Conrad     1

ELECTRONIC CULTURE AND THE FUTURE OF THE CANON
OF SCRIPTURE OR: THE HYPERREAL BIBLE
   George Aichele     8

O PAUL WHERE ART THOU?
   James Smith     24

SEMIOTICS, SCRIBES AND PROPHETIC BOOKS
   Edgar W. Conrad     41

THE SALVATION OF ISRAEL IN 'THE BOOK OF THE DIVIDED
KINGDOMS', OR, WAS THERE ANY 'FALL OF THE NORTHERN
KINGDOM'?
   David Jobling     50

READING MARK BACKWARDS: ESTABLISHING AN
INTERPRETIVE LENS FOR A FEMINIST-LIBERATIONIST
READING OF THE GOSPEL OF MARK
   Bernadette Kiley     62

READING THE SILENCE OF WOMEN IN GENESIS 34
   Julie Kelso     85

LOST IN PLACE: SOME PERPLEXITIES OF INTERTEXTUAL
ENTANGLEMENT
   Anne Taylor     110

WHO'S/WHOSE SARAH?:
JOURNEYING WITH SARAH IN A CHORUS OF VOICES
    Judith E. McKinlay    131

GENERATIVITY AND PLACE: THE GENEALOGIES OF GENESIS
1 TO 11 AND NEGOTIATING A SENSE OF PLACE IN AUSTRALIA
    Anne Elvey    144

SANCTUARY AND WOMB: HENRI LEFEBVRE AND THE
PRODUCTION OF ANCIENT SPACE
    Roland Boer    162

IT'S LONELY AT THE TOP: PATRIARCHAL MODELS, HOMOPHOBIC
VILIFICATION AND THE HETEROSEXUAL HOUSEHOLD IN LUTHER'S
COMMENTARIES
    Michael Carden    185

REDIRECTING THE DIRECTION OF TRAVEL: DISCERNING
SIGNS OF A NEO-INDIGENOUS SOUTHERN AFRICAN BIBLICAL
HERMENEUTICS
    Gerald West    201

Bibliography    226
Index of References    247
Index of Authors    252

## List of Contributors

George Aichele is Professor of Philosophy and Religion at Adrian College in Michigan. He is author of *The Control of Biblical Meaning: Canon as Semiotic Mechanism* (2001) and various other writings on semiotics and the Bible.

Roland Boer is Senior Logan Research Fellow at Monash University in Melbourne, Australia. Working in biblical criticism and Marxism, his current project concerns Political Myth and the Bible. He has recently completed *Marxist Criticism of the Bible* and *The Criticism of Earth*.

Michael Carden received his PhD in 2002 from the University of Queensland in Australia. His dissertation was a study of the reception of the stories of Sodom and Gomorrah and the outrage at Gibeah in both Christian and Jewish traditions up to the time of the Reformation. Michael has taught in the area of biblical studies and comparative religion at the University of Queensland and introduced a course on Religion and Sexuality. Michael has also had many years of involvement in LGBT and HIV/AIDS community organizations.

Ed Conrad is Reader and Director of Postgraduate Studies in the School of History, Philosophy, Religion and Classics at the University of Queensland. Along with other books and articles, he is the author of *Reading Isaiah* and *Zechariah*.

Anne Elvey is an honorary research associate in the Centre for Women's Studies and Gender Research at Monash University in Melbourne, Australia. She completed a PhD in Women's Studies in 1999 involving an ecological feminist approach to biblical criticism. Her research interests bring together ecological, feminist and postcolonial considerations of questions of origin and relationship to place.

David Jobling was the general editor for *Semeia* and has recently retired as Professor of Old Testament Language and Literature at St Andrews Theological College, Saskatoon, Canada. His most recent work, *I Samuel*, brings together Marxism, psychoanalysis and feminism, which he is now carrying on into the books of Kings.

Julie Kelso is a doctoral student in the School of History, Religion, Philosophy and Classics at the University of Queensland. Her work concerns Luce Irigaray and the book of Chronicles, exploring the way the presence of women in these texts is based upon their systematic absence, especially in terms of the mother–daughter relation and the maternal body.

Bernadette Kiley lectures in biblical studies and theology at the School of Education, University of South Australia. She has recently completed her doctoral dissertation on the Gospel of Mark.

Judith McKinlay has recently retired as Senior Lecturer in Biblical Studies in the Department of Theology and Religious Studies at the University of Otago, New Zealand. She is the author of *Gendering Wisdom the Host* (Sheffield Academic Press), and articles in *Pacifica*, *Semeia*, and *Biblical Interpretation*, variously exploring feminist, ideological, and postcolonial readings of texts. She is a member of the editorial board of *Seachanges*, the Asia-Pacific-based journal for Women Scholars of Religion and Theology.

James A. Smith teaches biblical studies at Cincinnati Bible College and Seminary. He specializes in Pauline Studies/Theology, Critical Theory and Cultural Studies.

Anne Taylor is a doctoral student at the Centre for Studies in Religion and Theology at Monash University. Her thesis concerns the work of Julia Kristeva and the function of intertextuality in the relation between biblical text, its versions (Septuagint, Vulgate, etc.) and the lectionary.

Gerald West teaches Hebrew Bible and African Biblical Hermeneutics at the School of Theology, University of Natal, Pietermaritzburg, South Africa. He is also Director of the Institute for the Study of the Bible and Worker Ministry Project.

INTRODUCTION: THE BIBLE AND CRITICAL THEORY

Roland Boer and Edgar W. Conrad

The essays gathered here are the first fruits of one of the most interesting developments in biblical studies in Australia and New Zealand for a long time, namely the Bible and Critical Theory Seminar. Since its first meeting in 1998, the seminar has set out to provide a forum in Australia for the exploration of the implications of critical theory for biblical studies. It actively works to engage in dialogue with specialists in literary theory and philosophy outside biblical scholarship. The programs have featured keynote speakers from overseas (George Aichele, Danna Fewell, David Jobling, Regina Schwartz, Susan Feiner and Judith McKinlay) and from Australia (John Docker and Kevin Hart).

We began organizing the seminar for a number of reasons: the absence of any group that dealt specifically with our interests in critical theory, here understood in the broad sense of the term, and biblical studies; the scattered nature of biblical studies in the antipodes; the increasing number of postgraduate students working in innovative areas in biblical studies; and the desire to have a good time.

Although we can think of only two organizations that focus on biblical studies in Australia, their tendency is very much for a certain status quo that has as its dual poles the context of the church and the tenacious hold of more traditional ways of doing biblical criticism in that context. This ossification of biblical studies that valorizes and preserves certain uses of the text in the context of pressing ecclesial politics and practice, along with a subservience to the perceived patterns of scholarship in the 'real' centres of learning, has a long history into which we will not delve here. This is not to say that all of the participants in the Bible and Critical Theory Seminar work precisely in such a situation. However, the seminar provides its members with a forum where they can ask the questions they wish to ask and probe them further, without the institutional constraints that would otherwise hinder their work.

Another feature of biblical studies in Australia and New Zealand, closely related to the previous point, is the oft-reiterated feeling of isolation in research, the sense that each person is the only one pursuing the work he or she does. This isolation may be due to the constraints mentioned in the preceding paragraph, but it is also due to the situation in Australia where a person will often take up an appointment as the sole representative of a discipline (here biblical studies) or of an approach. This situation is true of the universities and of the theological colleges. For many, one way of maintaining some sense of a collective activity, of finding intellectual interaction and discussion of ideas, has been to develop contacts overseas, travelling endlessly to the larger places in the northern hemisphere where the assumption is that one has at least a few colleagues interested in the same questions. This strikes us as strange. Another way has been to foster a number of postgraduate students who then form part of a small but vital intellectual group. The Bible and Critical Theory Seminar has in the last few years increasingly provided a forum where more and more biblical scholars, including postgraduate students, have found others who are interested in the same questions. Apart from developing connections with those working in other disciplines, one of the things the Seminar has achieved is the creation of an intellectual environment that many others take as a given.

Perhaps the most welcome discovery is the number of postgraduate students for whom the Seminar has become an important aspect of their own work. Ed Conrad has been by far the most effective in this respect, providing a situation at the University of Queensland where students can work in the most interesting areas of biblical studies for their postgraduate research. Others have come to Monash in Melbourne in order to take up doctoral studies in the intersections between the Bible and critical theory under the supervision of Roland Boer. At Griffith University in Brisbane Elaine Wainwright has supervised students working through similar concerns, and at Otago in New Zealand Judith McKinlay has provided a place to pursue innovative postgraduate study. Not only has the Seminar provided a wider sense of other postgraduates with similar interests, but it has also encouraged postgraduates to present papers in the earlier stages of their academic work. The energy of the Seminar is in many respects due to the presence and involvement of postgraduate students in its work.

Another aspect of the Seminar is that it has begun to influence the scholarship of those involved. Thus, John Docker, Mark Brett and Roland Boer acknowledge the role of the Seminar in the development of their own work, specifically Docker's *1492: A Poetics of Diaspora* (2001), Brett's *Genesis: Procreation and the Politics of Identity* (2000b) and Boer's *Marxist Criti-*

*cism of the Bible* (2003). Beyond the immediate circles of scholarship, from the meeting in Brisbane in 2002 Florence Spurling, the respected producer of the 'Encounter' program on ABC radio in Australia and now a senior director, invited Elaine Wainwright and Julie Kelso to be interviewed on the theme of feminism and biblical studies. The program, 'Elaine and Julie', went to air on two occasions to an audience of more than 100,000 listeners.

The essays in this volume were selected from a larger international meeting sponsored by the Bible and Critical Theory Seminar at Monash University in 2001. As the various papers were presented it became clear that a collection was emerging, for which Gerald West's paper, 'Redirecting the Direction of Travel', provided the underlying theme. The conference itself sought papers that addressed in one or another fashion the question: What if the direction of travel was reversed? What if biblical scholars travelled to the antipodes for an international conference instead of Europe or North America? And what are the implications for biblical studies of such a change in direction? But, like Deleuze and Guattari's well-known rhizomatic thought, the patterns of roots and warrens, the theme of redirected travel itself begins to move in a myriad of directions once the sense that one must travel to the metropolitan centres of the globe has gone, stopping in places that one would hardly expect. Thus, the essays gathered in this volume travel in a host of different directions, exploring the alternative journeys and places of biblical studies, developing connections in a rhizomatic fashion.

Such 'journeys' take a number of forms in these essays. They may be understood in terms of the consideration of other texts, whether those of biblical exegetes from Africa, or of the Reformation, or recasting our notions of the canon itself in light of new technologies. Or, these journeys may indicate other ways of reading the biblical texts, whether backwards, through superscriptions, the repression of maternal bodies, or as forms of literature not previously considered. Or, the question of alternative places may become the focus, whether reading for spaces in the text, or of the places in which the text has been appropriated outside the metropolitan zones. The methods used by the authors provide different paths, whether postcolonialism, feminism, Marxism, gay theory, semiotics, political theory or poststructuralism.

George Aichele, the keynote speaker at the first meeting of the Bible and Critical Theory Seminar in Melbourne in 1998, writes on the 'Hyperreal Bible', arguing that the technological changes brought about by electronic culture are as significant as those of codex and printing press. With his distinct ability to cast a global eye over biblical studies, he argues that in a fashion analogous to the effect of the codex on the formation of the canon itself, and of the new ability to print on the notion of canon during the Reformation, the canon by definition begins to slip away in the transition to the internet. Aichele suggests that in the ability to pick and choose, to construct one's own 'Bible' from the various electronic versions available, canon as a measure and boundary is no longer a viable way to speak of the Bible. Above all, the function of the Church as the controller of canon and of meaning dissipates with the hyperreal Bible. We would extend Aichele's argument to suggest that this process embodies one of the deepest paradoxes of the Reformation in that the basic tenet of people reading the Bible for themselves is beginning to be realized, much to the chagrin of a system that used such an ideology to impose its own control on the Bible.

We have juxtaposed Aichele's essay with the one by James Smith, in which he seeks a way beyond the impasse of Pauline studies. In 'O Paul Where Art Thou?' Smith brings together various moments of the Odyssey theme (Homer, the extraordinary Kubrick/Clarke film, and the Cohen brothers *'O Brother, where art thou?'*) to indicate what happens to the study of Pauline texts once the ontological assumptions about Paul's coherent theology begin to break down. What are the implications, asks Smith, if the determining force of an ancient logocentric environment is allowed its full reign?

Ed Conrad's essay follows, coming from a similar theoretical base as Aichele—semiotics, athough here specifically the work of Umberto Eco—to explore the implications for an alternative canonical reading of the prophetic books. What happens, asks Conrad, if we read the prophetic texts in light of their ordering in the Masoretic Text? The result is that the opening lines, the superscriptions, become crucial markers of the arrangement of the books themselves and that the texts are readable in terms of this literary context. The various terms used to describe the books suggest a range of different connections between books that have long been regarded as completely unrelated. Conrad is interested in how codes such as 'the words of' provide information for reading Amos and Jeremiah, how 'vision' provides information for reading Isaiah, Nahum and Obadiah, and how books that begin simply with 'and it happened' provide information for reading Jonah and Ezekiel. He argues that reading prophetic books involves the active role of the reader in configuring prophetic scrolls as a collage.

Like the previous three papers, David Jobling engages in a deductive reading, this time of the books of Kings, where he finds a 'divided consciousness': the overt negative understanding of the northern kingdom and their successors, the Samaritans, ends up fading away before an irrepressible positive depiction. Thus, the effort to provide theological reasons for the 'fall' of the north in 2 Kings 17 in terms of its sins fails to hold together when read against the earlier narratives, and the final narrative of the north's demise in this same chapter cannot but help in affirming its place and eventual salvation.

With Bernadette Kiley's essay, 'Reading Mark Backwards', there is a return to the New Testament, except that Kiley takes us on an alternative journey of her own, running like Jobling in the other direction from usual readings of Mark that read it in the conventional forewards direction of written narrative texts. It turns out that Mark is an untrustworthy text for women, one that offers the possibility of women's presence and involvement only to take it away time and again. For one who is keen to find a place for women in the institutional church, Kiley's text argues that Mark's Gospel provides little ground for women. Instead, what is required is a reading that goes beyond Mark's Gospel.

The next five essays focus on the Hebrew Bible, although with similar interests to Kiley's, namely the closures, absences, cooptations and possibilities for women. In her essay on Genesis 34, Julie Kelso makes use of one of the neglected theorists in biblical studies, the philosopher and psychoanalyst Luce Irigaray, to ask what happens to Dinah. Rather than siding either with Shechem or with Jacob's brothers, as so many readings of Genesis 34 do, Kelso argues that Dinah becomes an exchange object in the hom(m)osexual exchange between men. However, the violence of the text is not so much the 'rape' of Dinah itself, but the violence that closes down the glimpse of an alternative story, when Dinah goes 'to see into the daughters of the land'. Long regarded as a setting for the story itself, Gen. 34.1 threatens a leakage or journey away from the stories of men and into the repressed mother–daughter relationship (Leah and Dinah). From the second verse on, the story becomes a violent effort to deal with this threat, a cooptation of Dinah into exchange relations among men.

In her use of another well-known (although less well-known in biblical studies than she should be) French theorist and psychoanalyst, this time Julia Kristeva, Anne Taylor investigates a somewhat different form of leakage, namely the way the lectionary's perpetual effort at controlling intertextuality raises more questions than it answers. Focusing on Kristeva's work on intertextuality, Taylor explores the intertextual avenues opened and closed down by the rearrangements made in the lectionary for Deuteronomy 4, which is itself a selection of vv. 1-2 and 6-8, leaving out the 'problem' of Baal-Peor. If the intertextual connections to Numbers 25 and 31 as well as Psalms 106 are broken, the effort to link Deut. 4.1-2, 6-8 with Psalm 15, James 1 and Mark 7, with their themes of light, contamination, obedience to the commandments and inner cleanliness are no less problematic.

If Julie Kelso's essay is a lament for the lost possibility of Gen. 34.1, then Judith McKinlay's paper, 'Who's/Whose Sarah?: Journeying with Sarah in a Chorus of Voices', brings such a lament to the story of Sarah in Genesis 12. With a distinct and self-critical postcolonial turn, McKinlay relates the story of Sarah to those of Sarah Stephens, Charlotte Brown, Sara Maitland, Jenny Diski, colonial and postcolonial women in her own New Zealand/Aotearoa, as well as Miriam and Rahab in the biblical text. These form the 'chorus of voices' within which McKinlay reads the story of Sarah, closing with questions about the possibilities that are opened up by Sarah's own shifting collage of representations.

Anne Elvey echoes Judith McKinlay's postcolonial interest in how we should read the sense of place in a neocolonial space such as Australia. Taking up the burgeoning search for genealogies in Australia, Elvey relates these to the persistent concern with genealogies in Genesis. Seeking for both the possibilities and shortcomings of such genealogical concerns, Elvey focuses on the issues of colonial origin. Like the systematic effacement of the connections with land and the maternal body through the very act of genealogical construction in Genesis, Elvey argues that contemporary Australian genealogies remove any reference to country of origin, forgetting the material conditions of migration and preferring to begin with the moment of arrival. What might a pursuit of place look like if these repressions were acknowledged, a pre-history of migration and settlement, let alone one of birth itself?

A somewhat different concern with the womb and place appears in Roland Boer's essay on 1 Samuel 1–2. Employing the highly influential work of the French Marxist, Henri Lefebvre, on the production of space, Boer argues that the constantly shifting relations of space in this text render Hannah's womb the focus of ideological tensions. The initial opposition between her womb and the sanctuary and Shiloh fall under the next dialectical level of the contrast between Shiloh and Jerusalem and finally between Jerusalem itself and the imperial centre beyond Jerusalem. Rather than the independence of Hannah that so many read in this narrative, her apparent agency becomes a central element in the sacred economy of the text.

Journeying to another place, the 'top'—itself overlaid with various senses of place, be they patriarchal, heterosexual or erotic—Michael Carden provides a queer metacommentary on Luther's commentary on Genesis 12–14 and 18–19. Here we find that Luther's nervous affirmation of the heterosexual nuclear household, a necessary feature of the newly emerging bourgeois social landscape, relies upon homosexual panic in order to establish the godly, heterosexual society. Luther must engage in a systematic pattern of vilification that renders the Sodomites homosexual, Lot himself suspect, and the whole rotten system of Roman Catholicism, if not the occasional Reformer who disagrees with him, a modern day Sodom—all of which is based on a systematic misreading of the text that Carden seeks to uncover. In other words, Luther's militant heterosexual reading is based upon the identification and abhorrence of homosexuality, into which he then draws Genesis with little concern for the text.

Finally, Gerald West, one whose journey kept him this time in the Southern Hemisphere, investigates what happens when biblical scholars cease to be the experts and draw their methods from those who interpret the Bible without the tools of biblical scholarship. West's task is in part historical: what are the hermeneutic currents generated by African encounters with the Bible in the past? But the purpose of such a historical search is to look forward in (South) African biblical hermeneutics, and so West suggests, following the example set by Vincent Wimbush's investigations into early African American hermeneutics, that the earliest encounters with the Bible by Africans will turn out to be crucial for biblical interpretation in the present and for potential trajectories into the future. His particular example is the early encounter between the BaThlaping and the Bible, which then becomes crucial for understanding the hermeneutics of the African Independent Churches in South Africa and the hermeneutics of South African Black Theology.

As will become clear to anyone who runs through the list of contributors, most of the writers are from Australia (James Smith, Ed Conrad, Bernadette Kiley, Julie Kelso, Anne Elvey, Roland Boer and Michael Carden), a couple from New Zealand (Judith McKinlay and Anne Taylor) and the rest from South Africa, Canada and the United States. Or, if you like, two from the Northern Hemisphere and ten from the Southern Hemisphere. Given the title of this collection, it is worth registering such geographical information here, for apart from the methods and essays themselves, the redirection of travel is marked by a distinctly antipodal collection of writers.

A final note that relates to the current situation of Australian Research and government funding: all of the essays by Australian authors have been refereed and approved by an external referee, Professor Philip Almond, head of the School of History, Philosophy, Religion and Classics at the University of Queensland.

ELECTRONIC CULTURE AND THE FUTURE OF THE CANON
OF SCRIPTURE OR: THE HYPERREAL BIBLE

George Aichele

*Writing, Ideology and Canon*

Western culture is the Bible's way of making more Bibles (Pyper 1998: 74).

The Christian canon of the scriptures is a semiotic mechanism designed to control the meaning of its component texts. It is a list of books that is understood by the Christian churches to be an unchanging and complete repository of truths and values, an intertextual network that provides a reading context through which its component texts can be understood correctly—that is, in terms of Christian 'right belief'. The canon is a product of both technological innovation and ideological demand. The technology includes the mechanisms of writing and publication. The ideology arises from the desire for a self-explanatory, authoritative text, the 'word of God'.[1]

The canon is fundamentally a canon of the *scriptures*—that is, of written texts. In oral culture, the truth and authority of the spoken word is determined within the living, immediate encounter between speaker and audience. When the oral word is supplemented or even replaced entirely by the written word, some sort of external guarantee is required. Unlike an oral text, which exists only in the presence of its speaker, a written text cannot provide its own explanation. The written text is 'dead'. Writing removes the text from living memory and instead of the living, oral word, it leaves the reader with the task of deciphering inert letters. Written texts also proliferate uncontrollably. Once the text leaves its author's hands, the author no longer has any power to change it, or to prevent changes, or any effect on how the reader will understand the text's meaning. The possibility that readers will come to different and incompatible understandings of it is inherent in any written text. In addition, widespread dissemination of a

---

1. A more fully developed argument in support of these claims is made in Aichele 2001.

written text requires that it be copied by hand, and ancient authors often encouraged others to copy their books. Variations in the texts inevitably resulted from hand copying. These variations might be errors produced as a result of accident or incompetence, or they may be deliberate distortions or corruptions of the text.[2]

As a result, when writing first became known, people were suspicious of the new technology. Reading and writing seemed magical, and few possessed the secret of it. Socrates attacked writing as a 'conceit of wisdom' that would result in ignorance (Plato, *Phaedrus*, 1973: 96-97, 275). The written text cannot speak for itself, and it must be 'rescued' by its 'parent', the spoken word. Similar fears are reflected in various biblical texts. The story in 2 Kings 22 suggests that the scroll discovered during King Josiah's repair of the Temple had to be ratified by high priest, king, and prophet before its authority could be established. According to 2 Esdras 14, Ezra was inspired by God in order to recite and thereby rewrite the lost scrolls of the Torah. Using language remarkably similar to Socrates, the apostle Paul favored the writing of 'the Spirit of the living God, not on tablets of stone but on tablets of human hearts' over against the physical 'written code [that] kills' (2 Cor. 3.3, 6, RSV).

Despite these anxieties, the demand for the technology of writing continued to grow. Indeed, we only know about these ancient fears because they have been preserved in writing. The story in 2 Kings is set in Jerusalem just prior to the Babylonian exile, and it associates the newly discovered scroll with the exile. According to the story, the failure to heed the written law is the occasion for God's anger at the people of Judah, but the dispersion of people over great distances during the exile also made the use of written texts unavoidable. The concept of authoritative scripture arose under circumstances when writing became indispensable. The story in 2 Esdras is also set in a time of crisis and threat to community identity. In the ancient world, texts were written not only because the technology of writing made them possible, but also because circumstances such as exile and diaspora made them necessary. In the second century CE, Papias says that written texts are inferior to the oral traditions passed on by 'living and surviving' eyewitnesses to the words and deeds of Jesus and his disciples.[3] If those written texts were eventually accepted as the Christian scriptures because these witnesses had died, and because the return of Christ had still

---

2. See Gamble 1995; Ehrman 1993.
3. So says Eusebius in his fourth-century book, *Ecclesiastical History* (III, 39, 4).

not occurred, then that would suggest a different sort of exile, but one that required written texts nonetheless.

Canon requires not only the technology of writing, but also the technology of the codex. Although a single scroll could contain several short texts, such as the Minor Prophets, no useable scroll could contain the entire Tanak, let alone the Christian Bible. The codex form was already in nearly exclusive use for Christian texts as early as the second century, but it was only by the fourth century that the technology of manufacturing codices had developed enough to permit a single volume as large as the complete Christian Bible. Although 'single volume' is by no means equivalent to 'canon', the singleness of the Christian Bible codex is an important aspect of its meaning as canon.[4]

The different technologies of codex and scroll entail different types of reading. The codex permits the binding together of multiple texts, and it forces the bound texts into a specific sequence. The codex is also hypertextual. It allows the reader to skip back and forth between different books: prophecy and gospel, Elijah and John the Baptist, creation and apocalypse, Old and New Testament. The codex itself signifies something about the texts collected in it; it is an intertext produced by the canon, permitting the various texts to comment on each other and thus to control each other. The single codex of the Bible connotes to many people that the Bible is one single book, and that consequently it transmits a single consistent message—that is, that the two testaments and all of the writings in them are in total accord. The codex assembles a complete intertextual network in a format that can be easily used as such—that is, as a text that explains itself.

It is not clear when the canon was closed in any Jewish or Christian community, but that was probably not until the fourth century or later.[5] The fourth century was also the time in which 'early catholic' Christianity became the state religion of the Roman Empire. The canon is the product of emergent, imperial Christianity with its demands for a standardized, complete and authoritative scripture. Other forms of Christianity, of which there were many, were suppressed, and the ideology of a church that is united, universal and rooted in apostolic tradition became dominant.[6] One ideological function of the emergent Christian canon was to secure internal homogeneity (rejection of heresy) in an imperial religion, and another

---

4. Gamble 1997. See also Debray 1996: 141-44, and esp. Roberts and Skeat 1983.
5. Barton 1986: 28, 63. See also Aichele 2001.
6. See Bauer 1971; Wilken 1971.

function was to guarantee external legitimacy by identifying the church as the true Israel, the heir to the divine covenant.

Thus the concept of authoritative texts, or *scriptures*, arises from the need for writing in a world that mistrusts writing. However, no matter how authoritative they are, the scriptures remain written texts, and therefore they are unable to explain themselves. The desire for *canon* arises because the living oral texts have 'died'—that is, because they have become scripture. Canon responds to the desire to bring those dead written texts back to 'life'. The need for a canon arises from the inherent incompleteness of the texts, which becomes evident when they are 'translated' from living oral traditions into inert writings. The canon attempts to create a written text that explains itself, that transmits a clear message to the believing community. Canon also attempts to secure the texts, fixing their physical limits and maintaining them against change.

This understanding of canon as a mechanism that produces an authoritative, coherent and self-explanatory message is the ideal, the desire that the canon addresses. Insofar as it has ever really 'worked', the canonical Bible has created the illusion of a self-contained whole, a single, seamless text conveying a clear, already well-known message. Within the canon, each of the biblical texts is quoted whole, word for word, and translated into an organ of the larger entity.

However, no text can explain itself, and no collection of texts can explain itself, either. The Christian canon is at best a partial success. Additional, extracanonical commentary is required in order to control the meaning of the texts. In the ancient world, this commentary often took the form of allegorical reading. Allegory 'holds that the [text] has meanings contemporary with us which, quite possibly, an informed contemporary [of the writer] could not have discovered' (Kermode 1975: 75). Although other forms of interpretation were also known, most notably midrash,[7] ancient allegory played the canon to find the eternal, universal word of God lying hidden within the texts, a truth that does not crumble and fade, even though the physical texts themselves do. Quite unlike midrash, allegory served to establish a totalizing *imperium*, the eternal empire of the Christian canon, God's meaningful message to the eternal empire of universal Christianity.

---

7. See Hartman and Budick 1986, and Faur 1986. Marcion rejected allegory, but he also rejected the authority of the Old Testament (Barton 1997: 35-62). On orthodox Christian versus Gnostic use of allegory, see Ehrman 1993: 20-22.

## The Mass-Produced Bible

> The presence of the original is the prerequisite to the concept of authenticity (Benjamin 1968: 220).

The transformations involved in the shift from hand-written books to printed ones present a serious threat to the canon of scripture. In print culture, the security that canon provides for the biblical texts is replaced by other types of security, other semiotic machines. The technology of printing itself replaces important textual control functions of the canon. Unlike hand-written copies, in which textual deviations of all sorts are common, each printed copy of a book is exactly like every other one. Every page is exactly the same in each copy (and thus the page number becomes a useful way to reference citations). Scribal variations in the texts, whether accidental or deliberate, no longer occur. The technology of the printing press effectively protects the printed text from uncontrolled changes, whether they take the form of pirating, censorship or vandalism. The printing press produces lots of absolutely identical copies of the Bible, and thereby printing diminishes the need for a canon, because the need to secure the physical limits of the individual books and of the canonical list as a whole has been addressed by circumstances arising from the mechanical reproduction of the texts.

As the process of publishing a text becomes more technically elaborate, the scribal skills of reading and writing become more widely known. The printed text is intrinsically a mass phenomenon, and widespread literacy is required to generate demand for books, as well as systems of sales and distribution to supply that demand, on a scale much larger than the hand-written manuscript ever entailed. It is no coincidence that the Protestant reformation begins at the same time as print culture. The Protestant movements encourage each believer to be a reader, and therefore they generate demands for large numbers of printed texts, as does the rapidly growing urban middle class. Print culture mass produces not only books, but also readers. At the same time, reading becomes a silent, personal experience. Private reading loosens the authority of the text, for that authority is less and less dependent upon some commonly accepted creed or commentary tradition and more and more derived from the personal choice of the reader. As a consequence of print culture, the Bible loses its canonical universality, and the Christian empire dissolves into individualistic piety.

In addition, the ability to produce quickly and cheaply many copies of a book, and the availability of that printed book to many people, raise legal and economic questions of intellectual property. The mechanism of the canon initially appeared as a way to secure property of the church—that is, the Christian ideology, reflected in proper understanding of the scriptures —against heretics, Jews and other opponents of the Christian community. In print culture, the content and physical arrangement of the book fall more and more into the hands of the publishers, whose interests are more likely to be in sales and profits than in traditional theological matters. Economic incentives give publishers reason to guard against uncontrolled copying. Both the commercialization of publishing and the privatization of reading encourage the development of legal and ethical strictures concerning copyright and plagiarism (Eisenstein 1979). These rules provide a different sort of security for the printed texts, further usurping the canon's function as a guarantee of authority and completeness. As a result, the dissemination of the text in print culture is more tightly controlled that it was previously.

The mass production of the Bible by the printing press further deprives each of the copies of its 'aura', its unique existence. Walter Benjamin developed the notion of aura as a way to describe what happens to a work of art such as a painting when it is mechanically reproduced as a photograph in a poster or an art book. The aura of the original painting gives it authenticity and binds it to a tradition. 'The authenticity of a thing is the essence of all that is transmissable from its beginning, ranging from its substantive duration to its testimony to the history which it has experienced' (Benjamin 1968: 221). The aura expresses the power of the work of art as an 'original'. This aura functions in a primarily aesthetic manner in the modern world, but Benjamin stresses that the aura of the work of art originates in its ritual importance, and that this ritual significance remains attached in some vestigial way to the work's aura (1968: 223-24).

Benjamin's concept of aura may seem irrelevant to this discussion. Manuscript Bibles are copies just as much as printed ones are, and no original text of any biblical book has survived. Nevertheless, the concept is not irrelevant. The Bible continues to have important ritual uses, in which the canon plays an essential part. Furthermore, Benjamin also discusses the absence of aura in nature photographs and especially in the cinema, for which there is no original work of art, and he claims that mass produced, printed novels stand in a similar relation to traditional, oral stories. '[W]ithin the phenomenon which we are here examining, from the perspective of world history, print is merely a special, though particularly important, case' (Benjamin 1968: 219).[8] Although they are copies, manuscripts of the Bible are

---

8. This point is developed further in Benjamin 1968: 83-109.

of necessity produced one by one, by hand, like paintings, and even in large scriptoria where manuscripts were produced on an 'assembly line' basis, the relation of individual scribe to individual copy would be more intimate than that of printing press operators to the hundreds or thousands of copies that they generate. When printed books began to appear in the late 1400s, people feared that they were not as good as manuscript books were. Some early booksellers catered to readers who did not want to buy printed books, and early printed Bibles used typefaces that resembled handwriting.[9] We have long since forgotten that fear of the printed book, just as we have forgotten the anxiety about writing expressed by Socrates, Josiah, Ezra, Paul and Papias. Nevertheless, something fundamental changed in the reader's relation to the text when it was printed, and this includes the text of the Bible.

Just as the security provided by the canon is increasingly replaced in the modern world by the security provided by print technology and by laws defining copyright, so allegory as a way to read the Bible is increasingly replaced by modern scientific and historical methods of interpretation. These methods also challenge the imperial authority of the canon. As the Bible's religious authority declines—and as literacy spreads, due to print culture—it is replaced by the tendency to regard the Bible as a compendium of stirring narratives, moral and philosophical insights, and beautiful poetry. The texts' meanings are not eternal truths; instead, they are fallible (albeit important) ideas that have survived in the specific, contingent histories of human beings. The Bible becomes a 'classic'.

The growing importance of the silent, individual reader in print culture is accompanied by the emergence of the romantic ideology of the solitary author who writes in order to express her deepest thoughts and feelings (Kermode 1957: 43). Modernist hermeneutics identifies the author's intention with the single meaning of the text: 'the reader [must] use his learning in order to approximate to a reading of the [text] possible to an informed contemporary of the author's'.[10] This is a secular version of Luther's identification of the 'plain meaning' of the scriptures with the action of the Holy Spirit, the Bible's 'author', upon the faithful reader. Like the Holy Spirit, the human author's intention dictates how the text should be understood. According to this ideology, the writer (whether divine or human) 'owns' the text in a way that the reader cannot, and the reader is obliged to

---

9. See Eisenstein 1979/1: 32, 347, and Norton 2000: 82-83.
10. Kermode 1975: 75. See also Gadamer 1975. The theological dimensions of this belief, which is essential to modern biblical scholarship, have yet to be fully explored.

respect that ownership (Hesse 1996: 22). The text has been produced by its writer, and its truth must be the writer's truth.

Print culture understands that the written text lives in time, beginning at a definable point in the life of its writer and surviving the challenges of history until it reaches the present reader. The historically embodied truths of the Bible are not 'eternal' in the way that ancient allegory conceived the truth of the Bible. The distinction between appearance and reality, which in the ancient world defined the metaphysical difference between the realms of change and eternity, is realigned in print culture to define the historical difference between the reader's present consciousness and the author's past intent. The binary structure of signification, the difference between signifier and signified, has changed, although the underlying polarity remains.

### The Bible in Electronic Culture

> It is no longer a question of a false representation of reality (ideology) but of concealing the fact that the real is no longer real, and thus of saving the reality principle (Baudrillard 1994: 12-13).

The technologies of writing and the codex made the canon thinkable and feasible. The ideological demands of exile and empire made the canon desirable. Under these circumstances, the Christian Bible came into existence as a canon. The technology of printing, and concomitant cultural changes, presents a serious challenge to the canon of the scriptures. Nevertheless, the semiotic mechanism of the canon continue to be supported by the intertextual structure of the codex and by the material stuff of writing itself, both of which remained largely unchanged by print technology.[11] However, the challenge to the canon presented by print culture is only the beginning. The 500 year old culture of the printed text is now rapidly giving way to a new mediation of power and knowledge. Like print culture before it, but even more so, the new, electronic culture threatens the canonical control of meaning.

Until recent times, human cultures were limited in space by geography, language, and relatively primitive technologies of communication and transportation. That is no longer the case. Telephone and electric power lines now span the human world. Radio reaches into the most remote corners. The hardware and software that make possible the electronic transmission of culture themselves require the extension on a global scale of the

---

11. Paper was introduced in Europe around the eleventh century, but this change has had no apparent effect on the matters considered here.

economic and technological bases that make the electronic medium possible. Even the simplest computer requires a huge industrial and organizational support structure, both for its manufacture and for the software that runs on it. Nevertheless, electronic culture will not give rise to a single global, electronic empire. The old colonial empires, outmoded and despised, are rapidly disappearing. It is unlikely that monolithic empire in any form will ever again be possible. Instead, the multiple 'empires' of our time take the form of huge transnational corporations, such as Microsoft, Disney, McDonald's or Mitsubishi.

Electronic culture is neither the New Jerusalem nor the fiery pit. Because of it, our lives will certainly change, but they will not necessarily get better. The divisions between rich and poor, strong and weak will be realigned, but they will not be eliminated. Those who have access to the digital technologies will be privileged, just as those who have access to books and print technology have long been privileged, and still are. The biblical canon may very well continue to display a liveliness in communities that are marginalized in relation to electronic or even print culture. Yet although portions of the human population remain in effect trapped and isolated in circumstances typical of print or even oral culture, even this apparent isolation, and the seeming vigor of the canon within it, is also the product of electronic culture.

In this world, the old imperial forms of power and desire reflected in the biblical canon are less and less viable. Likewise, the traditional imperial metanarratives have been exhausted, and they are now replaced by countless local micronarratives, continually reassembled out of even smaller narrative fragments. Both traditional and modern societies and cultures are increasingly supplanted by nomadic, neo-tribal groupings, drawing on fragments of multiple belief systems, lifestyles and languages pasted together in new and quite fluid configurations. A polyvocal 'paralogy' of little narratives, a constantly changing multiplicity of stories, serves to destabilize the traditional metanarratives and to reveal what they have excluded, 'producing not the known, but the unknown'.[12] As Fredric Jameson says,

> We are left with that pure and random play of signifiers that we call postmodernism, which no longer produces monumental works of the modernist type but ceaselessly reshuffles the fragments of preexistent texts, the building blocks of older cultural and social production, in some new and heightened bricolage...[13]

12. Lyotard 1984: 60. See also Kermode 1975: 135-41.
13. Jameson 1991: 96. See also Lyotard 1984: xxiv.

This 'new and heightened bricolage' plays with both ancient and modern grand narratives, breaking them up and rearranging the pieces. Frank Kermode claims that this new situation encourages a plurality of readings of 'classic' texts—a plurality that will increase over time. An indefinite number of possible meanings may be attached to each text. In this context, allegory is reinvented as 'horizontal rather than vertical'—that is, fluid and amorphous intertextuality, a non-imperial, non-eternal network of texts that is flat and de-centered, not the antique hierarchical structure.[14] Indeed, postmodern allegory is curiously 'midrashic'. The texts overlap to form unstable networks of floating signifiers, endlessly deferring meaning, and thus making explicit the limitlessness of semiosis.

Postmodern thought collapses the binary polarity of reality and appearance that undergirds both ancient allegory and modern (print culture) hermeneutics, the difference that makes representation and thus interpretation possible. The hermeneutical tension between signified and signifier collapses, and the medium as such disappears, because everything has become medium. For postmodernism, there are no facts, only interpretations, as Friedrich Nietzsche intimated.[15] The so-called facts are referential illusions, produced by the ideological filters through which the world is perceived. Facts are the details that make the illusion convincing. Reality is the product of the 'reality effect' (Barthes 1986: 141-48), and no significant distinction can be made between an actual object and its image or simulacrum. Reality is replaced by realism, which is the illusion of reality —and which is always a fictional construct. '[T]he real is never anything but a meaning' (Barthes 1986: 140). No single, eternal truth underlies the text, nor does the author's intention govern its meaning. The author, indeed, is dead (Barthes 1986: 49-55).

Postmodernism is not the same thing as electronic culture. Numerous pre-electronic texts (including parts of the Bible[16]) are postmodern. Conversely, not all electronic texts are postmodern. Nevertheless, electronic culture does stimulate awareness of the 'postmodern condition'. Among other things, the emergence of electronic culture in the last century or so makes it possible to question the continuing viability of the canon of scriptures. Whether any canon of texts can speak universally or authoritatively in this brave new world is doubtful. Indeed, the Bible no longer has any genuine canonical hold over anyone today, no matter how loudly some people might protest.

14. Jameson 1991: 168. See also Deleuze and Guattari 1987.
15. 1968: 267, section 481. See also Nietzsche 1968: 47, section 70.
16. For an example, see Aichele 2001: 194-200.

Although millions of people still believe that the Bible is the 'word of God', the authoritative scripture, even for these people, the Bible no longer signifies *as a canon*. The loudness of the believing communities' protests on behalf of the canon is itself a symptom of the failure of the canon's authority. The Bible is no longer the canon of an imperial church. The text of the Bible is no longer the vehicle of a universal, apostolic message. Instead, if it signifies at all, or to anyone, it does so in other, non-canonical ways.

On one hand, the Bible becomes an index of authority, to be invoked by politicians, advertisers and newspaper psychologists, waved by televangelists and sports heroes, pounded by revivalists and businessmen, made the object of Sunday School games, sworn on in courthouses, set out on coffee tables or in motel rooms, and given to graduates and newlyweds. Church Bible study programs, TV Bible cartoons and 'simplified' Bibles present pre-cooked, easily digested explanations of the texts, so that one no longer needs the canon as self-commentary. The Bible becomes one more symptom of Christianity, along with Christian comic books, music and movies, Christian fitness centers, athletes, and amusement parks, 'WWJD' bracelets and crosses on chains, tattoos and earrings, Christian bumper stickers, T-shirts and billboards, dashboard Jesuses and back yard Marys, and other such paraphernalia.

In these ways, the Bible ceases to operate as a collection of texts, and it becomes instead a trademark of 'Christian family values', regardless of what it might actually say about anything. A biblical message is denoted in countless phrases that begin, 'The Bible says…', but what is important is not what some biblical text says, but rather the invocation of biblical authority itself—that is, what the words 'the Bible says' themselves connote. The Bible does not convey a message so much as it is itself the message. In these circumstances, the canon no longer serves as an intertextual commentary, for no commentary is required. The universal, orthodox meaning received through the channel of the biblical canon is reduced to a self-evident, self-explanatory image of cultural superiority, moral righteousness and personal salvation. This second level of meaning completely absorbs any other messages that might be derived from the texts. The importance of the Bible is reaffirmed even as the texts are emptied of meaning.

On the other hand, secular mass media freely take over and rewrite biblical texts. In popular films, TV shows, music and novels, the Bible is caught up in an endless shuffle and circulation of signs.[17] The textual body

---

17. For examples, see the essays in Aichele 2000 and Aichele and Walsh 2002.

is continually recycled—shattered, reassembled and re-contextualized—and its referential functions are suspended, split, or played out in a wide variety of ways. Again, although in a quite different way, the canon loses all control over the meaning of the texts. Secular media producers are willing to use biblical images, themes and entire stories, alongside material drawn from a wide variety of other sources, to create mixtures in which the biblical ingredients are not privileged as authoritative, universal or apostolic. The biblical text's status as a signifying channel is retained, but at the cost of its orthodoxy and univocity. Although some of these rewritings may appeal to Christians, others do not, and the plurality and fictionality of the phenomenon as a whole is disturbing to traditional faith. The texts cease to convey a single, canonical message—that is, they no longer denote a coherent reality of ultimate importance.

In either case, the Bible has ceased to function as a mechanism to control meaning. Indeed, the canon remains active within the discourse of both believers and non-believers only as a totem or talisman, an empty gesture. The Bible has become 'hyperreal', to use Jean Baudrillard's term.[18] Like everything else in electronic culture, the Bible has become virtual: a copy without an original, a map without a territory (Baudrillard 1994: 1). 'Simulation is precisely this irresistible unfolding, this linkage of things as if they had a meaning, so that they are no longer controlled or regulated except by artificial montage and non-sense' (Baudrillard 1992). In electronic culture, the Bible can only simulate a canon.

## The Hyperreal Bible

> God is not dead, he has become hyperreal (Baudrillard 1994: 159).

For Benjamin, literal translation makes manifest the 'translatability' of the original text (1968: 71). Likewise, digitized texts of the Bible make evident the hyperreality of the canon. The digitized Bible is a translation between media,[19] not unlike the translation from manuscript to printed text or even from oral tradition to written text. Indeed, digitization involves a kind of 'literal translation', in the sense that Benjamin uses that term (1968: 69-82), although no interlinear version is either possible or necessary for these texts. The digitized text is exactly the same, language for language and

---

18. 1994; see also Eco 1986, esp. pp. 1-58.

19. Intermedial translation is distinct from the three types of translation identified by Jakobson (1987: 429), although it is closest to what he called 'intersemiotic translation'. See also Landow 1996: 216-19.

word for word, as its written or printed source text, but it is not 'written' in the sense that the source text is—that is, inscribed upon a surface. Instead, the alphabetic signifiers have been transformed into binary code and stored as magnetic or optical patterns in an electronically accessed medium such as a hard disk or CD-ROM. Digital text cannot be read unaided, but instead it must be loaded into a computer's memory, manipulated by software and displayed electronically. Nevertheless, once this is done, the human operator can not only read the text, but index and search it thoroughly and rapidly, modify it easily, and transmit it almost instantaneously to others.

As a translation, digitized text is not as spectacular as dynamically equivalent multimedia translations of biblical or other texts in the cinema, television, video games or popular music. However, like literal translations generally, digital text raises fundamental questions about meaning and language far better than dynamically equivalent multimedia translations do. Digital text makes readers more conscious both of their own need for meaning and of the constructed character of meaning. Electronic reproduction of written texts such as the Bible produces greater awareness of the physical aspect of the signifier. The indispensability of the computer as a reading mechanism for the digital text interferes with the desire to think that reading is a natural process. It continually reminds the reader that reading and writing are themselves quite artificial technologies. The increased number of technological stages between the sender and the receiver of the digital message adds to the reader's consciousness of the frailty of the connecting media. Readers sometimes feel uncomfortable when confronted by digitized texts, just as the first readers of printed books, or the first scribes, were aware that something rather fundamental had changed. The Bible on a computer screen is a different Bible, just as printed Bibles are not the same as manuscript Bibles.

The Bible lends itself to digitization rather well, indeed more readily than most books do, for the texts have already been broken up into marked lexias (verses),[20] and the page number, that invaluable tool of the printed book, is generally useless in a Bible. Nevertheless, the copying of digital texts is a purely mechanical process, without scribal changes, and the uniqueness or 'aura' of the manuscript is gone forever. At the same time, the textual constraints provided by writing and especially printing are eliminated in the fluidity of the digital text. Furthermore, the digital text is not bound in a codex. Instead it takes the form of a computer 'file'

---

20. 'The [Bible] verse is an excellent working unit of meaning... For us, a verse is a lexia' (Barthes 1988: 229).

through which the reader 'scrolls' and in which 'pages' appear only as an anachronism demanded by print cultural reading habits.

The reader is physically able to rewrite the text once again, and both the codex and the material stuff of writing have been replaced by digital alternatives. The fixity of the individual text disappears, and the boundaries of the canon as a whole become permeable, for books can be effortlessly added to the directory of files or deleted from it. The canon becomes simply a by-product of a filing system, and it survives only as long as that system is convenient. The reader can prepare her own assemblage of texts and change it at will. However, the biblical canon has its roots in the beliefs and apostolic traditions of the Christian community, and thus it is not a personalized text collection. The digital text is an 'open' text, but there can be no open texts in a closed canon.[21]

Electronic media will not entirely replace print media, just as printing and writing have not entirely replaced talking. But just as we do not use talking in the same way that oral cultures do, and we replace it with writing for certain purposes, so electronic media will 'replace' writing and printed texts for many purposes. The digitizing of text makes it possible for nearly anyone to prepare, reproduce or distribute texts, skills that were formerly the property of a relative few. The control over the text exercised by the publisher decreases, and the individual reader's control reaches new heights. Just as the author has 'died' as the owner of the text's meaning, even so the print culture concept of intellectual property is also threatened by the new technology. As the World Wide Web increasingly replaces traditional hard copy sources for texts such as the Bible, something rather like 'scribal drift' appears again. Altered copies of popular texts, including the Bible, are as likely to proliferate online and via user downloads as are unaltered copies, unless some way is available to discriminate between them. The concept of the 'original text' loses all value in such a situation.

Digitizing the texts makes it apparent that the canon already is hyperreal. Now we can recognize that the canon was never actual, that it was always virtual. The list of book titles is real enough, but the canonical collection can only be an 'artificial montage' of texts. The Christian Bible has always been a simulation, and perhaps 'this linkage of things as if they had a meaning' is even the archetype of all simulation. Electronic, digital text simulates printed text, which in turn simulates handwritten text. However, no written text can ever simulate an oral text, and that is Socrates' point. It is the canon as an intertext that attempts to simulate living, oral

---

21. See Hesse 1996: 31; Debray 1996: 144-48; Simone 1996: 250.

text. The Christian Old Testament simulates the 'written Torah' of Judaism, and the New Testament simulates Christian 'oral Torah', without which the written Torah makes no sense. Just as mass-produced media simulate the canon of the Bible, even so the Christian Bible itself simulates the unique living word of God—the powerful, authoritative, oral word of prophet, psalmist, messiah or even deity.

Once its virtuality has been recognized, the canon can no longer function at all. Today belief in the divine and apostolic authority that undergirds the canonical message has been seriously eroded. Many continue to fight vigorous rearguard actions against this alleged postmodern nihilism. Most evident in this battle are those who still maintain that the Bible refers clearly to some extratextual, theological truth, which is often identified with actual historical events. The canon guarantees the validity of the believers' access to this salvation history. Institutions and academies of biblical scholarship also remain committed to preserving the value of the canon, and thus they too reject the hyperreality of the Bible. Scholars and believers are sometimes uncomfortable in one another's company, not because their interests are fundamentally opposed, but rather because they are all too similar. This becomes most evident when the lines between theological commitment and scholarly method become blurred, for example, in controversies regarding the synoptic problem or relics such as the shroud of Turin—not to mention descriptions of the 'historical Jesus'.

Biblical scholars and believers alike maintain that the ideal, original text possesses a purity that may be diminished in its copies. The existence of hypothetical scriptural autographs, 'original texts', is thought to ground the authority of the existing textual copies. The scholarly attempt to uncover the earliest forms and functions of the texts, like belief in the autograph, seeks to restore the lost, Benjaminian aura of the scriptures. However, the struggle to defend the canon has already been lost. Both scholars and believers have forgotten Benjamin's point: that once it has been photographed, the *Mona Lisa* has lost its aura forever. Even Da Vinci's painting then becomes just another copy. Likewise, once the biblical texts have been printed and then digitized, then every manuscript, no matter how ancient, becomes a simulation.

The Christian canon attempts to satisfy the desire to secure the biblical texts against the threat of loss, and especially to control their meaning by severely limiting and directing the intertextual play between them. It is an exercise of power, the power to control the meaning of the scriptures. The canon of the Bible is among other things an oppressive institution, one that *prevents* people from reading these diverse and ambiguous books, or that so controls the reading of these texts that people are in effect blinded and crippled by the canonical constraints. In the world of electronic culture, the biblical texts will sink or float on their own in the secular, cultural currents of the times, just like non-canonical texts do. Some of these texts will probably disappear forever into the ever-growing trash heap of forgotten texts. However, others will continue to be of interest, even to secular readers. These formerly canonical texts will remain in circulation and they will be read and rewritten in all sorts of ways, but they will no longer be consulted for 'canonical' reasons. The biblical canon can hold no residual authority for these readings and writings, and the formerly canonical status of any of its texts is simply left behind it, a part of its past that no longer matters. As humanity moves deeper into electronic culture, the biblical canon, itself the product of premodern imperialism, will disappear, because it no longer controls the meaning of the biblical texts.

O Paul Where Art Thou?

James Smith

*Overture*

Stanley Kubrick begins the film-version of Arthur C. Clarke's Odyssean tale with a first movement provocatively entitled OVERTURE. What is interesting about this title, is that an 'overture' is not a beginning at all. It is rather an 'opening', even 'nothing'; hence the Overture's soundtrack contains the disharmonic strains of nothing in particular. The Overture is therefore not a starting point as much as it is a moment through which passes already existing reality that has not had the values of human thought attached to it—the 'disharmony' is 'music' prior to the conventional force of human values. Indeed, creating confusion around the concept of a beginning and the subsequent unconscious expectation of inherent value and meaning is one of the overtures made by 2001: A Space Odyssey as it takes us into that which is without beginning and end: infinity: everything: nothing.

In considering our own Odyssey, it appears that we have the same complex of confusion operative within the various movements of biblical studies. While the disharmonic strains of Kubrick's introduction scrape against our sense of harmonic convention, we are transported to view the dark side of the moon. Its bleak blackness momentarily consumes the screen, just as a sunlit earth slides silently over the moon, soon followed by the sun rising magnificently over the earth's now diminutive horizon: moon, earth, sun, all dangling in the universe like a cosmic mobile. It is the 'Dawn of Man'. To what is it attached? To what are we attached?

While it is obvious that this initial vantage point is not from earth, its real importance is that it is not really from anywhere in particular. Kubrick forces us to become illocal, voiceless voyeurs watching the celestial rhythms of moon, earth, sun dance to the strains of, well, noise, unless that's really the sound of nothing. As the strains of Strauss's *Thus Spake Zarathustra* commence, we are suddenly transported to a new perspective of the very same sunrise; we see it now through the eyes of the earth's inhabitants. Thus, while we commence with the apparent permanence of a beginningless, pre-existent, non-foundational perspective of the earth, it is quickly thrown into relief by the subsequent earth-bound foundationalist perspective of the Ape-Man, named 'Moon-Watcher' for whom witnessing births and grizzly deaths is a commonplace.

For Arthur C. Clarke, Moon-Watcher is the ancestor who bears our own genetic predisposition to wonder about the world around us. He is the one who begins a history of overcoming the self. Thus the name 'Moon-Watcher' is first of all descriptive of his curiosity, since he, in fact, watches the moon. Within Clarke's narrative, moon watching is something more significant than just noticing the moon, or even reacting to it like a baying dog. It is supposed to indicate some curiosity towards the Other. Moon watching in this sense is not the province of your average australopithecine; it is rather the activity of a superior-ape-man, a super-ape-man, a super-man, or more pointedly, Nietzsche's *Übermensch*.

For Nietzsche, the complex of the *Übermensch* is both a critique and solution for his view of humanity. He has famously suggested that humanity is fraught with four errors. The first of which is that we have never seen ourselves, other than imperfectly; the second is that we attribute to ourselves imaginary qualities; the third, that we assume a false position within the order of rank with animal and nature; and the fourth is that we continually invent new tables of values and periodically assume each to be eternal and unconditional; with the result that a given human drive and state took first place and was consequently ennobled (Nietzsche 1910: §115). In other words, Nietzsche does not exactly take a high view of us mortals (but then he literally went mad, and then he died, which just goes to show that not even God likes a smarty pants).

The four errors represent the guts of Nietzsche's nihilistic perspective at which he had arrived before writing *Thus Spake Zarathustra*, which in many ways is presented as a solution to the human condition. Thus we hear Zarathustra announce: 'I teach you the Superman: Man is something that should be overcome' (Nietzsche 1969: 41). Of course, by 'man' Nietzsche refers to the amalgam of the four errors. 'Man' insofar as it embodies these four errors is something that needs to be overcome. Kubrick and Clarke, as a sort of critique/embrace of Nietzsche, posit Moon-Watcher as fully endowed with the genetic predisposition and physical capability of the *Übermensch*, the will-to-overcome and evolve beyond those human frailties.

Regardless, Moon-Watcher remains primitive and so is his hermeneutic. Kubrick's initial two scenes are designed to contrast Moon-Watcher's foundational perspective with the already existing non-foundational perspective. That is, Kubrick precedes Moon-Watcher's earth-up view with an ungrounded, placeless view of the threefold rise of moon, earth and sun, and thus demonstrates that while Moon-Watcher sees the moon, he does not see that he sees the moon from earth. He does not see that the earth is as detached, as suspended by nothing as is the moon. He does not see an earth at all, he does not even see himself; he just looks away from himself taking unconscious comfort in the foundation on which he squats.

A gradual realization has occurred in biblical studies that has awakened us to the fact that we have been taking unconscious comfort in an assumed foundational perspective. Hence the first error observed by Nietzsche: 'we have never seen ourselves, other than imperfectly'. The gradual realization I refer to here, however, has not evolved from biblical studies, as much as it has from critical theory and has adapted itself to the needs of biblical scholars. One could go a long way by describing critical theory as a means by which we begin to see ourselves, and thus establish critical theory as a true mark in the evolution of human thought.

In spite of the obvious forward-movement of critical theory, we still find that within biblical studies there abides a pervasive antipathy towards it. Historical criticism, while genuinely offering a great deal, remains a hegemonic structure that assumes a panoptical position in order to govern and maintain an asymmetrical relationship to alternative means of acquiring knowledge. One of the best examples of this is Pauline studies, or rather 'institutional Pauline studies'. We shall therefore consider two kinds of problematic privileging located within Pauline studies, not to suggest an end to historical criticism, but rather to question its dominance.

Above everything else, the problem I observe in 'institutional Pauline studies' is its mono-critical approach to Paul and his texts. Inherent within this mono-critical perspective is again the aforementioned first error of humanity: 'we have never seen ourselves, other than imperfectly'. Historical criticism rose up out of the Enlightenment, and in a desperate dash to divest itself of subjectivity, it effectively pretended not to notice itself, embracing a philosophical position all-too-close to the absurdity of logical positivism. Historical critical analysis was designed for and applied to the search for an aboriginal biblical and theological reality—which has otherwise been obscured by copious layers of human history, culture and interpretation—in order to provide some kind of 'authentic' meaning. Yet while providing genuinely beneficial analysis of historical objects, and then moving on to provide an evaluation or interpretation of those analyses, it sustained the very same flaw located within Moon-Watcher's primitive, vacant stare. While gazing intently at the past, historical criticism consistently failed to investigate itself and its gazing practices. A significant feature of this mono-directional investigation has been the omission of the question concerning the nature of writing. Linguistics, yes; writing, no. This is especially pertinent since writing has been both the object and the means of investigation, yet never really consciously investigated.

Pauline studies has generally assumed both the benefits and the inadequacies of historical criticism to such a degree that the two are virtually synonymous. And so Pauline studies has become a discipline entirely characterized by a mono-critical, even monocular view of the biblical text. This tension between a monoculist Pauline studies and a polycritical set of alternatives is an old, if not one of the oldest stories.

In the first line of Homer's *Odyssey*, we are informed that Odysseus is a *polytropon*, literally a man of many ways, but used by Homer in the metaphoric sense as well: Odysseus is a man of clever twists and turns, a versatile fellow whose thinking is multifaceted; he eschews singularity and embraces plurality. This multifarious man finds himself up against the great cyclops, Polyphemus, who is confined both literally and figuratively to the familiar monocular view of the world around him—though as *polyphemos* he apparently has a lot to say about what he sees or indeed, fails to see.

Odysseus lands on an island and discovers that a great cyclops lives there. He bids the cyclops for the assistance due to a stranger in the name of Zeus. With his great cyclopic eye, Polyphemus gazes at Odysseus and his men and sees only a meal. He snatches two of Odysseus's men and slowly eats them for dinner. Polyphemus is a great, hulking figure, possessed of incredible strength and his mortal enemies are nothing but his meals. Yet his talent is fundamentally limited by a lack of vision. Odysseus is able to overcome the singular strength of the cyclops by virtue of his multifarious, *polytropos* nature when he eventually tricks him and puts out his great eye altogether. So sits Pauline studies, a great cyclops peering down from its centralized panoptical position, fanatically and monocularly embracing a single critical approach to the biblical text. It was quite a delight then to discover that the Cohen brothers' retelling of Homer's *Odyssey* in *O Brother Where Art Thou?* has reincarnated the cyclops in the form of an unscrupulous, one-eyed, mid-western Bible salesman, named Big Dan Teague.

Within the cyclopic monolith of Pauline studies there are two kinds of privileging at work: canonical privileging (by which I refer to the *Hauptbriefe*, and Romans in particular) and methodological privileging (by which I refer to historical criticism). I cite, in particular, the fact that, when discussing Pauline literature, the 'great epistles'[1] or the *Hauptbriefe* (Romans, Galatians, 1 and 2 Corinthians) if not explicitly stated, lurk in the background as a dominant and, more importantly, a delimiting force.[2] This 'lurking' occurs not simply by virtue of the fact that the term both normalizes and marginalizes the various Pauline texts, but also by virtue of the way in which that normalizing process writes itself into the *institution* of Pauline Studies at the very point which provides the possibility of discussing Pauline texts as something in particular.

*Aperture*

The opening statement in the article on Romans in the *Dictionary of Paul and His Letters* claims that

> Romans is both the least controversial of the major New Testament letters and the most important… It is most important as being the first well-developed theological statement by a Christian theologian which has come down to us, and one which has had incalculable influence on the framing of Christian theology ever since—arguably the single most important work of Christian theology ever written (Dunn 1998: 838).

The question begging to be asked here is to what degree does that assumption influence our treatment of other Pauline texts and, consequently, Pauline theology? The study of the theology of Paul has traditionally privileged Romans in a way that is good neither for the study of Romans nor

---

1. For all practical purposes this privileging process started with F.C. Baur although he bases his own discussion partly upon on Eusebius's history and analysis of the formation of the canon in which there were said to be two classes of Pauline epistles: the Homologoumena and the Antilegomena. 'In the Homologoumena there can only be reckoned the four great epistles ['*Hauptbriefe*', p. 276 of German edition] of the Apostle, which take precedence of the rest in every respect, namely the Epistle to the Galatians, the two Epistles to the Corinthians, and the Epistle to the Romans' (Baur 1875: 1.246, 247).

2. It is far more common these days for people to employ the phrase 'undisputed epistles' and by that title refer to Romans, Galatians, 1 and 2 Corinthians, Philippians, 1 Thessalonians and Philemon. We note, however, that the title 'undisputed' refers primarily to authorship and not perceived value. The idea of a 'big four' remains a somewhat prominent feature on the noetic landscape of Pauline studies, both theological and historical.

for that of Paul. The privileging of Romans has a somewhat solid pedigree: note, for example, F.C. Baur's own panoptical vision of Romans: 'only from the standpoint of the Epistle to the Romans do we survey the rich treasures of the spiritual life of which the Apostle was the depositary and the organ' (Baur 1875: 2.308). Günther Bornkamm understands it to be 'Paul's last will and testament' (Bornkamm 1995; 1971: 88-96); Kümmel labels the epistle as 'the theological confession of Paul' (Kümmel 1975: 312-13).

As Calvin Roetzel notes 'once Romans is established as the goal and quintessential expression of Paul's theology, then every other letter of Paul can be read as a preliminary or provisional statement of a Pauline theology that receives its most adequate expression in Romans. This letter then becomes the canon of Paul's mature theology' (Roetzel 1999: 93). Of course this is exactly what has happened. I cite the classic centralizing of certain theological *topoi* which subsequently place hegemonic, interpretative demands on our reading of the Pauline epistles in general.

The problem here is primarily with the way Paul's letters, and Romans in particular, are thought to function. It is not with the answers theologians have produced,[3] it is rather with the questions being asked—not prior 'theological' assumptions, rather prior assumptions about Paul and the nature of his letters. Hence the significance of Stanley Stowers's observation in the opening of his *A Rereading of Romans*:

> Romans has come to be read in ways that differ fundamentally from ways that readers in Paul's own time could have read it. More than any other writing of earliest Christianity, Romans, especially in the West, came to bear the major economies of salvation. These systems of sin and salvation reshaped the frame of reference that determined the reading of the letter (Stowers 1994: 1).

To be sure, the problem with privileging Romans is not a superficial one; yet there is a genuine need to consider the reality of a difference between what has come to be the 'normal' or 'institutionalized' way of reading Paul's letters and the way Paul would have expected his letters to be read.[4]

---

3. How could we question the skill with which the likes of Bultmann crafted ingenious responses to the questions presented to them?

4. I am not here overturing towards an original, authorial reading. It is rather the case that there appears to be a significant difference between traditional Pauline theology which seeks to represent the ideas of the historical Paul, and the sorts of assumptions we can make about the expectations someone like Paul would have had about the way his texts would be read.

James Dunn provides an excellent example of methodological and canonical privileging in his recent and rather corpulent text *The Theology of Paul the Apostle*.[5] In his discussion on how we can move toward a theology of Paul (Dunn 1998: 23-26), Dunn posits a question, which is not really a question at all because the answer is already deeply engraved upon the cornerstone of institutional Pauline Studies. Dunn feigns that 'one final point needs to be decided before embarking on the enterprise, that is, where one should best locate oneself within the flow of Paul's thought in order to begin the dialogue with it'. After a relatively short discussion, the answer is said to be easily made, 'for there is one letter of Paul's… And that is Romans'.

Now this is perfectly legitimate in many respects. Nonetheless, a complex of assumptions has led Dunn to the same point to which many others have come and which I find to be quite problematic. To begin with, let us observe that Dunn's ultimate and rather visceral goal is 'first of all…to get inside the skin of Paul, to see through his eyes, to think his thoughts from inside as it were' (Dunn 1998: 24). Now, if we can drag our minds away from this rather startling image, then we may note here that Dunn's ultimate goal is really quite underwhelming in its claim to do what virtually everyone who approaches Paul attempts to do, since it is has been rather well demonstrated that culture, time and language conspire to create a significant, perhaps impenetrable, barrier between us and *understanding Paul on his own terms*.

Dunn wants 'to get inside the skin' of the Apostle in order to locate himself in some Pauline *primordium*, and the suggestion is that Romans is the aperture through which he plans to enter into that activity, but herein lies our problem. What Dunn actually attempts to 'defend' is whether Romans is a sufficiently stable text which represents a 'statement of Paul's own theology by Paul himself' (Dunn 1998: 25). He does not defend Romans as the point through which he may enter into and begin to possess the Pauline corpus. There is an important and crucial difference here: it is not a given that the status of Romans as a stable text and its function as a privileged, primordial hermeneutical aperture are the same thing. The fact that Dunn assumes or suggests that they are is a problem, since at the very

---

5. Dunn's status within the realm of Pauline studies, the proliferation and excellence of his writing and thinking on Paul allows him to be used as representative of traditional Pauline studies. It should therefore also be noted that the subsequent focus on Dunn's work is really a focus on the institution of Pauline studies and not on Dunn in particular.

point of real decision in this process, the point at which even Dunn thinks a reading of Paul is made possible, he glosses the most important question with a statement on the text's apparent relative lack of historical interest.

Dunn's desire for possession of the Pauline corpus is hardly rare and really quite typical of all writing about writing. It is especially true of writing about biblical writing, since so much seems to be at stake. The traditional approach to Paul is one of domination over the text; indeed, the desire for possession is the desire to dominate. So what do we say to such a writing, or rather to such a desire? In his discussion on Moses, Freud notes that the delineation of JEPD (Yahwist, Elohist, Priestly writer and Deuteronomist) is an act of priestly mediation or distortion [*Entstellung*], and 'not unlike a murder' in which 'the difficulty lies not in the execution of the deed but in the doing away with the traces' (Freud 1951: 70; 1937: 411). The concept of distortion [*Entstellung*] is an important one for Freud and refers to a fundamental mechanism of his psychoanalytic theory. Essentially, it is a reference to 'the modification of forbidden thoughts, impulses, or experiences to make them more acceptable to the ego' (Goldenson 1984: 229), or 'the disguising or modification of unacceptable impulses so that they can escape the dream censor' (Chaplin 1985: 134-35).

Freud himself notes that he desires to bring into our understanding of his use of the term 'distortion', 'the double meaning to which it has a right… It should mean not only "to change the appearance of", but also "to wrench apart", "to put in another place". That is why in so many textual distortions we may count on finding the suppressed and abnegated material hidden away somewhere, though in an altered shape and torn out of its original connection' (Freud 1951: 70). Furthermore, it serves us well to marry Nietzsche's classic suspicion of 'any manifestation which someone has permitted us to see' (Nietzsche 1911: §523) with Freud's sense of 'distortion'. That is, Nietzsche suspects that when someone presents information to us, that the presentation involves a prior distortion of something that at one point was 'unacceptable' to the presenter but is now rendered in an 'acceptable' form. It is such moments or acts of (Freudian) distortion that Nietzsche seeks to uncover in his genealogical project.

While biblical criticism in general is an attempt to isolate difficulties and smooth them over so as to 'manifest' the text as comprehensible and coherent, it is thus an act of *Enstellung*. The desire for possession of and dominance over the Pauline corpus is thus also the desire for 'distortion'. Pauline theology seeks to precede, displace, and eventually replace the Pauline text in favor of itself. It requires a 'dissatisfaction with the work (conscious or unconscious)' (Sontag 1997: 253), it 'conceal[s] an aggression' towards the work (Sontag 1997: 251), manifests a desire 'to replace it by something else' (Sontag 1997: 253), invokes a 'radical strategy for conserving an old text, which is thought too precious to repudiate, by revamping it' (Sontag 1997: 251). It is a classic manifestation of the Nietzschean will to power, especially given Bloom's observation that 'no critic can evade a Nietzschean will to power over a text because interpretation is at last nothing else' (Bloom 1986: 21). And insofar as this *locus classicus* of Nietzschean thought is true of theology, so is Freud's *Enstellung*, since theology, through acts of replacement, necessarily 'distorts' the text to make it acceptable and comprehensible. Could we go as far as Freud and call it a murder?

The failure of writing for Plato was that ideas could be accessed by anyone while the 'father' of the ideas represented in writing is absent: 'Every word, once it is written, is bandied about, alike among those who understand and those who have no interest in it, and it knows not to whom to speak or not to speak; when ill-treated or unjustly reviled it always needs its father to help it; for it has no power to protect or help itself' (Plato, *Phaedrus*: 275E).[6] Plato fears losing possession of the text, which is always too ready to forget the father, and situates the act of reading within the violence of patricide. The fear of patricide—of someone else's desire to possess and dominate his text—drives Plato to castigate the possibility of a bastard text[7] which knows not its father: writing. Yet, it is not the conveyance of knowledge that feeds Plato's fears, rather the possibility of interpretation, or, not to put too fine a point on it, a theology of the text, since a theology of the text can never be the author-father's legitimate heir and remains the bastard child. Theology seals the father's fate.

As an interloper, Pauline Theology seeks fatherhood over the text. It is a hunter, collecting texts, stuffing and mounting them in trophy rooms, pathetically presenting the stuffed carcasses with their glazed eyes and ominous postures as the things themselves. It transforms texts in the same way that 'the approach of the Other prevents the real from being disclosed as merely something in itself' (Rapaport 1995: 98-103, 108). It is thus a parasite, siphoning its existence from what cannot be manifested as merely

---

6. Phaedrus then, following Socrates' lead, goes on to announce that the written word (ὁ γεγραμμένος) is merely the 'image' (εἴδωλον) of the 'living and breathing' (ζῶντα καὶ ἔμψυχον) word (Plato, *Phaedrus*: 276A).

7. Plato has Socrates argue that only speech is the legitimate child (γνήσιος) and writing desires a father, but has no one to help it (Plato, *Phaedrus*: 275E–267A).

something in itself. It is always necessarily a distortion. Hence the imperative that theology, as commentary, must 'include an interpretation of its own existence, must show its credentials and justify itself' (Jameson 1988: 5). But, 'even if in principle we cannot get outside our conceptual frameworks to criticize and evaluate, the practice of self-reflexivity, the attempt to theorize one's practice, works to produce change, as the recent history of literary criticism amply shows' (Culler 1982: 154). Self-reflexivity, a form of suspicion about the self, another kind of Nietzschean *Hinterfrage*, is thus necessary, if we are to make progress in our Odyssey.

The problem here is the expectation of the ontological within the text. Much to Plato's chagrin, patricide is ultimately the only way in which a text can have a life outside of the father. To sound somewhat confessional, unless there is some severance—some space between the father and the text—there can be no text; and thus, of course, the existence of text is precisely the absence, or death of the father. Yet theology (of the text) is still very much desired.

Let us say that (biblical) theology, in general, has been the process and product of the attempt to pry the ontological out of the text. It has sought to remove the veil from the letter of the text, and reveal the essential truth that only comes from the spirit: 'for the letter kills, but the spirit gives life'. The revelation of the spirit though an attack on the letter is the ontic idol towards which theology bends itself. But is it even possible? Eugene Peterson heads up a seminar on how theology is mass-produced—that is, a seminar on the writing of commentary. He describes the process: 'The writing of a commentary is a conspicuous (and sometimes dazzling) act of ministry to the church of Christ. But it is done inconspicuously' (Peterson 1990: 386). The product is manifest but the process is immanifest: a striking statement on the nature of theology. Again, Nietzsche: 'When we are confronted with any manifestation which someone has permitted us to see, we may ask: what is it meant to conceal? What is it meant to draw our attention from? What prejudice does it seek to raise? and again, how far does the subtlety of the dissimulation go?' (Nietzsche 1911: §523).

Pauline theology attempts to manifest itself as the man himself. Yet regardless of the degree to which, à la Dunn for example, one may attempt to don the apostle's ancient skin—to stretch it over one's own body, to peer through the aperture of dried-up eyes, to squeeze one's own head inside that skull—to assume that one may then even remotely resemble the Apostle is, at best, unfortunate. The goal, of course, is to come to possess a more immediate form of the truth of Paul, 'to think his thoughts' (Dunn

1998: 24). Quite an obvious impossibility, yet consider the even more grandiose goals of F. Dale Bruner who confesses to his 'sheer delight to be rummaging in the thoughts and words of God' (Bruner 1990: 401):

> Suddenly…a new idea occurs to him one day, *his* idea; and the entire blessedness of a great personal hypothesis, which embraces all existence and the whole world penetrates with such force into his conscience that he dare not think himself the creator of such blessedness, and he therefore attributes to his God the cause of this new idea and likewise the cause of the cause, believing it to be the revelation of his God. How could a man be the author of so great a happiness? ask his pessimistic doubts. But other levers are secretly at work: an opinion may be strengthened by one's self if it be considered as a revelation; and in this way all its hypothetic nature is removed; the matter is set beyond criticism and even beyond doubt: it is sanctified (Nietzsche 1911: §62).

Such a patricide is unworthy of us, the author-god is dead and we have killed him, and 'who will wipe this blood off us?', cries Nietzsche (Nietzsche 1910: §125). The response: 'we will'. But how? We must ourselves become gods simply to be worthy of such a crime! (Nietzsche 1910: §125). We must become creators ourselves, engaging in acts of creation; we must become theologians.

### *Reverture*

> All letters forge absence.
> Thus, God is the child of his name.
> (Reb Tal cited in Jabès 1963: 164)

The journey begins from its destination. We sojourn through the desert—'the garden is speech, the desert, writing' (Jabès 1963: 164). We happen upon a book. We read. We write: An oasis rests upon the horizon. We are drawn to its refreshing splendor. Our spirit is weak, but our flesh is crawling: where is the horizon?—a mirage. Footprints! We trace them. We are so careful. In the distance we can just make out our hope. We run. We are closer. We are jubilant—we write faster. Our hope turns to face us; we have come upon ourselves reading the book we are writing. We are again alone, alone with the book, but look, a theology, there, on the horizon…

*Theology: a comedy of absence. O Paul, where art thou? Or should we cry out:* Eli Eli lama sabachthani? *It's the same question, isn't it?*

Let us journey in reverse. A weakness with the sort of approach typified by Dunn's seeking possession of the Pauline corpus is that it fails to consider ancient assumptions about the nature of language. An investigation into the *assumed* nature of language in the first century reveals that, for the most part, Western theology, in an effort to move forward, has lost its grip on what was paramount to ancient writers when they wrote. It appears that in the first century the chief concern of language was the function it performed. In the historical development of biblical and theological investigation, this chief concern shifted away from the function of the language and moved to the search for a metaphysical nugget of truth buried within the text. Thus the quest for an unveiled spirit or 'theology' was pursued in such a manner so as to forget the very means by which the writers assumed the text would work, which is made problematic by virtue of the intentions and assumptions of a theology that generally seeks to know what the author was trying to 'say'.

Functionality, rather than serving as a footnote to ancient literary practice, was indeed the framework of that practice. Thus Jane Tompkins observes that 'all modern criticism…takes meaning to be the object of critical investigation, for unlike the ancients we equate language not with action but with signification', furthermore, 'the equation of language with power, characteristic of Greek thought at least from the time of Gorgias the rhetorician, explains the enormous energies devoted to the study of rhetoric in the ancient world' (Tompkins 1980: 203, 204). There are copious examples of this from both ancient theorists and practitioners alike: to summarize them, both ancient writers and theorists assumed that functionality, or consequentiality was primary; the real mark of good communication was to generate an effect upon the audience, sometimes this was reduced simply to the goal of persuasion.

When it comes to Paul, and thus 'Pauline theology', we find that in the ancient epistolary tradition the emphasis on function was maintained. Letters, before anything else, generate the effect of the surrogate or fictional presence of the author.[8] In order for any letter to work and perform other functions, this function must already be operative. One need only to observe that the standard descriptive names given to the various genres of ancient epistles employ transitive verbs; that is, they are defined by what they *do*. Thus Stanley Stowers, in his work on Greco-Roman letter-writing, consistently points out that it is upon the *function* of the epistles that we must focus our attention.

---

8. See discussions in the following: Berger 1984: 25.2.1329; Koskenniemi 1956: 38-42; Stowers 1988: 79; Thraede 1970: 95-106 where he analyses three uses of the 'presence-motif' in the New Testament.

> From the modern perspective, it is natural to think about letters in terms of the information they communicate. The interpreter, however, should resist the temptation to overlook the great multiplicity of functions that letters performed and to speak only of the communication of information. *It is more helpful to think of letters in terms of the actions that people performed by means of them* (Stowers 1986: 15, emphasis added).[9]

In spite of the historical data, it remains the case that in the contemporary (institutional) study of Paul, the 'meaning' or 'value' of Paul's letters is still construed in terms of the information they communicate. Importantly, the difference that the critical theorist, Jane Tompkins, and the classicist, Stanley Stowers, have both drawn is that contemporary assumptions about texts are preoccupied with 'information' rather than with the functional interests of the ancient writers.

The contemporary preoccupation with an inherent textual metaphysic is to be offset by the ancient preoccupation with a grubby, this-world functionality. Thus to treat Paul as a fairly normal first-century writer, we are required to shift from the obsession with the metaphysical and to embrace a textual operation delimited to and by itself. Perhaps we could entertain the idea of a 'genuinely logocentric' operation of the text—that is, we could take possession of the term 'logocentric' as a description of the fact that we really do reduce everything to language, rather than as Derrida's adjective for how philosophy/theology relies on language while pretending not to. The point would be to emphasize the etho-poetic features of the text that reciprocally operate upon—defining and being defined by—the radically immanent social code which gives rise to the text's ability to perform in the first place. Thus, again, the problem with Pauline theology is the obsession with arriving at an 'authentic' text that provides some prior metaphysical meaning which is then stabilized as *the final* reading of the text. The textual operation is then abrogated and the assumption seems to be that theology is left to exist in some unsullied, glorified state.

The mechanism of theology is typically fuelled by the historical-critical desire for a final, totalized reading. Thus theology is the means by which the text is then, as mentioned, abrogated, since by attempting to 'interpret' the text, it seeks to become the text in other words, displacing the text in favor of itself: echoes of *Entstellung* abound. Theology, as the distortion

---

9. Subsequent to Stowers's exhortation to focus on function, he lists 19 specific functions which ancient letters were designed to perform upon the reader. The important point to note from Stowers's list is the transitive nature of each item (see Stowers 1986: 15-16).

of the text, then attempts to invest itself as the text's supplement, which as Derrida has made quite clear '*is nothing* neither a presence nor an absence... It is precisely the play of presence and absence, the opening of this play that no metaphysical or ontological concept can comprehend' (Derrida 1976: 244). This is not to suggest that theology 'is' nothing, rather that its supplemental logic and the 'play' invoked by it precedes the object of its force: the text.[10] Thus, like Rousseau's supplement, theology is a point of metaphysical undecidability; it seeks to be both a part of and an addition to the text, wavering between presence and absence, never quite one or the other, never quite the text, never quite theology.

All very good, but just how do we embrace a genuinely logocentric text and thus emphasize the etho-poetic features of the text, rather than a chimeric inherent metaphysic? Analysis of the radically immanent, socially discursive structures which both enable and constrain the conditions of thought and expression is obviously required. One outstanding feature of Paul's culture which precedes his writing practices is the general adherence to the priority of language's function, not to the detriment of information, but certainly not subordinate to it.

That Paul was a product of his environment is scarcely novel; thus Alexander notes:

> If we have learned anything from the last twenty years of New Testament scholarship, it is that 'thought' does not operate in a kind of disembodied noetic sphere independent of personal and social structuring. Thought is an activity of thinkers, and thinkers are tied in to certain patterns of behaviour, restricted to certain specific forms of communication, by the society they live in (Alexander 1994: 60).

Importantly, the fact that Paul was a product of his environment necessitates that his culture formed not only the conditions of possibility for his thought and expression but also the conditions of impossibility, the constraints. Thus, the consideration of Paul's culture has been high on the agenda of Pauline studies for some time. For example, Abraham Malherbe's labeling of Paul as at once *Paulus hellenisticus* and *Paulus christianus* (Malherbe 1989: 8-9) is a helpful and typical description of the dynamic relationship between Paul's theology and culture which gives rise to the shape of his letters. It is, however, perhaps too egalitarian, since *Paulus christianus* is clearly preceded and enabled by *Paulus hellenisticus*—it was not an axiom of Christianity to employ Hellenistic ideas and structures of activity, by contrast, to 'Hellenize' non-Greek ideas and structures

---

10. For comments on the property of man, see Derrida 1976: 244.

of activity was essential to the identity of Hellenism as a phenomenon.[11] Paul can only understand himself and his beliefs in terms of the cognitive, psychological and social structures available to him, which include any religious beliefs, and those structures which make up his culture, which was Hellenistic. Hellenistic structures provide the framework which locates Paul at a particular point in the fabric of human social history, his structures of communication—that by which he articulates and conveys his ideology—his theology, and thus also our ability to know something of this person.[12]

Importantly, therefore, a reference to the constraint of Paul's discourse is also a reference to the constraint of Paul's theology to its genuinely logocentric complex rather than the desired ontological realities. Paul's thought and expression are bounded on all sides by the cultural conditions present to him during the creative acts of thinking and writing, and those conditions are fundamentally 'logocentric' insofar as they derive their currency from a social economy and not a metaphysical one. Furthermore, Paul's pragmatic focus on the gospel and his use of proclamation as an ethical reference point[13] brings genuine logocentrism to the fore as a structuring force in our own thinking about the nature of Paul's texts. This naturally fails to satisfy the lust for a traditional theological reading, a reading which is unconsciously metaphysical in its desires, yet always remains just that: *desire* for the grammatical apprehension of the metaphysical in the text, 'a kind of ontological inferiority complex' (Jameson 1988: 4).

The increasingly common emphasis placed upon Pauline paraenesis is something of a testimony to the important shifts taking place in Pauline studies. Paraenesis is more than simply ethical exhortation, it is rather a movement from the indicative to the imperative. In other words, it conforms somewhat to the is-to-ought approach to ethics. Thus, a focus on Pauline paraenesis, while headed in the right direction, does not actually satisfy the ontological desire, and neither is it intended to. It simply articulates a difference between Paul's idea of the 'general order of existence'

---

11. This is a generally accepted point, however see Hengel 1989; also Walbank 1993: 14-16.
12. Hence, not simply 'pre-Christian' in Hengel's sense of the term, which amounts to the pre-Damascus road Paul with an emphasis on his relationship to Judaism (i.e. Saulus, not Paulus); see Hengel 1991.
13. Both of these are discussed at length in Smith 2000.

(is) and 'establish[ing]...moods and motivations' to live out that order (ought) (Geertz 1973: 90-91).[14]

The value of a focus on ethical exhortation is that it keeps the exegetical significance of Paul's texts in terms of how they work in this world—hence the need to read Paul's texts as etho-poetic products and not as theological products. Yet paraenesis itself is problematic for two reasons: first, it relies on the text's metaphysical gestures being available to the reader before it goes on to create the ethical requirements, and second, it is actually a fairly standard Greco-Roman convention for exhorting people to do one thing over another. Both of these reasons subsequently conform to a common structure by which the culturally constrained etho-poetic nature of Paul's text is effaced by a theological procedure that assumes that the indicative features of Paul's text are forged in a transcendent, cultural vacuum.

There is a cause and effect problem operating here. The indicative features of Paul's texts are typically assumed to be that section of the Pauline corpus which expresses the ontological state of affairs. The expression of those affairs, however, can only ever be conceived and executed in terms that are already present to Paul and to those to whom he writes; culturally constrained ways. The 'is' that they express is thus not a metaphysical gesture, rather an expression of the immanent principle, an expression of that which a priori constrains Paul. To then move on from this as the basis for an ethical imperative is clearly the theological crafting of the same illusory distortion discussed earlier. Herein lies the confusion between cause and effect: rather than a state of being giving rise to a certain set of practices, we find that a certain set of practices gives rise to the expression of a state of being. And this is always the problem with Pauline theology: *it is always being structured by that which constrains it.*

### *Closure*

Given that the significance of Paul's texts is confined to a genuinely logocentric environment, let us then say that what Paul's texts do in that environment 'is' their 'theology'. Even if Paul's texts gesture towards the metaphysical, then the significance of that is not in fact the metaphysical (which is unattainable anyway), rather the act of doing so along

---

14. Here Geertz hesitates a definition of religion which is essentially about moving from an 'is' to an 'ought'.

with what that act does to those who are being acted upon. Thus, the new theology of Paul's texts, one that actually takes account of where we have come in our ability to begin to see ourselves, must begin and end with seeing Paul's texts for what they really are, etho-poetic products, and relinquishing the *idée fixe* of the past, the transcendent within the text.

Where to next in our biblical Odyssey? Homer has it for us:

> But as my men were going on their journey I spoke among them, saying: 'You no doubt think that you are going to your journey's end; but our travel has been redirected towards yet another journey, a journey to the house of death'... So I spoke, and their spirit was broken within them, and sitting down right where they were, they wept and tore their hair. But no good came of their lamenting (Homer, *Odyssey*: 10.561ff., modified).

# Semiotics, Scribes and Prophetic Books[1]

## Edgar W. Conrad

The so-called superscriptions of prophetic books, that is, the Latter Prophets (Isaiah, Jeremiah, Ezekiel and the Twelve) provide an interesting array of information. The beginning of Isaiah informs the reader that this is the 'חזון [vision] of Isaiah, the son of Amoz'. This חזון is something which he saw (חזה) concerning Judah and Jerusalem. The חזון is dated generally in the days of Uzziah, Jothan, Ahaz and Hezekiah, kings of Judah.

The beginning of Jeremiah provides the reader with similar but considerably different information. Here the reader is informed that what follows are 'the דברי [words] of Jeremiah'—not a חזון as in Isaiah. While Jeremiah is also identified as 'the son of Hilkiah' in a similar manner to the idenification of Isaiah as 'the son of Amoz', additional information is given, which has no correspondence in Isaiah. Jeremiah is among the priests (מן־הכהנים) who were in Anathoth in the land of Benjamin. The 'words' of Jeremiah like the 'vision' of Isaiah is dated, but the words are now identified as 'the דבר [word/thing] of Yahweh', and the dates are given with more precision than they are in Isaiah:

> The word of Yahweh came to him in the days of Josiah, the son of Amon of Judah, in the thirteenth year of his reign. It was also in the days of Jehoiakim, the son of Josiah, the king of Judah until the completion of the eleventh year of Zedekiah, son of Josiah, the king of Judah until Jerusalem went into exile in the fifth month.

The opening of Ezekiel provides the reader again with similar but rather different information. The superscription opens by informing the reader

---

1. I want to express my thanks to the Institute for Advanced Studies in the Humanities at the University of Edinburgh. My time as an elected Research Fellow at the Institute (January to July 2001) enabled me to reflect on these matters. I am particularly grateful to Professor John Frow, Director of the Centre and to Professor Graeme Auld of the Divinity School whose conversations with me on these matters were particularly helpful.

about what happened: 'and it happened' (ויהי). What happened is dated with even more precision than in Jeremiah to 'the thirteenth year, in the fourth month, on the fifth day of the month'. This date apparently was the period of time he was in exile. There is no mention of Judaean kings at this point and no mention of his ancestry. The beginning of this book also is distinctive in that Ezekiel speaks in the first person and his name is not immediately mentioned as in Isaiah and Jeremiah. What happened he says took place, 'when I was among the exiles by the river Chebar, the sky was opened and I had מראות [visions] of god'. It is interesting to contrast this with Isaiah. The חזון of Isaiah is singular but is dated over a long stretch of time, in the days of Uzziah, Jotham, Ahaz and Hezekiah, kings of Judah. In contrast, what happened to Ezekiel is not identified in the singular as a חזון of Ezekiel but in the plural as מראות of god that came to him in a very specific period of time, the thirteenth year, the fourth month and the fifth day of the month. In 1.2-3 Ezekiel is referred to in the third person. This fifth day of the month is further clarified as the 'fifth year of the exile of Jehoiachin'. Interestingly, Jehoichin is not identified as the king of Judah. Just as the 'words' (דברי) of Jeremiah are referred to as 'the דבר [word/ thing] of Yahweh', so the 'visions' (מראות) that came to Ezekiel are referred to as 'the דבר (word/thing) of Yahweh'. Ezekiel is now acknowledged as the son of Buzi and like Jeremiah he is associated with priests. Ezekiel is not among the priests as was Jeremiah, but he is 'the priest' (הכהן). While Jeremiah was among the priests in 'the land of Benjamin', Ezekiel is 'the priest in the land of the Chaldeans'. The opening information in Ezekiel concludes by saying that 'the hand of Yahweh was upon him there'.

The question I want to raise is: What does a reader of a prophetic book do with this opening information encountered at the beginning of prophetic scrolls such as Isaiah, Jeremiah and Ezekiel? Is it information placed at the beginning of these scrolls arising at the end of a process of the redactional growth of prophetic books as they developed through time so that its significance is of secondary importance? This has been the general historical critical evaluation of this information in superscriptions. While this material was often viewed mimetically as providing data about the prophet named, little value was given to the material for reading what follows.

The secondary importance of the superscriptions for reading is associated with the notion that prophetic books are unreadable. In the past prophetic books were viewed as a collection of prophetic words that were deemed to be meaningful only when the words were situated in an oral context. Present literary context and the limits set by the structure of prophetic books are credited with little value. This is the position advocated, for example, by Hermann Gunkel. In his well known essay, 'The Prophets as Writers and Poets' (1987: 24) he says,

> The prophets were not originally writers but speakers. Anyone who thinks of ink and paper while *reading* their writings is in error from the outset. 'Hear!' is the way they begin their works, not 'Read!' Above all, however, if *contemporary readers* wish to understand the prophets, they must entirely forget that the writings were collected in a sacred book centuries after the prophets' wrote. *The contemporary reader must not read their words as portions of the Bible but must attempt to place them in the context of the life of the people of Israel in which they were first spoken* (italics mine).

He goes on to argue that literary context is of secondary importance and that the reader should question whether there is any such thing as the structure of a prophetic book. He observes (1987: 31) that

> in interpreting as well as in criticizing the prophetic books one must use the criterion of 'context' only with great caution; and also that in attempting to indicate the structure of prophetic books such as Amos or Deutero-Isaiah one must first investigate whether such a thing exists at all.

In this paper I want to contest Gunkel's notion that prophetic books are simply deposits of once spoken words and, as a consequence, readers should ignore literary context and treat the information at the beginning of prophetic books as being only of secondary importance. In some ways, my approach has affinities with an increasing number of studies of prophetic books during the 1990s, which argue that prophetic books evince signs of structure and design (see for example Collins 1993). However, many of these studies understand this configuration in terms of the text's inception. Redactors are understood as authors and the aim of these studies is to uncover the intention(s) of the author(s)/redactor(s) against specific historical background(s) surrounding their origin. My aim is different. I am concerned with the reception of the text. Rather than focusing on the recovery of the intentions of an actual author/redactor, I am concerned with reading. In particular, I am interested in both the role of the reader and the role of the text in interpretation.

My approach to reading prophetic books has affinities with Umberto Eco's theory of semiotics. According to Eco, for communication to take place an author will compose a text for a Model Reader employing codes and subcodes to decipher the text's intention. Eco says (1981: 7),

> To organize a text, its author has to rely upon a series of codes that assign given contents to the expressions he uses. To make this text communicative, the author has to assume that the ensemble of codes he relies upon is the same as that shared by his possible reader. The author has thus to foresee a model of the possible reader (hereafter Model Reader) supposedly able to deal interpretatively with the expressions in the same way as the author deals generatively with them.

For Eco, the Model Reader is not a real reader but exists in the mind of the author. In turn what is accessible for the real reader is not the real reader but an encoded text, which is limited by codes employed by the sender (author) for the envisaged Model Reader. Just as a real author can envisage a Model Reader so a real reader can envisage a Model Author who has encoded a text for reading.

But herein lies a problem. 'In the process of communication, a text is frequently interpreted against the background of codes different from those intended by the author'(Eco 1981: 8). It is for this reason that Eco would say that meaning is indeterminate. The author's intention is no longer available to the reader. What is accessible is the encoded text. This situation is precisely the case with prophetic texts whose envisaged Model Reader is imagined against a different social context than that of a contemporary reader of a prophetic text. Such texts according to Eco 'obsessively aim at arousing a precise response on the part of more or less precise empirical readers...and are in fact open to a possible "aberrant" decoding. A text so immoderately "open" to every possible interpretation will be called a *closed* one' (1981: 8).

My concern in reading prophetic books can be defined in terms of Eco's semiotics of reading. I understand information provided at the beginning of prophetic books in superscriptions as coded information that the Model Author has provided for the reader of prophetic books. While I understand prophetic books to be closed texts and open to all sorts of aberrant decoding, I am arguing that it is legitimate for contemporary readers to focus on coded information provided by a Model Author.

Before discussing how the superscriptions in Isaiah, Jeremiah and Ezekiel can provide codes employed by a Model Author, I want to speak a bit more about how I imagine the Model of Author of prophetic books. I understand that prophetic books have a compilational unity although they do not have the compositional integrity expected of authored works. Prophetic books are the result of scribal activity of ordering, arranging and archiving material as well composition not unlike that described in Philip Davies *Scribes and Schools*. However, unlike Davies, I assume that this ordered arrangement arose at a point in time rather than resulting from a diachronic development through time. I am not interested in how the particular text I am reading came to be, but how the codes employed at the beginning of prophetic books provide information for the reader.

I understand a prophetic book (ספר) not only to refer to the scrolls of Isaiah, Jeremiah and Ezekiel but also to individual writings within the scroll of the Twelve. For example, Nahum is identified as 'the book [ספר] of the vision [חזון] of Nahum'. Indeed, it is the twelve ספרים of the Minor Prophets that provide the opportunity for gaining insight into the coded information at the beginning of Isaiah, Jeremiah and Ezekiel. By reading Isaiah, Jeremiah and Ezekiel together with the twelve ספרים of the Minor Prophets, it is possible to gain a kind of 'intertextual knowledge' (Eco 1981: 21) that can be used for reading.

In the remaining part of this paper I want to consider how 'the חזון of Isaiah', 'the דברי of Jeremiah' and what happened to Ezekiel (ויהי) can be seen to provide coded information for these prophetic books when they are read intertextually with other prophetic ספרים from the minor prophets.[2] 'The דברי of Jeremiah' is matched only by the ספר of Amos, which begins in exactly the same way as Jeremiah, 'the דברי of Amos'. The superscription to Amos, like the superscription to Jeremiah, also identifies Amos as belonging to some group other than the prophets. Just as Jeremiah was 'among the priests' of Anathoth so Amos was 'among the shepherds [נקדים] from Tekoa'. The significance of the coded information of 'the words of' associated with a figure who comes from a non-prophetic group will become apparent below. For now it is important to note that both Amos and Jeremiah are books about the 'words' of these two characters and also that they are associated with groups other than prophets. Amos is dated in the days of Uzziah, the king of Judah, and unlike Jeremiah he is also associated with a king of Israel, Jereboam. Like Jeremiah, Amos's words are also dated with precision. However, rather than linking the precise date with the reign of kings his words are dated as happening two years before the הרעש. This word is normally translated 'the earthquake', but for reasons I will detail later, I think it is better translated as the 'rumble' associated with war.

The significance of 'the words of' is more clearly seen by focusing on what follows in Amos and Jeremiah rather than focusing simply on the superscription. While the superscription informs the reader that Amos

---

2. A far more detailed account will appear in late 2003 in my forthcoming book, *Reading Prophetic Books*, to be published by Continuum.

'saw' (חזה) 'words' concerning Israel, Amos's words, like Jeremiah's words, are never identified as a חזון, like Isaiah, nor as מראות of god, like Ezekiel. Seeing in Amos and Jeremiah is of a different kind. When Amos and Ezekiel see 'words', they see them in the visual world around them. Jeremiah sees such things as 'a branch of an almond tree' (1.11), 'a boiling pot facing away from the north' (1.13), a potter's house (18.2), a potter's earthenware jug (19.1), two baskets of figs (24.2), among other things. Amos sees two people walking together (3.3), a lion roaring (3.4), birds falling into snares (3.5), trumpets blowing in the city (3.6), locusts (7.1), fire burning the land (7.4), a plumb line (7.7), and a basket of summer fruit (8.1). Furthermore when these prophets see these things they take their words to the temple where they are confronted by priests since their words are a threat to kings. Amos goes to Bethel where Amaziah the priest says to Jeroboam. 'Amos has conspired against you in the very center of the house of Israel; the land is not able to bear all his *words*' (7.10, emphasis mine). Jeremiah is instructed by Yahweh:

> Take a scroll and write on it all the *words* that that I have spoken to you against Israel and Judah and all the nations, from the day I spoke to you, from the days of Josiah until today. It may be that when the house of Judah hears of all the disasters that I intend to do to them, all of them may turn from their evil ways, so that I may forgive their iniquity and their sin (36.2-3).

Baruch is instructed to take this scroll and read it in the temple (36.5; see Jer. 7 and 26).

There is one other way in which 'the words of Amos' and 'the words of Jeremiah' introduce prophetic 'books' that illumine one another when read together intertextually. Both 'books' speak of Yahweh roaring (שאג) and uttering his voice (נתן קולו) (Amos 1.2 and Jer. 25.30) with the consequence that this will bring devastation to all the nations of the land. These unconventional prophets (one from among the priests and the other from among the shepherds) have the extraordinary role of prophesying the end of kingdoms and temples where Yahweh was present. Amos announces the end of the northern kingdom of Israel, including the sanctuary at Bethel, and Jeremiah announces the end of Judah and its temple in Jerusalem.

This raises an important feature of my thesis on reading prophetic books coded for the Model Reader that I do not have time to develop fully. Amos and Jeremiah are unconventional prophets who prophesy in extraordinary times concerning Yahweh who has made the decision to abandon his people, his land and his house (temple). Conventional prophets (like Isaiah whom I will look at below) receive vision (חזון) from Yahweh who is present in the temple. Conventional prophets go out from the temple with words of comfort and consolation, unconventional prophets come to the temple deserted by Yahweh to announce the end.

Amos and Jeremiah are joined by Ezekiel, the other non-conventional prophet who is identified in the superscription as 'the priest in the land of the Chaldeans' (1.3). Ezekiel will return to his role as a priest writing the torah of the temple at the end of the book (43.10-12; cf. Ezek. 7.26-28; Jer. 2.8; 18.18). It is in his role as a non-conventional prophet that we should understand the encoded information at the beginning of Ezekiel, 'and it happened' (ויהי). What happened was that Ezekiel had 'visions [מראות] of god' in the land of the enemy, the land of the Chaldeans. Unlike Isaiah he did not have a 'vision' (חזון) in the temple.

The only other prophetic book to begin with the phrase, 'and it happened' (ויהי) is Jonah. Although Jonah is not an unconventional prophet and does not have 'visions [מראות] of god', a similar thing happened to him that happened to Ezekiel. Yahweh appeared to him in Nineveh, the land of the enemy.

I want to turn now to the three prophetic 'books' concerning extraordinary times: Amos, Jeremiah and Ezekiel. These three prophets are portrayed as being indentifed with groups other than prophets (נביאים) and are, themselves, presented as extraordinary prophets. The language of the books, which follow, back up this observation. The verbal form of the root נבא 'prophesying', which occurs in both the Niph'al and Hithpa'el *binyanim*, is not evenly spread throughout the so called Latter Prophets. It occurs once in Joel (3.1) and twice in Zechariah (13.3-4). In both cases it has to do with prophesying in the future and does not relate to the activity of either Joel or Zechariah. All the other references are found in the three books of the unconventional prophets Jeremiah (over 40 times), Ezekiel (over 30 times) and Amos (6 times). Each of these 'books' uses the verb to emphasize that Jeremiah, Ezekiel and Amos are engaged in prophesying. Only in these three prophetic 'books' is the point emphasized that these three individuals are prophesying. In the other prophetic 'books' prophesying appears to be taken as a given.

This concentration of the verb 'prophesying' is significant for understanding the encoded information in the 'books' of Jeremiah, Ezekiel and Amos for reading. In each 'book' the superscription emphasizes the non-conventional origin of the figure and each 'book' itself makes repeated emphasis that each of these individuals (Amos, Jeremiah or Ezekiel) is prophesying. These unorthodox characters are prophesying, and this point is stressed in what follows by repeatedly drawing attention to the activity of prophesying.

Isaiah, as a prophet of חזון is a more conventional prophet. Other prophetic books, which have this similar information in the superscription, are Obadiah ('The חזון of Obadiah') and Nahum ('An oracle concerning Nineveh. The book of the חזון of Nahum of Elkosh'). But I would also understand that 'the oracle that the prophet Habakkuk saw' to be a חזון. Habakkuk is told,

> Write down the חזון;
>   make it plain on tablets,
>   so that a reader may run with it.
> For there is still a חזון for the appointed time;
>   It speaks of the end, it does not tarry (Hab. 2.2-3).

These words in Habakkuk outline the main characteristics of a חזון. It is written down to be read out by a messenger who reads it. A vision is also something on which one waits. I understand that the vision of Isaiah shares these characteristics. See, for example, Isaiah 8.16 where Isaiah gives instructions to record his vision and to wait for it.

The notion that a חזון is written down so that a reader may run with it helps explain words immediately following the superscription in Isaiah. The announcement that this is the חזון of Isaiah in 1.1 is followed in 1.2 by imperative verbs summoning the sky and the land to 'hear' and to 'give ear'.

> Hear [שמעו], O sky, and give ear [והאזיני], O land, because Yahweh has spoken.

While I do not have time to develop the argument in any detail, I think that these words following the superscription of Isaiah helps explain similar words following the superscription in Joel and Micah.

> Hear [שמעו] this, O elders, and give ear [והאזינו] O inhabitants of the land (Joel 1.2).

> Hear [שמעו] O peoples, all of you, and hearken [הקשיבי] O land and all that is in it (Mic. 1.2).

Also these prophets of vision are associated with the temple in which Yahweh is present as in Isaiah 6 (see 1 Sam. 3). They do not see things in natural imagery as do Amos and Jeremiah, nor do they have 'visions' מראות of god in a foreign land as does Ezekiel.

I have covered a lot of material here regarding the superscriptions in a rather hurried fashion. However, I hope that I have done enough to indicate how the openings of prophetic books provide coded information for the reader to understand the compilation of materials that follow. At the very beginning of Isaiah, Jeremiah and Ezekiel, the reader is given information about how to read what follows. The חזון of Isaiah is introducing specific information for the reader that distinguishes it from either the דברי of Jeremiah or the מראות of Ezekiel.

THE SALVATION OF ISRAEL IN 'THE BOOK OF THE DIVIDED KINGDOMS',
OR, WAS THERE ANY 'FALL OF THE NORTHERN KINGDOM'?

David Jobling

This essay falls within a larger program of research on a part of the books of Kings. My aims and intentions in this research are much the same as those that directed my book on 1 Samuel (1998).

The scope of the text with which I am working requires explanation. In *1 Samuel* I made a particular point of asking how our reading of the Deuteronomic History is changed when we divide it not according to the familiar canonical books but according to the major editorial passages (sometimes called 'historical summaries' or 'sermons'; e.g. Judg. 2.11-19; 1 Sam. 12; 2 Sam. 7) that intrinsically organize it. I defined 'books' that begin and end with these passages, and gave them names. My purpose was to let these 'books' problematize and be problematized by the canonical books, which have shaped the reading of the History much more than its readers are generally aware.[1]

The part of the History to which I have now turned I call 'the Book of the Divided Kingdoms' (BDK), and posit it as extending from 1 Kings 11 to 2 Kings 17 (both the beginning- and the end-point are, of course, debatable). My starting point is the end of the reign of Solomon (1 Kgs 11), perceived in the History as the cause of the division of the kingdom, and I end with 2 Kings 17, which tells of the fall of the Northern Kingdom and explains it in a long and famous 'sermon'. Free from the constraint I was under in the *1 Samuel* book, to privilege the canonical book because I was writing for a commentary series, I here choose to privilege a Deuteronomic 'book'.

---

1. I want to say *both* that the 'Deuteronomic' divisions (and hence the resulting books) are probably an intentional compositional strategy, *and* that it does not ultimately matter to me whether this is so or not. See my *1 Samuel* (1998: 36) for a longer consideration of this question.

I read the Deuteronomic History in terms of how it might have functioned in the creation of Israelite identity in the postexilic period (cf. the subtitle of Linville 1998). Though I do favour a late date for the composition of the History in its present form, It is not very important for me whether it actually originated in the postexilic context; in any case it existed then and functioned as an authoritative text. Nor do I at all care if the line becomes blurred between ancient identity-formation and our own identity-formation, as we have been formed by the Bible. I believe that such lines inevitably become blurred. On the other hand, I am not an advocate of reading the text as a 'literary work' detached from any history. I continue to take an interest in the postexilic period as a likely historical referent of my text.

In regard to identity-formation, the special issue in BDK is, of course, the 'doubleness' of Israelite identity; Yahweh's people is divided into nations north and south. Will the postexilic Judaeans see themselves reflected only in Judah, the Southern Kingdom, or somehow also in northern Israel? Do we have a situation something like Scottish identity formation, which seems to fluctuate between narrowly Scottish and broadly British according to which is more productive in a given case? What, from the point of view of postexilic Jerusalemites, does it all have to with those embarrassing others, the northerners of their own time, the Samaritans? The point of these questions is sharpened when we note that BDK has very much *more* to say about northern Israel than about Judah.

I believe, and have often argued (e.g. 1998: 5-7), that meaning is to be sought in biblical narrative *first* at the level of the very large narrative—the whole Deuteronomic History and ultimately the whole 'Primary Narrative' (Genesis to Kings). My method is deductive, examining the meaning of the parts in relation to a developing model of the whole. That is my procedure here; this essay is a first attempt to say what BDK—as a sub-unit of the Deuteronomic History—is all about.[2]

---

2. This bland statement cloaks a history. I intend to organize my work on BDK, as I did on *1 Samuel*, according to the great triad of ideological criticism: class, gender and race. I have, in fact, already written several papers along these lines, and gone so far as to publish one of them (1999). But as I was working on my paper for the Monash University conference out of which this volume came, I realized that I had been breaking my long habit by trying to work inductively. I had no sense of the whole; I was trying to create one—quite randomly—out of the parts. Those earlier pieces will now need to be recast in the light of this one.

I do not, in this essay, engage very much with earlier scholarship. The question I ask in Part 1 has, indeed, been addressed by a considerable number of readers, and I will make some comment on their views. So far as I know, no one has addressed the texts that I look at in Parts 2 and 3 with questions like mine, nor brought together the issues I raise in all three parts in anything like the way that I do.

*Part 1: The Economy of Sin in The Book of the Divided Kingdoms*

I begin at the end, with the enormous list of sins of which northern Israel is accused in 2 Kings 17.7-17, the sins for which it was given up to defeat and exile. This list suggests a settling of accounts, an 'economy' of sin. All Israel's sins have been enumerated, and the exile constitutes the punishment of them in the aggregate.

I asked myself, to what extent is this list a fair account of the sins committed by Israel in the long chapters of BDK? The answer, it turned out, was: almost completely not. There is very little correspondence between the sins in the list and the sins said in the preceding chapters to have been committed by the people of the north. Some items have never been mentioned at all, as committed by *anyone* during that time (e.g. 'divination and augury'),[3] while others have been ascribed to *Judah* or its kings, but never to Israel (e.g. making children 'pass through fire', or atrocities 'on every high hill and under every green tree'). Even some of the sins that *have* been ascribed to the kings of Israel (e.g. the building of 'high places') have been referred much more often to Judah.

Scholars have explained these observations in different ways, of which Linville provides a handy summary (1998: 202-12; in his discussion points of interest to me are intricately mixed with historical-critical observations foreign to my concern, so I summarize him only very generally). Some see the sermon of 2 Kings 17 as directed against the *whole* people of Yahweh, both Israel and Judah. They rest their case in part on vv. 19-20 (reading the 'Israel' of v. 20 as the whole people of Yahweh). From a literary point of view, this seems perverse. The explicit purpose of 17.7-18, 21-23, as v. 7 clearly indicates, is to answer the question of why the event in vv. 1-6 happened, namely the fall of the *Northern* Kingdom. The later part of the chapter (17.24-41) also deals exclusively with the north. Explanation for the later fall and exile of *Judah* will be separately attempted, in various

---

3. All biblical quotations are from the NRSV.

ways, in the final chapters of 2 Kings. (2 Kings 17.19-20, which are parenthetical to the rest of the chapter, pointing out that Judah eventually shared Israel's fate but also taking the opportunity of claiming that Judah fell because it imitated Israel's behaviour.)

Other scholars look for a theological point in the ascription to northern Israel of the sins of southern Judah. I find this line of inquiry useful, and cannot help but think at this point of the scapegoat of Leviticus 16. Northern Israel was, as it were, driven off into the wilderness of exile loaded with all the sins of Judah—with *our* sins, from the perspective of the postexilic community. I believe this is an important possibility, but it is not in this direction that I want to pursue my observations here.

To ask my earlier question again in an extreme form, are there *any* sins in the list in 17.7-17 which are associated *wholly* with northern Israel as a people? To pursue this question usefully, we need to press the distinction between the *people* of Israel and its *kings*. BDK is famously riddled with repetitions of the statement that some king of Israel 'did not depart from the sins of Jeroboam [Jeroboam I, the first king] which he committed and caused Israel to commit' (or the like). Yet in spite of this emphasis throughout the preceding chapters, that it was the *kings* who were most to blame for Israel's sin (and in spite the strong tendency throughout the Bible to blame instigators to sin more than the sinners themselves), the only hint in 17.7-17 of blaming the kings is at the end of verse 8, '[the people of Israel walked] in the customs that the kings of Israel had introduced'—a statement that is unspecific, grammatically odd, and not unanimously attested in the textual tradition. I have to conclude that 17.7-17 exculpates the kings of Israel in order to inculpate the people. If the sins of Judah are loaded onto Israel, so also are the sins of the kings loaded onto the people. Detailed examination of the earlier chapters does, in fact, confirm that several of the sins for which Israel is blamed in 17.7-17 are ones which the kings, but not the people, are said to have committed (e.g. building high places, serving idols).

To answer the question of the preceding paragraph, I believe there are just two sins in the list which the *people Israel*, as opposed to kings, and as opposed to Judah, have ever been said to commit. The first is '[they] served Baal' (17.16). But this seems at first sight a very odd example. Surely this is a classic instance of Israel being led astray by its kings! All the references to Baal in Israel fall within the long chapters devoted to the house of Omri, and it is made abundantly clear that it was King Ahab and Queen Jezebel who introduced the Baal cult. Nonetheless, beginning here is justified, and helps me to organize my evidence.

The point is that to serve Baal or not is sometimes presented as an individual choice for Israelites, regardless of what kings and queens may be doing (classically in the account of Elijah on Carmel; see 1 Kgs 18.21). Slight as this point is, it would seem to offer a legitimate basis for including 'serving Baal' among the sins that stand to the people of Israel's negative account with Yahweh. But this possibility is immediately undermined from a different direction. For it is made abundantly clear in the account of the fall of the house of Ahab (2 Kgs 9–10) that Jehu ridded Israel not only of the royal family but also of *all* the individual Baal-worshippers in Israel —and that Israelites faithful to Yahweh helped him to do it! How then can Baal-worship possibly *still* stand to the negative account of the Israel of ch. 17? Those who sinned in this way were long ago exterminated, and by the people of Israel themselves!

This first example thus proves to be a fake one, though for reasons different from what we expected. I begin with it because it raises a key new issue, that of the royal *dynasty*, or 'house'. Aside from keeping accounts with the people of Israel—the accounting on which 2 Kings 17 is based— Yahweh also keeps accounts with kings. However, the operative unit for this accounting is the dynasty rather than the individual monarch. Ahab's sons, for example, share his fate (1 Kgs 21.20-24), though their implication in Baal-worship is not altogether clear—in fact the punishment falls on them more than him (v. 29). The *house* (of Omri, or Ahab) which introduced Baal must be removed in favour of a new house, that of Jehu.

I turn, then, to the second case, in fact the *only* sin in the list in 2 Kgs 17.7-17, so far as I can see, whose presence there is fully justified. The issue of dynasty proves just as relevant to this case as it was to the last. The sin is the making of 'sacred poles', or Asherim.[4] The reference is to 1 Kgs 14.15, a verse that comes at the end of the oracle announcing the end of northern Israel's very first dynasty, the house of Jeroboam I. In vv. 7-14 this oracle has detailed Jeroboam's sins and announced the end of his house without reference to the people of Israel. But the oracle continues for two further verses:

---

4. The similar reference in v. 16 to 'an Asherah' (singular) is rather complicated. Nowhere (other than in 1 Kgs 14.15) are the Israelites said to have made *any*. Ahab made *one*, according to 1 Kgs 16.33. Perhaps this was the one which the Israelites failed to remove in 2 Kgs 13.6. This seems to be the only possible referent for the accusation in 2 Kgs 17.6. But failing to remove is not the same as making, so the accusation cannot, by a literal accounting, be reckoned a legitimate one.

> The LORD will strike Israel, as a reed is shaken in the water; he will root up Israel out of this good land that he gave to their ancestors, and scatter them beyond the Euphrates, because they have made their sacred poles, provoking the LORD to anger. He will give Israel up because of the sins of Jeroboam, which he sinned and which he caused Israel to commit (14.15-16).

Ahijah's oracle suddenly turns from announcing doom on Jeroboam's house (fulfilled already in the next chapter, 15.27-30) to projecting a distant future. The national exile of which 2 Kgs 17 tells is here anticipated from afar. Yahweh's accounting with the kings, at the level of dynasty (vv. 7-14), and with the nation, over the whole period of its life (vv. 15-16), are here immediately juxtaposed.

Two reasons are given for Israel's coming exile (rather than the twenty or so of 2 Kgs 17). One is that their first king led them astray—with perhaps the implication that they were to blame for *following* where the king led. The other is a sin of the people's own, independent of the king, the making of Asherim. This sin appears in 1 Kgs 14.15 quite out of the blue; there has been no earlier reference to any such thing.

All the *real* content of 2 Kgs 17.7-17 is contained *in nuce* in 1 Kgs 14.15-16. Israel is doomed first for the sins of its kings, to the extent that accounts have never been settled over these sins. These sins boil down to the sins of Jeroboam I, and specifically to the making of the golden calves (1 Kgs 12.28, 32). The calves were never got rid of, even by Jehu (2 Kgs 10.29). So there is some show of plausibility in including the making of the calves among the sins of *Israel* in 2 Kgs 17.16, and in holding them still to Israel's account. But the text seems to betray embarrassment over its own procedure. In 2 Kgs 17, as in 1 Kgs 14, such an explanation for so total a doom is felt to be a bit thin, especially when in 2 Kgs 17 (unlike 1 Kgs 14) it involves so radical an exculpation of the kings (see above). Can a sin not be found of Israel's very own, to add to what originated with its kings? 1 Kgs 14 pulls out of thin air the making of Asherim, and 2 Kgs 17, for all its piling of sin on sin, can really do no better.

To summarize: The first part of the sermon in 2 Kgs 17 (vv. 7-20, including the list of sins), fails to make a very good case that the fall of northern Israel was justified.[5] In reaching this conclusion, we have come upon

---

5. I do not have space to consider in detail the much briefer and seemingly independent passage which follows (vv. 21-23). This passage places the stress differently, greatly emphasizing Israel's guilt in 'continuing in all the sins' of Jeroboam. But it gets into a different kind of theological difficulty by claiming that Israel made Jeroboam king, when 1 Kgs 11 makes it clear that Yahweh did!

the key importance of the northern *dynasty* in the theological dynamics of BDK. The next stage of my argument will develop this concept of dynasty.

*Part 2: The Dynasty of Jehu and the Salvation of Israel*

Yahweh's keeping of accounts with the kings of Israel, then, works by dynasty. For its sins, Yahweh casts down each royal 'house' and another takes its place, usually by Yahweh's own initiative. There are four northern dynasties which achieve a clear profile, those of Jeroboam I, Baasha, Omri (more often called 'the house of Ahab'), and Jehu. Yahweh is directly said to establish all of these dynasties except Omri's, and to bring down all except Jehu's.

As I began to see the importance of the dynasties as sub-units of Deuteronomic theologizing, a sort of parallel crossed my mind between these dynasty-units and the judge-cycles in Judges and 1 Samuel (extensively discussed in Jobling 1998: 43-53). In both cases history falls into a cyclicality from which there is no obvious egress. Once my mind was set on this track, I was able to notice—as I should have noticed long before—that the Deuteronomic account of the last significant northern dynasty, that of Jehu, is cast precisely as a judge-cycle!

My attention was caught first by 2 Kgs 13.2-5. I don't know how many times I must have passed over these verses in my reading, without grasping that the entire judge-cycle, both the conceptuality and the terminology, is presented there. A judge-cycle falls into six parts:

- A. The Israelites do what is evil in the sight of Yahweh.
- B. Yahweh is angry and punishes Israel with foreign domination.
- C. The Israelites cry out to Yahweh.
- D. Yahweh raises a deliverer or saviour.
- E. The deliverer defeats the foreign oppressor.
- F. The land has peace during the deliverer's lifetime (generally 40 years).

So, for example, in Judg. 3.7-11:

1. The Israelites did what was evil in the sight of the LORD.
2. Therefore the anger of the LORD was kindled against Israel, and he sold them into the hand of King Cushan-rishathaim of Aram-naharaim; and the Israelites served Cushan-rishathaim eight years.
3. But when the Israelites cried out to the LORD,
4. the LORD raised up a deliverer for the Israelites, who delivered them, Othniel son of Kenaz, Caleb's younger brother.
5. the LORD gave King Cushan-rishathaim of Aram into his hand.
6. So the land had rest forty years.

Likewise in 2 Kgs 13.2-5:

1. [King Jehoahaz, son of Jehu] did what was evil in the sight of the LORD.
2. The anger of the LORD was kindled against Israel, so that he gave them repeatedly into the hand of King Hazael of Aram, then into the hand of Ben-hadad son of Hazael.
3. But Jehoahaz entreated the LORD.
4. Therefore the LORD gave Israel a savior,
5. so that they escaped from the hand of the Arameans;
6. and the people of Israel lived in their homes as formerly.

There are, of course, some difficulties with this 'judge-cycle'; it could hardly be otherwise, since the passage refers to a time when there weren't any judges! The first problem is that the role of Israel in the old judge-cycle is here divided into two parts, one played by Israel but the other by the king (Jehoahaz):

The *king*, not the people, does evil in Yahweh's sight (A);
The *people* are punished by foreign domination (B);
The *king*, not the people, cries to Yahweh (C);
Peace is restored to the *people* (F).

A second problem is that in 2 Kgs 13 the foreign oppression is a repeated, not a single event ('repeatedly', v. 3). A much bigger problem, thirdly, is that the saviour is not named, and no specific acts are ascribed to him—we are only told very generally that by whatever he did Israel 'escaped'. Finally, the peace at the end seems to have no duration—it gives way instantly to an even more total disaster (v. 7).

Most of these problems become very much less acute (or at least take on a quite different character) if we understand the 'cycle' as extending beyond these four verses and as referring, in fact, not just to the reign of Jehoahaz but to the whole time of 'the house of Jehu'. Looking first *backward* from 13.2-5, we find that acute Syrian intrusion into Israel (point B in the cycle) began not with Jehoahaz but in Jehu's time. Already within the theological summary of Jehu's reign we learn that 'in those days the LORD began to trim off parts of Israel' by the agency of the Syrians (10.32-33); in this formulation, the word 'began' implies a process continuing into the time of Jehu's successors. Looking then *forward* from 13.2-5, we find that Israel's recovery (points D and E) actually begins not with Jehoahaz but with his son Joash, who wins some partial victories (13.25), and that it is completed only by Joash's son, Jeroboam II (14.25). Our judge-cycle finds its deferred completion and conclusion, in the most specific, terms in 14.27: 'he saved them by the hand of Jeroboam' (point E).

It seems to me that this 'judge-cycle', so laboriously mapped onto the account of the house of Jehu, functions, as in Judges and 1 Samuel, as a powerful theological expression of salvation through punishment. The last substantial dynasty in northern Israel (brought into being by Yahweh to wipe out the house of Omri and the cult of Baal) has been made to function as an emblem of a final salvation of northern Israel through punishment. This is the way out of the in principle endless cycle of dynasties—it is made to conclude with a dynasty which *signifies* national salvation. Two clear formulations in the account of Jehu's house reinforce this message. In 13.23 we read that Yahweh refused to destroy Israel on account of the covenant with the ancestors, 'nor has he banished them from his presence until now'; while in 14.27 the salvation by Jeroboam happened because Yahweh 'would not blot out the name of Israel from under heaven'.

It is true that the clarity of this picture is muddied by the many short-lived kings of the north who reign after Jeroboam II (2 Kgs 15.8–17.6). The first of them, Zechariah, who reigns for just six months (15.8), is even said to be Jeroboam's son, so that he is a fifth king of Jehu's line. This certainly seems to spoil my pretty picture, but there is more to be said. The promise made to Jehu (10.30), later said to have been fulfilled (15.12), is that his 'sons of the *fourth* generation' will sit on his throne. In the Bible's inclusive reckoning, this can only mean the fourth generation counting Jehu himself as the first, and hence his great-grandson Jeroboam as the last. The 'saviour' Jeroboam has been rhetorically turned into the *last* king of Jehu's line, while Zechariah is removed from the salvation theology, and thrown among the other odds and ends of kings in Israel's declining years. Zechariah does, though, serve a necessary purpose. All the dynasties of Israel end with the killing of a king by his usurping successor. But the message of salvation carried by the account of Jehu's house would be entirely spoilt if the 'saviour' himself were murdered by a usurper. So Jeroboam is allowed to die in peace, and his fate is transferred to his son (a mere six months later).

The kings after Jeroboam II, even his own son, do not belong to the *significant* history of the north, which ends, as it began, with a Jeroboam. As by Jeroboam came Israel's death, so by Jeroboam comes its resurrection from the dead (see 1 Cor. 15.21, and compare 1 Kgs 14.16[6] with 2 Kgs 14.27).

---

6. It is a nice curiosity that 14.16 in 2 Kings announces the accession of Jeroboam the saviour!

*Part 3: When is a Foreigner not a Foreigner (2 Kings 17.24-41)?*

The final part of this essay takes us back to 2 Kings 17. Most readers end their reading of the Deuteronomic 'sermon' at v. 23, and see the following verses as returning to the historical account. But verses 34b-40, at least, have a heavy sermonic cast, and I believe that the whole section 17.24-41 must absolutely be included with vv. 7-23. I shall show that the later verses, while at first sight they seem (and are intended) to agree with the theology of vv. 7-23, in fact give further evidence of the text's divided consciousness as to the fate of northern Israel.

Verses 24-41, which I take as the Deuteronomic conclusion to 'the Book of the Divided Kingdoms', tell how the north was completely depopulated by the Assyrians and repopulated with foreigners. However, because the new population 'did not worship the LORD' they encountered problems. To cope with these problems, the Assyrians sent back one exiled northern priest who taught the new population 'how they should worship the LORD'. Then, seemingly, they prospered, even though they did not worship Yahweh aright.

In this strange account we hear two distinct voices. The first (vv. 24-34a, 41) gives the facts and then describes the result, as it has persisted 'to this day'. For this voice, the worship of the north is syncretistic: 'they worshiped the LORD but also served their own gods'. From this voice one fails to hear any strong note of condemnation. Its matter-of-fact quality belies its extraordinary content—that a large population of non-Israelites have become, on a long-term basis, Yahweh worshippers, if not very good ones. Having just paraphrased 1 Corinthians, I think at this point of Romans, Paul's vision of Gentile stock grafted onto the true Israel (Rom. 12.17-24). How on earth is the reader supposed to view this new population of the north, introduced by the Assyrians? Is it in any sense 'Israel'? What does its existence have to do with the salvation of Israel?

Such questions are too much for the second voice, which we hear in vv. 34b-40. It directly contradicts the first—'They do not worship the LORD' (v. 34). It goes on to give a definition of 'Israel', as 'the children of Jacob' (v. 34), which seems to rule out the possibility that the new population could be 'Israel' in any sense. Yet something very odd happens in these few verses, something which makes me wonder—not for the first time—how people imagine they can read biblical texts without help from psychoanalysis.

It is all in the pronoun 'they'. The second voice begins by picking up the 'they' of v. 34a—'they continue to practice their former customs'—clearly referring to the imported population of the north. The rest of v. 34, beginning 'They do not worship the LORD', is naturally read as still referring to this new population. But the 'they' of the next verse, 35—'made a covenant with them', etc.—is a different, indeed an opposite 'they'. Its antecedent is 'the children of Jacob' (v. 34) and it refers to the old covenant community. However, when this second 'they' reappears (after several verses of direct speech by Yahweh) in v. 40, it is in the words *'they continued to practice their former customs'*. Exactly the same form of words that had been used about the 'they' of v. 34a, the imported population, is now used about the 'they' of v. 40, the old covenant community of Israel (the NRSV's paragraph division makes the parallel prominent). We have a perfect case of the 'condensation' of diametrical opposites, turning on a phrase and a pronoun. The second voice, the one which set out to be utterly negative to the new population of the north, turns out to be rhetorically unable to distinguish this 'new' population from the old Israelite one, and so ends up giving the reader cause to doubt that there ever was a 'new' population.

Such doubt is very much confirmed by 2 Kgs 23.15-20. Here King Josiah of Judah carries out his purge of the religion of the territory of the former Northern Kingdom (which he is trying to reclaim). We get no sense from this passage that the population with which he has to deal in the north (some of whom he even consults in 23.17) are in any sense new, or different from the former Israel. He deals with them as Israelites in continuity with their ancestors. Doubtless he invites them to his Passover.

## *Conclusion*

The obsession with kings and the theological problems they create, which I found in 1 Samuel and even Judges (1998: 41-104), is at least as strong in the Book of the Divided Kingdoms. Everywhere we turn the question crops up, in new forms, of whether the fundamental problem before the Exile was with Israel or with its kings. What are we to make (see Part 2, above) of a royal dynasty presented in the guise of a 'judge-cycle' in which kings are cast in the roles of sinner, supplicant to Yahweh, and saviour? Is Israel to be saved from, despite, or by kings? And what relevance do such questions have in the postexilic time, when there *are* no kings?

This agenda remains over from the earlier parts of the Deuteronomic History. But Book of the Divided Kingdoms (BDK) has another agenda more immediately critical to postexilic identity-formation: how to understand the Israelites of the old Northern Kingdom and their successors, the Samaritans. On this issue, we find in BDK a dominant, negative understanding which is in the end completely undermined by traces of an opposite understanding.

2 Kings 17 seems at first sight to report the complete death of northern Israel as a people, to justify this fate theologically, and to draw a lesson from it. But in Part 1 of this essay we found the theological justification to be a failure, and in Part 3 we found, reading between the lines, that the report of Israel's demise undermines itself. In between (Part 2, on the house of Jehu) we discovered what can only be described as a powerful and programmatic affirmation by the Deuteronomists of the permanence and the ultimate salvation of northern Israel.

Was there any 'Fall of the Northern Kingdom'? *As a kingdom* it certainly fell, but did this entail any discontinuity in the covenant community of the north? Does the Deuteronomic History claim any such discontinuity? Over this question, the Book of the Divided Kingdoms turns out to be a book of divided consciousness. In terms of identity-formation, any special purity or uniqueness that the Jerusalem community might base on BDK proves to be illusory. The Other which must be excluded to achieve an assured purity insists on continuing to be included. The scapegoat won't stay in the desert. The claims of the Samaritans inhabit and finally suffuse the canonical text.

READING MARK BACKWARDS: ESTABLISHING AN INTERPRETIVE LENS FOR A FEMINIST-LIBERATIONIST READING OF THE GOSPEL OF MARK

Bernadette Kiley

Most Gospel readers are essentially 'familiar' or 'second-time' readers. When they encounter individual passages or even whole sections of a Gospel, they effectively hear or read that text 'backwards'—that is, through the lens of the story of Jesus' resurrection, the Gospels' concluding narrative. The resurrection of Jesus provides the interpretive key for understanding all that precedes it, shaping the reader's understanding of Jesus and her evaluation of those who either follow or reject him. More, it effectively neutralizes the suspense the writer creates for the first-time reader because the familiar reader knows how the story ends. This does not mean that the Gospels' meanings are fixed. On the contrary, perspective and repetition lend new insights to the second-time reader, as Togovnick argues for readers of fiction:

> Since first readings involve the continuous remaking and revision of guesses, first readings are like the process of living from moment to moment in the present. Second or subsequent readings—when the question of 'what happens next' no longer pertains with urgency—differ fundamentally from first readings and resemble the ways in which we experience the past. Upon rereading, pattern and rhythm—connections between beginning, middle and end—may be more easily discerned and more fully understood by the reader. Appreciating such connections through retrospective patterning provides the primary pleasure of rereadings, just as reliving the facts or perceiving the patterns in our lives forms the basis on which we regard our pasts (Torgovnick 1981: 8).

Torgovnick argues further that before a reader becomes an effective familiar reader, she must carefully investigate the ending of the narrative so that it can act as the lens through which her rereading will be done. Many Gospel readers, however, are not attuned to the different nuances of each Gospel's conclusion, and tend to read a particular Gospel via a generalized conclusion that incorporates both the discovery of the empty tomb as well as aspects of Jesus' post-resurrection appearances and his promise of an enduring presence with the disciples.

Where the Gospel of Mark is concerned, however, a careful reading shows that the sudden and dramatic ending (16.8) provides a quite different interpretive key for the familiar reader. Silence, terror and an empty tomb hold few of the consoling elements of the resurrection narratives contained in the other Gospels, and the reader of Mark must reread the Gospel without supplying them. When the familiar reader of Mark is also one who reads from a feminist-liberationist perspective, the process of rereading is compounded by the fact that those who are terrified at the discovery of the empty tomb of Jesus and who refuse to announce the message of his resurrection are three women who have been constant witnesses to the last events of Jesus' life. The feminist reader must deal with the reality that the conclusion of Mark's Gospel, and therefore its chief interpretive key, relies for its credibility on the failure of the women to do as they have been commanded. This feminist-liberationist investigation of Mk 16.1-8 takes this reality seriously but also seeks other possibilities for understanding the women's roles in the final chapter of the Gospel.

I have a vested interest in feminist-liberationist appropriations of the Gospels of the Second Testament. I am a middle-class, well-educated woman, who teaches scripture to tertiary students. I call the Catholic tradition my spiritual home, though I consider that its view of women mocks the gospel message. Similarly, as a non-indigenous Australian who loves this land, I am also painfully aware that I am implicated in the gross injustices experienced here both by indigenous Australians and by refugees and asylum-seekers who have made their way to these shores. In my view, interpretations of biblical texts that attempt to restore the voices of those who have been silenced can help to call attention to the voices that remain silenced both in the churches and in society.

*Part A: Preparing to Read the Markan Ending*

*A.1. Reading the Markan Text Via the Lens of the Ending: A Matthean Model*

In a 1987 article, Frank Matera considered the plot of Matthew's Gospel in terms of the 'kernels' (major turning-points) and 'satellites' (elaborations on, and reflections of, the kernels) that guide the reader's experience of the text. Time and causality, he argued, are two significant factors in the shaping of the plot and are reliable indicators of the Matthean author's unique theology. The Gospel of Matthew does not begin and end with the birth and resurrection of Jesus but is rather positioned within the broad sweep of history: the genealogy (1.1-17) points backwards to Jesus' location within the community of Israel, and the so-called 'great commission' (28.16-20) looks to a future time when the gospel will be preached beyond Israel's borders. The story between these two 'bookends' is a careful construction of related and interdependent events that produce in the reader the emotional response desired by the author. Thus, time and causality are the scaffolding on which the story of Gospel of Matthew is built, and they guide the reader in determining the kernels and satellites of the text.

When Matera comes to the task of isolating kernels and satellites, he argues that these are best appreciated once the reader has understood the great commission with which the Gospel ends:

> [W]e recognize kernels retrospectively. Once we have come to the ending, we realize the major events which have brought us to the narrative's inevitable conclusion. In Matthew, this inevitable conclusion is found in the great commission. How is it that Jesus has received all authority? How is it that the Gospel has passed to the Gentiles…? (Matera 1987: 243-44).

The conclusion of Matthew's Gospel becomes the lens through which familiar readers can appreciate the particular emphases of the Matthean author. From that vantage point, they can see clearly the sweep of time from Abraham to the parousia in which Matthew has located the story of Jesus' life, death and resurrection. They can also identify the strategies he has used to tell the story, the building blocks on which the story has been based and the progression of events leading to the inevitable conclusion. Readers can trace the origins of the authority of Jesus' claims at the Gospel's end, and can see how the mission to the Gentiles has been prefigured in the narrative. They can appreciate that the Gospel is both firmly founded in the past (Jesus' life and ministry) while being open to the future (the preaching of the gospel beyond Galilee). They can easily answer the question, 'How did the story come to this?'

Jesus' claim to authority, his commissioning of the disciples to preach the gospel to the nations and his promise to remain present until the close of the age are also intended by Matthew to engender responses of worship and confidence in the readers. Matera argues that such 'affective responses' are hinted at in the infancy narrative, where the angel proclaims Jesus as 'God with us', and where the Gentile Magi worship Jesus as King of the Jews. It is in the Gospel's conclusion, however, that worship of Jesus as Israel's Messiah and confidence in him being forever present to the community are confirmed as the appropriate starting-point for familiar readers of Matthew's text. They are the emotions that will lead readers to reflect on the identity of Jesus as Matthew understands him.

*A.2. The Significance of the Markan Ending: Applying Matera's Model*
What happens when Matera's argument and his insights into the Gospel of Matthew are applied to a feminist-liberationist reading of the Gospel of Mark? Can Mark's conclusion (16.1-8) offer the same interpretive tools to the feminist reader as does Matthew's? Matera's two categories of time and causality deliberately ignore the role of character in shaping the plot of Gospel narratives. Given that the terrified silence of the women brings down the curtain on Mark's narrative, how might a feminist analysis understand these three characters?

At first glance there seem to be few points of similarity and many of contrast when the Markan ending is viewed in terms of Matera's model. At the conclusion of Mark's Gospel, when the reader's expectations have been shattered by the women's fear and silence, the reader is likely to feel confused at best or cynical at worst. Matera notes that familiar readers of Matthew have a broad historical sweep within which to situate and understand the life and ministry of Jesus. They also have the Gospel's future clearly spelled out in the instructions of Jesus to the male disciples on the Galilean mountain. The reader of Mark has few such indicators. The story is truncated, both at its beginning and at its end. The ending is unsettling and theologically provocative, and there is no vast panorama against which the story of Jesus is set. Unlike the emotions generated in the reader at the conclusion of Matthew's Gospel, there are no grounds here for confidence or worship. Nor, unlike Matthew's Gospel, is there any sense of an 'inevitable' ending, one that clearly emerges from the plot as it has been constructed. Instead, where the reader has been led to expect a resolution to the problem that Jesus' death poses, and a confirmation that his resurrection is God's new word to the world, there is instead only terror and silence and a refusal to obey.

David Hester suggests that nothing really prepares us for the way the Gospel ends: 'The ending is not an ending, and it comes completely at the expense of every narrative expectation, causing the breakdown of the story world which only the actual reader can rescue' (Hester 1995: 62).

His sense of the shock of the ending echoes the responses made by both scholars and readers of Mark's Gospel. It also asks the question about the legitimacy of endings that leave so much to the reader. Frank Kermode comments on such endings in other narratives:

> The books which seal off the long perspectives, which sever us from our losses, which represent the world of potency as a world of act, these are the books which when the drug wears off, go on to the dump with the other empty bottles. Those that continue to interest us move through time to an end, an end we must sense even if we cannot know it; they live in change until, which is never, *as* and *is* are one (Kermode 1967: 179).

What Kermode sees as the power of endings that engage the reader in continual interpretation is precisely the power of the Markan ending. It urges the reader back through the narrative to its beginning, to begin the reading process anew. It also requires of the reader an ability to take the narrative out of the text and into the present and indeterminate future of the reader's own historical reality, and to test there the story's powerful claims. Whether or not the Markan text can 'live in change', as Kermode proposes for works of similar type, will depend on how the reader rereads the text in terms of its conclusion.

*A.3. A Feminist-Liberationist Reading of the Markan Ending: Adding Characters*

For feminist readers, the open-ended nature of the conclusion of Mark's Gospel would seem to provide the necessary space for evaluating the transformative possibilities of the Markan text. If the author of Mark hands back the story to the reader for the reader's own processes of meaning-making, then feminist readers, too, can participate in such an activity, bringing the text to closure in their own ways. Yet it is immediately obvious that the Markan ending, like the Gospel as a whole, cannot be appropriated unreflectively. In telling of the discovery of the empty tomb by the women who come expecting to anoint Jesus' dead body, Mark constructs characters whose actions are problematical for feminist readers. Ironically, the news of Jesus' resurrection can be proclaimed by Mark only by rendering the women silent, and readers who take seriously Mark's offer of completing the story in their own ways can do so only by countering the women's act of disobedience. Where does this leave the feminist reader who seeks new ways of understanding the life, death and resurrection of Jesus?

A feminist-liberationist reading of Mk 16.1-8 could begin by seeking to fill the gap created by Matera's work on the ending of the Gospel of Matthew. In his study, Matera does not consider the question of characterization, focusing instead on the categories of time and causality as they shape the Matthean narrative. However, current Markan scholarship on the ending of the Gospel (including feminist scholarship) acknowledges the women characters as important players in the story, hence a consideration of how characters can be seen to function in Gospel texts can open up the final story in Mark to more thorough feminist analysis.

Recent studies on characterization in Second Testament texts have been concerned with understanding the role that characters are intended to play in first century literature that includes the Gospels. Much has been made of the argument that twenty-first century notions of characters and character development are an inappropriate starting-point for appreciating the nature and role of characters in ancient texts. Where contemporary reader-critics are keen to identify with the inner journey that characters make, Greco-Roman writers and readers were more interested in plot and consequently adopted a more functional attitude to characters. While characters were undeniably individuals in particular historical circumstances, they were nonetheless employed to point to the universal realities with which the literary text was concerned. Mary Ann Tolbert (1997) develops this argument and applies it to the Gospel of Mark. She argues that all the characters, 'regardless of their traditional or historical roots' (1997: 73), serve the bigger story that Mark tells. First-century audiences saw Gospel characters not as personalities but as 'pointers' to the contours of the story. Thus they had no interest in the characters' psychological development, and nor did they seek to identify with them in what Tolbert describes as a 'profoundly postromantic style of reading' (1997: 73).

Not everyone agrees, however: contemporary scholarship suggests that the debate on characterization in Second Testament texts remains lively. While Tolbert's caution about reading Gospel characters in twenty-first century ways is instructive, it is not clear to me whether and to what extent contemporary readers can in fact read texts as first century readers/hearers received them. Contemporary readers have learned to balance plot and character in their assessments of the power of narratives, and it is inevitable that they will bring such practices to their reading of the Gospels. In addition, scholars such as Burnett (1993) and McCracken (1993) suggest not only that the ancients had a greater interest in characters as personalities than we have hitherto thought, but also that contemporary readers of first-century narratives appreciate the dynamic relationships that exist between character and author and between character and reader in ways that do not do violence to the text. Feminist biblical scholar Alice Bach offers a way of rereading female characters in biblical texts that challenges the power of the so-called 'omniscient narrator'. She argues that a 'suspicious narratee' should replace the 'ideal reader' and should be wary of reading the characters simply as the narrator intends:

> [A]n irritable or suspicious narratee could question the story told through the narrator's fixed gaze and surreptitiously glance around the fictive landscape to pick up clues about the story ignored by the narrator. In the biblical narrative, irritable voices, like Miriam questioning Moses' power as sole prophet of Israel, are quickly silenced. Their cause must be taken up by the equally suspicious or irritable reader (Bach 1993: 67).

Bach wants to prevent female characters from 'oozing away' as they surely would if real readers simply followed the cues of the implied author/narrator. Instead, feminist readers can respond 'actively' to characters and sometimes 'even appropriate them'. She argues that characters are not fixed entities within narratives whose influence is limited to the roles assigned by the implied author/narrator. Rather, they can take on an existence in the mind of the reader that, while grounded in the narrative, is at the same time also grounded in the real reader's own historical reality. Such a view of characters offers the feminist reader a map for reading the women characters in Mark's story.

In the following study of Mk 16.1-8, I will explore the text from a feminist-liberationist perspective, using socio-rhetorical strategies. Unlike Matera's study of Matthew's concluding story, this one will take account of the three women characters in order to assess the text's capacity to act as an interpretive key for a rereading of Mark's stories of women.

## Part B: The Text

### B.1. The Characters

Mark begins the narrative of the empty tomb by linking the Sabbath's close with the reference to its day of Preparation in 15.42. The careful attention to the passing of time has characterized Mark's Passion Narrative since the reference to the 'two days' before the Passover with which the narrative opens in 14.1. In this way, Mark creates a space between the burial of Jesus' body by Joseph of Arimathea and the discovery of the empty tomb by the women during which (the reader assumes) the women observe the Sabbath rest. When Mark begins the story of the women's journey to Jesus' burial place, however, all notions of rest are quickly laid aside. The narrative picks up pace, increases the level of tension in the reader and focuses clearly on the activity of the women. Every activity described, except the message of the young man, refers to the women. They 'bought'; 'went'; 'had been saying'; 'looked up'; 'saw'; 'entered'; 'saw'; 'were alarmed'; 'went out'; 'fled'; 'said nothing'; 'were afraid'. They are clearly central to the telling of the story.

But how has Mark constructed their characters? The women named are Mary Magdalene, Mary the mother of James, and Salome. Mary Magdalene and Salome have been referred to earlier in the Gospel of Mark, in 15.40-41, where Mark names them among the women who used to follow and serve Jesus when he was in Galilee. The use of the Greek imperfect (ἠκολούθομν; διηκόνουν) suggests a habitual following and serving rather than a reference to their having followed after Jesus on his way to Jerusalem. In Mark's description of the women, the reader hears echoes of the particular discipleship terminology employed in the Gospel where those invited by Jesus follow him (1.17-18), and where Jesus spells out the necessity for the disciple not only to follow but to serve (10.41-45). Commentators and translators alike have sought to interpret the women's activity in terms of women's work traditionally understood, and have argued that the women followed Jesus for the purpose of 'looking after him' or 'attending to his needs' (see, for example, Witherington 1984). While it is true that in the dominant narrative no woman is described as a disciple, a resistant reading of 15.40-41 opens up the possibility that women can be counted among Jesus' Galilean disciples (see Munro 1982; Malbon 1983; Schüssler Fiorenza 1983; Myers 1990; Kinukawa 1994; Schottroff 1993; Dewey 1994).

'Mary the mother of James the younger and of Joses' is identified as the third woman in the group that witnessed Jesus' death from afar (15.40), and it is not clear that 'Mary the mother of James' in 16.1 is the same person. Mary Magdalene and Mary the mother of Joses had witnessed the burial of Jesus (15.47). Hooker (1991) suggests that Mark may have combined several traditions in the telling of the death, burial and discovery of the empty tomb of Jesus. Whatever about the history of the text, Mark places three women at the empty tomb, at least two of whom had been named (belatedly) by the evangelist as having been among those who used to follow and serve Jesus in Galilee. At least two, and possibly three, form a narrative link between the death and resurrection of Jesus, so that, as Hester notes, they are 'entrusted by the reader with the success of the story' (Hester 1995: 62).

Yet the feminist reader of Mark cannot be as confident as Hester in assuming that women characters already constructed by Mark as trustworthy and faithful will necessarily remain so. While I agree that the immediate context of the ending (the faithful ministry of the women disciples at the cross and burial—15.40-47) prepares the reader to expect that they will be faithful to the end, the Markan conclusion shares with so many other aspects of Mark's Gospel the sense that nothing is inevitable. The reader has already discovered that the crowds, disciples, religious leaders, family members and hometown friends who *should* have comprehended who Jesus was and followed him, fail to do so. Early in the Gospel, the narrator begins to destabilize the reader's expectations, and continues to destabilize them to the end. In the story of Jesus' cure of the paralysed man (2.1-12) Mark first intimates that some of the religious establishment will object to Jesus' claims and plot his destruction; his mother and family accept that Jesus is out of his mind and attempt to remove him from the public sphere (3.21); and the people of his hometown object to his wisdom and power (6.1-6). Where the disciples are concerned, the see-sawing image of their relationship with Jesus convinces even the most superficial reader that expecting a neat outcome to this subplot flies in the face of the evidence Mark assembles. Initially enthusiastic (1.17-20), the disciples become fearful of Jesus (4.41) and increasingly unable to understand him (6.52). While they continue to follow him, most of them ultimately desert him (14.50), though the promise of a reunion in Galilee remains (14.28). The young man at the tomb reminds the women of this meeting (16.7), but it is not reported in the story. There is an instability in Mark's narrative that is evident from the beginning, carefully developed in the body of the narrative, and confirmed in the ending. It cautions against expecting a positive resolution to the story, and guides the reader through what Sternberg (1990: 94) describes as 'pockets of darkness and ambiguity' to the end.

For the feminist reader of Mark, the instability of the narrative has an added dimension. What I have described above as the see-sawing effect of Mark's story of Jesus becomes a veritable roller-coaster when the stories of women are considered. Women first appear in Mark's Gospel in the context of Jesus' proclamation of the Reign of God and his invitation to the four male disciples that immediately follows. Jesus then sets about defining the Reign of God by a frenetic round of exorcism and healing. The healing of Simon's mother-in-law constitutes the first such action Jesus performs in Mark's Gospel. She is healed on the first 'day' of Jesus' ministry in Capernaum, and her response to her healing is to 'serve' (διηκόνει) Jesus and those with him (1.29-31). Soon after, however, Jesus ascends a mountain and summons 'those whom he wanted' and names them apostles. Their mission is to 'proclaim the message and to…cast out demons' (3.13-15). No woman is named among the group of twelve specially chosen by Jesus to share his ministry of preaching and healing.

As the narrative unfolds, Mark begins to deal with those who fail to accept Jesus and his message. Among them is Jesus' mother. In 3.21 Jesus' 'family' including, we can assume, his 'mother and brothers' referred to later in the pericope (3.31), attempt to 'restrain' Jesus on the basis of reports that he was out of his mind. His mother, therefore, is depicted by Mark as among those who do not understand Jesus, and Jesus uses her presence to affirm a new family structure for his own followers that does not include her (3.34-35). In chapter five, by contrast, Jesus claims as 'daughter' a woman he restores to health. In the intercalated stories of the healing of the haemorrhaging woman and the raising to life of the daughter of Jairus, the woman who is healed knows something of Jesus' power and believes she can access it for herself. Jesus interprets her healing as the result of her faith (5.34)—remarkable because of the lack of faith evident in the disciples (4.40) and in the hometown crowd (6.6), whose stories frame the woman's own.

Positive images of women quickly fade, however, when Mark follows the stories of the women's healing with that of Herod's daughter, Herodias. The young girl and her mother (also named Herodias) conspire to have John the Baptist executed when Herod offers to reward her for her dancing (6.17-29). The women in this story have become widely recognized as prototypes of the evil seductress (see Anderson 1992), and while they are not directly linked with the activity of Jesus, their presence in the narrative is a stark reminder of the power of misogynist texts to shape interpretation. In the following chapter, Mark tells the story of Jesus' encounter with a Syrophoenician woman. Here, a Gentile woman bests Jesus in a theological debate and wins healing for her daughter (7.24-30). Set in the context of Mark's exploration of the place of Gentiles in Jesus' mission, the story poses the question of their inclusion and answers it affirmatively via a woman's voice. In terms of the roller-coaster image already proposed, feminist readers have experienced both the 'heights' and the 'depths' several times over as they approach the mid-point of Mark's Gospel.

In the critical central section of the Gospel (8.21–10.52), Mark's Jesus journeys towards his suffering and death in Jerusalem. On the way, he three times predicts his fate in Jerusalem and follows each prediction with instructions to his uncomprehending followers about the nature of true discipleship (8.27-33; 9.30-37; 10.32-40). Included in this section of the Gospel is the story of the transfiguration of Jesus in the presence of the three male disciples, Peter, James and John (9.2-9). They see a vision of Jesus' divinity that they are commanded to keep secret until after his resurrection (9.9). In this climactic part of the Gospel there are no stories of women (Dewey 1994: 496), and references to them are confined to Jesus' teaching about divorce (10.2-12), his quoting of the commandments (10.19), and the inclusion of 'sisters' and 'mothers' among all that the follower of Jesus must leave in order to be a disciple. Moreover, readers have to deal with the notions of servanthood and suffering offered here by Jesus as characteristics of the faithful disciple. The images of 'tak[ing] up their cross' (8.34) and of being 'servant' (10.33) and 'slave' (10.34) require considerable deconstruction by contemporary feminist readers (Dewey 1994: 496).

When a woman next appears in Mark's Gospel it is almost at the end of Jesus' time in Jerusalem, when he has spent considerable time teaching in the Temple. The widow is an enigmatic character in Mark. Jesus never meets her, and she doesn't speak. Jesus observes her putting money in the Temple treasury, and laments that the very institution that should be supporting her is, in fact, reducing her to a pauper (Myers 1990: 322).

By the time the feminist reader arrives at the beginning of the Passion Narrative in Mark, she could be forgiven for expecting little in the way of women's stories in the climactic final chapters. However, not only do women appear in the Markan Passion Narrative, but they also have significant roles to play in the events that unfold there. The story of the woman who anoints Jesus at Bethany (14.3-9) functions as the prologue to the Passion Narrative and finally resolves the question of Jesus' identity: he is the Messiah who will suffer and die. Images of women in the Markan Passion Narrative are not uniform, however. The story of the servant girl who taunts Peter (14.66-72) could appear at first as an anti-woman story in a similar way to the story of Herodias. However, there is a sense in which the servant girl effectively puts Peter on trial and brings to fulfilment Jesus' prediction that Peter would deny him three times. Her persistent accusations challenge Peter to acknowledge the discipleship he had vowed at the Passover meal (14.31), but he is unable to answer her truthfully.

In contrast to Peter and the other disciples who run for their lives after Jesus' arrest and trial, women disciples watch his crucifixion from a distance and witness the last moments of Jesus' life (15.40-41). Two of them are present at his burial, observing 'where the body was laid' (15.47). The women become the thread that weaves together the events of Jesus' death, burial and resurrection. Three of them appear again in the closing stages of the narrative where Mark tells the story of the discovery of the empty tomb.

It is possible to argue, then, that when the feminist reader arrives at the conclusion of Mark's Gospel and discovers that women will play a central role in it, she is already uneasy about the way women's stories have functioned in the dominant narrative. She has never really felt comfortable as a real reader of Mark. While Hester (1995: 62) argues that real readers '…see no duplicity on the part of the implied author or implied reader' the feminist reader has wandered around in the Markan text and located the androcentric bias of its author. She has noted the positive images of women in several Markan stories, but she has also questioned the worldview that has either presented women as being of marginal importance to the story of Jesus, or that has demonized them as clearly antithetical to it. If general readers of Mark are constantly made aware of the instability in the narrative, the feminist reader has had to contend not only with a story that constantly challenges her sense of the inevitable but also with her own deep suspicion of the way in which this Gospel has used stories of women. For her, the women in Mark's Gospel are clearly at his mercy.

However, as I have noted, several scholars working on characterization in Second Testament texts have proposed ways of breaking the narrator's stranglehold on the characters that feature in the narrative. At the point in Mark's Gospel where the feminist reader most fears for the fate of the women characters that feature in the last days of Jesus' life, she can do as Bach suggests and take up their cause. She can give them a context and a voice: she can imagine their key roles in the Jesus movement as disciples and co-workers in Galilee, and she can fill in the gaps in the story of their journey to Jerusalem with Jesus in anticipation of his suffering and death. She can imagine the scenario that leads to their witnessing his crucifixion and burial and can write the script (as Mark does not) for their determination to anoint his body. In the mind of the feminist reader, the women characters thus have a story to tell that goes beyond the narrative but is nonetheless grounded in it. Their appearance in 15.40-41 and 15.46 and their reappearance at 16.1 provide the grounds for such a story. Further, the feminist reader knows that at the beginning of the empty tomb narrative, Mark's story of Jesus is about to be resolved, and the women will somehow be central to its resolution. They will take the reader to the heart of the questions Mark has posed throughout the narrative and will invite a response from the reader.

*B.2. The Characters as Female Disciples*
As the story of the empty tomb begins to unfold Mark notes that the women bought spices so that they might go and anoint (ἀλείφωσιν) the body of Jesus (16.1). Careful readers of the Gospel might logically conclude that there will be no anointing because there has already been a proleptic anoint-

ing of his body by the woman of Bethany. However, Mark's use of the Greek ἀλείφωσιν to describe the intended anointing is instructive. In the story of the Bethany anointing (14.3-9), Jesus refers to the woman's action as an anointing (μυρίσαι) for burial (14.8). In the story of the empty tomb, however, the women's action is described in the same way as Mark has described the teaching and healing ministry of the twelve in 6.12-13: 'So they went out and proclaimed that all should repent. They cast out many demons, and anointed [ἤλειφον] with oil many who were sick and cured them'. This is the only other occurrence of the verb in Mark.

In the Graeco-Roman world, ἀλείφω was generally associated with healing and exorcism, rather than with the anointing of the dead body. Hence, its use to describe the activity of the Twelve is particularly appropriate. As Schlier notes, 'The apostles heal in connection with their preaching of repentance and their expulsion of demons, and in this regard they are messengers and bearers of the inbreaking kingdom of God' (1965: 229).

Its use in 16.1, however, is unusual. The narrator has already demonstrated that the women know Jesus is dead. Why would they not be described as intending to anoint (μυρίζω) his dead body? Mark's use of ἀλείφωσιν here is both unusual and provocative in view of the fact that the narrator has already described at least two of these women as having *followed* and *served* Jesus while he was in Galilee (15.40-41). Despite the fact that Mark has nowhere referred to women disciples in Jesus' company, the picture that emerges from 15.40–16.8 (at least for the feminist reader) suggests a very different reality for women from that prevailing in the narrative as a whole. To following and serving is now added the disciple's ministry of healing. In 16.1 Mary Magdalene, Mary the mother of James, and Salome intend to anoint Jesus' body perhaps in the same way as they had anointed the bodies of the living while they were his disciples in Galilee. And as they healed with oil, they also engaged in the proclamation of the kingdom of God, as Schlier explains in his reference to the apostles. In the story of the empty tomb, their intention to anoint Jesus' body will also involve them in the work of proclamation, another of the disciple's roles. This time, however, it is not the kingdom of God that they will be instructed to announce, but rather Jesus' resurrection, the kingdom's most powerful symbol.

On the way to the tomb after sunrise the women talk to each other about the problem of rolling away the stone, acknowledging that they would not be able to do this themselves (16.3). On the level of the narrative, their failure to enlist the help they need to ensure access to Jesus' body makes little sense, but it is no doubt intended by Mark to create the suspense necessary for their encounter with the young man in the tomb. When the women enter the tomb in search of Jesus' body they see a young man, 'dressed in a white robe, sitting on the right side; and they were alarmed' (16.5). The young man attempts to reassure them, reveals to them the news of Jesus' resurrection, and charges them with its proclamation.

While numbers of Markan scholars see the young man in the tomb as linked to the young man in Gethsemane who flees naked from the scene of Jesus' arrest (14.51-52), it seems that another parallel might be found in Mark's story of the transfiguration (9.2-10). In the story of the empty tomb, three women disciples encounter a messenger dressed in white. In the earlier story, Jesus is transfigured in the presence of three male disciples, Peter, James and John. Mark describes Jesus' clothing as 'white' (λευκά) with the same adjective as for the young man's (λευκήν), but accentuates the whiteness of Jesus' apparel to underscore the male disciples' experience of theophany. Moses and Elijah speak with Jesus as the disciples look on. Peter, like the women walking to the tomb, chatters nonsensically. Peter, James and John are frightened (9.6—ἔκφοβοι καὶ ἐγένετο) at the vision of Jesus transfigured, and the women respond similarly when charged by the young man with the message of Jesus' resurrection (16.8—ἐφοβοῦντο γάρ).

While the parallels between the two stories are interesting, it is clear that the empty tomb story, unlike the story of the transfiguration, is not told as a theophany. The women receive no vision of Jesus and, importantly, no interpretation of such a vision that links it with his resurrection. The women encounter a young man, not God or an angel. Their fear is not a response to what they see but rather to what they are told by the messenger. While the young man's presence causes the women to be 'alarmed' (καὶ ἐξεθαμβήθησαν), Mark reserves the stronger descriptors of fear and terror for the women's reaction to the young man's revelation that Jesus had been raised from death. In the narrative of the transfiguration, by contrast, the three male disciples are privileged visionaries of the divine Jesus. Jesus chooses them to accompany him to the mountain (the traditional location of theophanies), reveals himself to them as the beloved of God, and then associates their experience with post-resurrection proclamation: '…he ordered them to tell no one about what they had seen [μηδενὶ διηγήσωνται ἃ εἶδον…], until after the Son of Man had risen from the dead' (9.9). The story concludes with the disciples obeying Jesus' injunction but continuing to wonder about the meaning of 'rising from the dead' (9.10).

In the context of the Markan narrative, the revelation of Jesus to the three male disciples is of particular interest. They first appear as a trio in the story of the raising of the daughter of Jairus from death (5.37). Here, they act as witnesses, together with Jairus and his wife, to Jesus' power to restore the young girl's life (5.42). They are 'overcome with amazement' (ἐξέστησαν [εὐθὺς] ἐκστάσει), a response similar to, though less intense than, that of the women at the tomb who were seized by terror and amazement (εἶχε δὲ αὐτὰς τρόμος καὶ ἔκστασις) in response to the young man's message (16.8).

They are witnesses again in the latter stages of the narrative when Jesus suffers in anticipation of his death (14.32-42). Summoned by him to 'keep awake' (14.34), Peter, James and John are overcome by sleep each time Jesus looks to them for support.

In the significant middle portion of the Gospel (8.21–10.52), Mark has Jesus three times predict his passion, death and resurrection, and three times his disciples fail to understand him. After the first passion prediction Peter remonstrates with Jesus, only to be banished as one who thinks 'human things' rather than 'divine things' (8.33). On the second occasion, the disciples do not understand Jesus' prediction, and are too frightened to ask him (9.32); and after the third prediction, James and John, looking to their own future, ask Jesus for exalted places in his kingdom after the predicted events are concluded (10.37).

The three male disciples who are named as witnesses both to the raising to life of the daughter of Jairus as well as the transfiguration, and who have been led by Jesus to link it with his resurrection, obey Jesus' command to silence but do not comprehend the passion predictions. Not only are they unable to accompany Jesus in Gethsemane despite his plea for their support, but also with the exception of Peter they run from the garden when Jesus is arrested. Peter follows as far as the house of the high priest but finally falters when challenged to acknowledge his connection with Jesus. On the other hand, the women who are commissioned to announce his resurrection have been long-standing disciples of Jesus since the time of the Galilean ministry. They have come up to Jerusalem with Jesus and have been the only disciples to witness his death and burial. All the narrative indicators suggest that they will do as they have been instructed but, amazingly (so it seems), they fail in their task. According to Mark, the women are beside themselves with fear, run from the tomb and say nothing to anyone (καὶ οὐδὲν εἶπαν), 'for they were afraid' (ἐφοβοῦντο γάρ). As Donald Juel (1994: 115) concludes, '[N]either the stirring words of the divine messenger nor the empty tomb succeed in making evangelists of the women who have come to do their duty to a corpse.'

Juel suggests that had the women obeyed the young man's directive, they would have been preachers of the Gospel (evangelists). His assumption is borne out by the text. The young man's instruction to the women to tell the other disciples of Jesus' resurrection is given clearly and strongly, with two successive aorist imperatives used by the narrator to underline the seriousness of their mission: ἀλλὰ ὑπάγετε εἴπατε…(16.7). The verb, εἴπατε (tell), the aorist imperative form of λεγω, links the women's mission with others in Mark's narrative who have taught or proclaimed. Preaching was one of the activities to which Jesus calls the Twelve when he first invites them to be with him (3.14). The word κηρυσσω, employed in 3.14 and in 1.4, 1.45, 5.20 and 7.36, describes the preaching activity not only of the Twelve but of John the Baptist, the leper, the demoniac and the crowds who witness Jesus' healing acts. It is also used to describe Jesus' own announcement of the kingdom of God (1.14, 38) and his understanding of its future proclamation (13.10; 14.9). While it is true that the verb used to describe the preaching mission given to the women is not κηρυσσω, it is also true that both the activity and the content of proclamation are not always conveyed by forms of the verb κηρυσσω but are in fact described in various ways in the Second Testament (Friedrich 1965: 696). Mark frequently uses the theologically charged λογος (Debrunner 1965: 100-102) to refer to Jesus' teaching (2.2; 4.14, 15, 16, 17, 18, 19, 20, 33; 7.13; 8.32, 38; 9.10; 10.22, 24; 11.29; 12.13; 13.31; 14.39), and to describe the preaching activity of both the leper (1.45) and the Syrophoenician woman (7.29). Thus, it is appropriate that when the women are commanded to 'go and say', both the content of their message and the activity they are instructed to perform fit the category of preaching as Mark has understood it. Juel is quite right to describe them as evangelists. He also describes them as failed evangelists: at the very moment when the women are called upon to exercise the disciple's role of preaching, Mark silences them and constructs them as failures. The women's silence is the element of the ending that virtually every Markan scholar describes as 'shocking' or 'unexpected'. It is also the element that gives the Gospel its unique hard edge by handing the narrative back to the reader for completion.

I would argue, however, that for the feminist reader the ending, far from being shocking, is in some sense anticipated. In the course of her reading of Mark, the feminist reader has become suspicious of Mark's treatment of women, and has seen the cavalier way in which they have been both incorporated and omitted from the dominant narrative. If Mark can deal in such fashion with the serving, following and healing ministries of women, as he seems to in 15.40-16.1, then it comes as no surprise that he can deal in like manner with their role as apostles and proclaimers of the gospel.

Is the silence of the women at 16.8, then, the final word about their discipleship, even though a resistant reading of their roles in the Passion Narrative reveal them to be long-time followers and ministers of Jesus (15.40-41) who had probably also been engaged in a discipleship ministry of healing and preaching (16.1, 7)? Is Mark's reader meant to understand from the transfiguration narrative that the proclamation of the resurrection belongs after all to the male disciples beyond narrative time, even though within the narrative they fail to understand Jesus and ultimately desert him?

*B.3. The Failure of the Women*
The theme of the women's failure at 16.8 is taken up by many scholars of Mark's Gospel, including feminist scholars. Writing recently on the relevance of Mark, Telford assesses the role of women in the Gospel and concludes that the picture is decidedly negative. He refers to the women at the tomb as 'disobedient' and argues that they fail as witnesses to the resurrection: 'In this respect, then, they are no better than their male counterparts, for whom, indeed, in narrative terms, they act as 'stand-ins' (Telford 1999: 234).

Telford's view that the women fail is shared by numbers of scholars, including van Iersel (1998); Hooker (1991); Kelber (1985); and Schweizer (1981). Among feminist scholars who share this view are Luise Schottroff (1993) and Joanna Dewey (1994). Schottroff, while acknowledging that the women's response could be explained by their fear in the presence of the numinous, nonetheless describes the women's flight and silence at 16.8 as 'probably the gravest failure of the disciples in the Gospel of Mark' (1993: 187). Joanna Dewey agrees that the women fail, though her stance is somewhat different. She argues that Mark leaves feminist readers with little option than to conclude that these women disciples, like all the other disciples, including the men, fail as faithful followers of Jesus. She goes further and suggests that Mark, too, has failed: 'He has failed to overcome his androcentric perspective, his assumption of male privilege. He has failed to dramatize the egalitarian way of discipleship that he teaches. Rather he uses the women, as he uses children, slaves, and foreigners, as models for discipleship, as examples for the men' (Schottroff 1993: 508).

Another group of Markan scholars wants to see the women's failure in a more positive light. Some, for example, attribute their silence to the awe generated by an experience of the numinous and not to cowardice or fear (for example, Malbon 1983; Sabin 1998; Mitchell 2001). However, this argument must rely on interpreting the young man's encounter with the women as an apparition of the divine. While the young man's presence in the tomb is entirely unexpected and his clothing unusual, a comparison with the telling of the transfiguration has shown that Mark does not describe the empty tomb story in the language of theophany. Still other scholars (including feminist scholars) want to argue that the women's silence was only temporary or that their silence was restricted to outsiders (for example, Schüssler Fiorenza 1983). This view, too, is problematical because in its attempt to rehabilitate the women and conclude the story as the other evangelists have, it appears to be trapped in a historicist reading, and claims more for the Markan text than the text itself can argue.

Where does this leave the feminist reader of Mark? Is there no viable alternative to interpreting the women's failure at 16.8 as the definitive evaluation of their role in the Gospel? Dewey argues that '[w]e must go beyond Mark, to envision and create a true discipleship of equals…' (1994: 508), but this suggests that for those who commit themselves to shaping such a reality the Gospel might be more of a liability than an asset. And where does the challenge to 'go beyond Mark' leave the second-time (familiar) feminist reader who re-listens, rereads and must continue to reinterpret the characters and roles of women as Mark has constructed them in the Gospel?

The question of how a feminist reader deals with the ending of Mark's Gospel, and by extension, with all of the stories of women contained there, is a vexed one. The assumption of failure (the majority view) is hard to resist because the text at 16.8 seems to insist on it. Hester (1995: 68) has suggested that at the conclusion of Mark's Gospel the reader must enter the story and 'rescue' it. What kind of 'rescue' might a feminist reader consider, since 'rescuing' texts is anathema to the feminist biblical enterprise? Hester, I think, is not suggesting the kind of rescue that erases the Gospel's difficulties but one that claims its central premises as a dynamic text for now. For feminist readers this is a hazardous undertaking because it must include a reading of the Gospel that not only tests the narrator's reliability (as Hester advises) but also analyses the rhetoric of the text and its constructions of women's characters to see if the Gospel can be liberating for women and all oppressed people today. Is there a way through this impasse?

*B.4. The Failure of Mark*
At this point it is helpful to return to Joanna Dewey's notion of Mark (the evangelist's) failure. She has argued that Mark 'has failed to dramatize the

egalitarian way of discipleship that he teaches' (Dewey 1994: 508) and has instead used the women as examples for the men, indeed even to shame the men of Mark's community 'into doing better'. I agree with Dewey that Mark does not treat women as the equals of men in the Gospel. I think she is right to insist on their lesser status in the narrative, particularly where discipleship is concerned. I disagree, however, with her conclusion that Mark uses stories of women to teach the men about being better disciples. I don't think this is clear in the narrative. Nor do I agree that women are 'substitutes' for the men, because where they appear in strong roles, as, for example, in the Passion Narrative, there is nothing in the previous behaviour of the male disciples that leads the reader to expect that they would have behaved so faithfully had they been able to last the distance.

Dewey's notion of Mark's failure, however, is interesting, though I would want to describe it in more specific terms. I think Mark's real failure is in regard to the women at the empty tomb. There is a sense in which, had these women been allowed by the writer to proclaim the news of Jesus' resurrection to the other disciples, and had the male disciples been portrayed as too frightened to speak, the narrative would retain something of its hard edge while at the same time being true to the picture of male discipleship (particularly that of Peter, James and John) that Mark had constructed. In reality, Mark has not succeeded in papering over the evidence for the discipleship of these women, but has still managed to deliver the ultimate insult of using them as silent and terrified females to goad his audience into being (unlike them) brave proclaimers of the Gospel. Feminist readers, then, must deal with the two-edged sword that this story is: while the resistant reader claims the true discipleship of women in Mark, the dominant narrative has both silenced their proclamation and reduced them to inaction. How will the second-time feminist reader of Mark deal with the rest of the Gospel, reading through the lens of the conclusion? Perhaps 'retelling' rather than 'rescue' better describes the kind of activity required.

*B.5. Strategies for Rereading/Retelling The Gospel of Mark*
The re-telling of Mark to which every reader is summoned at 16.8 could consist for the feminist reader not only in a critical and resistant rereading of the text but also in a rediscovery of the powerful roles of women in earliest Christianity as they have been remembered beyond the text of Mark and, indeed, of the Second Testament itself. Contemporary feminist biblical scholarship is increasingly paying attention not only to biblical and extra-biblical texts but also to epigraphs, papyri, icons, and coins and

other archaeological finds to shed light on the lives of women in the early centuries of the Common Era (Kraemer 1988, 1992; Cardman 1999; Eisen 2000). They argue that epigraphical and other evidence, like literary evidence, does not offer positive proof of women's activities in the ancient world of Judaism and emerging Christianity (Eisen 2000: 20). However, it does constitute another piece of the jigsaw and, unlike the texts of the Second Testament, is sometimes the work of women themselves. Tomb inscriptions, personal letters, legal documents and contracts have not passed through the censorship of a male writing elite in the way that biblical texts probably did. They represent a way in which women tell something of their own stories unhindered.

This new research has produced some surprising results. First, it confirms the fluidity of (in this case) early Christianity, its local variations and cultural differences:

> [T]hose who write about practical questions of church constitution must always keep in mind what Firmilian wrote in a letter to Cyprian of Carthage, namely that not everything was true in Rome that was the rule in Jerusalem, and that in most of the other provinces as well a good many things diverged according to the differences of the locality and the people (Eisen 2000: 6).

Secondly, it shows clearly that in such a context women often thrived as members of Christian communities. Women's lives in early Christianity were as varied as the places in which they lived them. Eisen argues that it is not possible to trace a simple line from an early egalitarianism to a creeping patriarchalism and explain the differences in women's religious lives accordingly. Christian women throughout the Mediterranean region often exercised considerable religious and economic independence not only in earliest Christianity but also for several hundred years after Christianity had become the official religion of the Roman Empire. Despite what the texts of the Second Testament say concerning the roles from which women were excluded, women's lives demonstrated a vastly different reality:

> It is clear that women were active in the expansion and shaping of the church in the first centuries: they were apostles, prophets, teachers, presbyters, enrolled widows, deacons, bishops and stewards. They preached the Gospel, they spoke prophetically and in tongues, they went on mission, they prayed, they presided over the Lord's Supper, they broke the bread and gave the cup, they baptized, they taught, they created theology, they were active in care for the poor and the sick, they were administrators and managers of burial places (Eisen 2000: 274).

Where women's apostleship (or discipleship) is concerned, it is not epigraphical but literary evidence that proves valuable to the feminist reader of Mark. Within the Second Testament itself, Paul acknowledges Junia, the apostle (Rom. 16.7), and the early church writers, Origen and Hippolytus, give the title 'apostles' to Mary Magdalene and the women at the tomb (Eisen 2000: 55). Beyond the canon, however, can be found the most telling evidence for the discipleship of women and for the controversies it evoked. While it is true that stories of women in Gnostic and apocryphal texts are neither frequent nor uniformly positive, it is also true that they can act as important commentators on women's religious experiences in the early Christian world and can thus contribute to the formation of contemporary feminist theologies. The *Acts of Thecla*, together with some of the Gnostic texts, affirms women's roles as upholders and guarantors of the community's traditions concerning Jesus of Nazareth. The *Acts of Thecla* (dated to the mid-second century CE) is usually set within the text of the *Acts of Paul*, but, as McGinn argues, it creates a 'nearly perfect reversal' (1994: 806) of the pro-Paul and anti-women stance of the *Acts of Paul*. While the *Acts of Thecla* reveals the hallmarks of early Christian apocalyptic thinking and its emphasis on virginity and asceticism, it nonetheless paints a remarkable picture of a second-century woman apostle who appears both stronger and more committed to the Gospel than does Paul. In Cardman's view, Thecla could represent numbers of late first-century/ early second-century women who preached and baptized, claiming Paul's authority. Yet, as she notes, Tertullian blames Thecla for the profusion of women's ministries in second-century Christianity, and later interpretations of Thecla's story attempted to reduce its power by portraying her as martyr and virgin, even though there is no evidence for this in the text: 'Thus reduced to more familiar proportions, the transformed image of Thecla furthered the exclusion of women from ministry by erasing the memory of her as a woman who had preached and baptized' (Cardman 1999: 302).

Where the Gnostic texts are concerned, the *Gospel of Mary* addresses the same controversial question of the leadership and authority of women in early Christianity. In this text, Mary Magdalene is depicted not only as the ideal disciple but also as a leader within the discipleship group. Interestingly, in the light of the problematical conclusion to Mark's Gospel, in the *Gospel of Mary* Mary Magdalene proclaims certain teachings to the disciples Peter and Andrew, but is not believed. Mary's response is to challenge Peter, and she convinces him of the authenticity of her teaching by aligning it with the Saviour's own words (McGuire 1999: 257-59). Salome, too, makes an appearance in the Gnostic tradition as a disciple: in the *Gospel of Thomas* she challenges Jesus' teaching and then claims to be his follower:

> Jesus said, 'Two will recline on a couch; one will die, one will live.'
> Salome said, 'Who are you, mister? You have climbed onto my couch and eaten from my table as if you are from someone.'
> Jesus said to her, 'I am the one who comes from what is whole. I was granted from the things of my Father.'
> 'I am your disciple.'
> 'For this reason I say, if one is [whole], one will be filled with light, but if one is divided, one will be filled with darkness' (Log. 61).

In the same text, Jesus says clearly that in order to enter 'the Father's domain', both male and female require transformation, yet in the final saying of Jesus in the *Gospel of Thomas* he resolves to make Mary Magdalene 'male' in order to save her. This is in reply to Simon Peter's request to 'them' to have Mary banished 'for females don't deserve life' (Log. 114).

Mark's story of the women who discover the empty tomb suggests a line of continuity from the emerging Christian communities to the practices of the earliest church. In Mark, as in the Gnostic and apocryphal texts, the evidence of women's pivotal roles in the telling of the story of Jesus' life, death and resurrection surely reflects their pivotal roles in the communities that followed him. On the other hand, what I would argue to be the deliberate suppression of women's agency in earliest Christianity, evident in Mark and in the extra-biblical texts, testifies to the battle over women's participation in the church that the women of Mark's community knew and that is still being waged today. At the level of the narrative, 16.1-8 need not be seen by the feminist reader as evidence of the failure of the women as disciples of Jesus. Instead, it can be seen as evidence of Mark's failure as a writer to produce characters (the three women) that are in the end believable.

## Conclusion

Kermode argued that the best texts are those that do not 'sever us from our losses', and that 'live in change' into an indeterminate future (Kermode 1967: 179). For feminist readers of Mark, the ending of the Gospel that effectively discounts the discipleship of women touches a raw nerve that will always remind us of what we have lost. When the Gospel is retold through the lens of the conclusion it will require a particular retelling. This cannot be one that simply weaves together the threads of the story as Mark has left them strewn across the narrative landscape. Rather, the retelling must include new threads drawn from our own historical realities of oppression in church and society, our experiences of injustice and marginalization, or our resolution to dismantle the structures of oppression in which we are implicated. Such a stance will not only enable us to call Mark to account for the stories of women in the Gospel, but will also give new voices to the ones so dramatically silenced.

READING THE SILENCE OF WOMEN IN GENESIS 34

Julie Kelso

> The Old Testament does not tell us of a
> single happy mother–daughter couple,
> and Eve comes into the world
> motherless. (Luce Irigaray 1994: 100)

It is rather difficult to challenge Irigaray's matter-of-factness when it comes to the happy mother–daughter relationship and its conspicuous absence in the Hebrew Bible. This statement about the Old Testament, given as the epigraph of my essay, was made in a lecture in Syracuse, Palermo in 1989 titled 'The Forgotten Mystery of Female Ancestry' (Irigaray 1994). Even a sideward glance at her work to date confirms that Irigaray is clearly fonder of Greek myths and tragedies such as Aeschylus's *The Oresteian Trilogy*, where Clytemnestra murders her husband Agamemnon to avenge his sacrifice of Iphigenia, their daughter, for military purposes. In 'The Forgotten Mystery of Female Ancestry' it is the various versions of the Demeter–Persephone/Kore myth that Irigaray pursues.[1] In these stories, she argues, we can still see what once was a powerful bond between women, a bond that has its own history. Demeter is the mother of a daughter, and she is a mother who 'agrees to be fertile *with her daughter*' (Irigaray 1993: 79). Unlike the Hebrew Bible, these Greek myths have not yet managed to drain their literary universe of that once-revered bond between women. While these Greek myths and their different versions mark the process of the erasure of female ancestries or maternal genealogies, it seems that as far as Irigaray is concerned, the Hebrew Bible leaves us only the legacy of that very success, albeit on different cultural turf. So what are we to make of the appearances of mothers and daughters in the Hebrew Bible?[2]

---

1. For an in-depth discussion on the shifts in Irigaray's thinking on the theme of female genealogies through various readings of Greek myths, see Muraro 1994.
2. For a survey of the mother–daughter relationship in the Hebrew Bible, see Bronner 1999.

What are we to make of Dinah and Leah? The question itself seems strange at this point because, apart from the afterthought-like note of Leah's birth of a daughter in 30.21, Dinah's brief story in ch. 34 has, on the surface, little if nothing to do with her being the daughter of Leah. However, the story does open with Dinah given the genealogical epithet that ties her to her mother: 'And Dinah, the daughter of Leah, whom she bore for Jacob, went out to see into the daughters of the land' (34.1). She is בת־לאה, 'the daughter of Leah'. It is this feature of Genesis 34 that has always intrigued me, and gives me the question that drives my reading of Genesis 34. Why is Dinah introduced as בת־לאה, 'the daughter of Leah', rather than as בת־יעקב, 'the daughter of Jacob', particularly given that this is quite clearly a text operating under patriarchal cultural assumptions which include the control and ownership of the daughter by the father? To insist on asking this question of Genesis 34, however, generates a number of other problems that need to be addressed. First of all, why is the silence of women so deafening (despite the relative lack of critical attention given to this silence) in a story about their exchange? And how are we to translate הילדה (34.4), especially since the usual translation of 'the young girl' or 'marriageable girl' conceals the social functionality of birthing (ילד, the verbal root of הילדה) specific to women's bodies? Why does the story need to change Dinah's genealogical arrangements, effectively expelling the mother from them as the story progresses? And what has the figure of the prostitute got to do with any of this? These are the questions that need to be addressed along the way if we are to understand the importance of Dinah's and Leah's connection in 34.1, and indeed the importance of this verse for the story as a whole. But before I state my thesis, I need to summarize the story itself.

Genesis 34 goes something like this. Dinah, the daughter of Leah whom, we are told, she bore for Jacob, sets out to visit the women who live in the land (lit. to see into the daughters of the land; לראות בבנות הארץ) in which Dinah's family have recently settled. On the way, however, something happens to her. Shechem and Dinah are involved in an illicit sexual act, traditionally interpreted as rape but more recently as consensual sexual misconduct (Fewell and Gunn 1991; Bechtel 1994; Camp 2000; Brett 2000b).[3] And this is where the trouble starts, even though Shechem is

---

3. All of these recent discussions of Genesis 34 focus at some point on whether Dinah was raped or not. Whereas these studies analyse the key verbs in the text, I concentrate on the significant nouns and genealogical epithets. As will become clear, the

taken with Dinah and asks his father to get her for him for a wife. Unfortunately, Shechem is understood by Jacob and his sons to have defiled Dinah. When Hamor, Shechem's father, and Shechem himself make their offer to Jacob and his sons, suggesting they live together in their land and exchange daughters with each other, and ask any bridal price whatsoever for Dinah, the sons of Jacob's response is that all the men of Shechem must be circumcised. Only on this condition will they give their consent.

Having returned to their city, Hamor and Shechem convince all the men to circumcise themselves so that Jacob's family might live and trade with them. But three days later, while the men of Shechem are still recovering, Simeon and Levi, two of Jacob's (and Leah's) sons come to the city and kill all the men and remove Dinah from Shechem's house. Then they (and their other brothers?) ransack the city, taking all the dead men's possessions, including their women and children. Jacob is not impressed. He breaks his silence at this point to berate Simeon and Levi for bringing trouble to them by potentially enraging the peoples who inhabit the land (Canaanites and Perizzites). Jacob fears that they may gather together and destroy him and his family. But the brothers remain firm, attempting to justify their actions by questioning whether their sister should be treated as a prostitute. This is the official end of the story of the Dinah–Shechem encounter, though in Gen. 35.5, Elohim steps in to ensure that the people living in the cities do not pursue the sons of Jacob.

My argument is that in Genesis 34 the maternal body constitutes what Michelle Boulous Walker claims is 'the site of a radical silence' (Boulous Walker 1998: 1). This story about the struggle between two systems of exchange (endogamous and exogamous) fails to conceal the very condition for the existence of this religio-political struggle in the first place: the subordination of (re)productive nature to its socially inscribed function *for men*. That no women enter into the narrative's dialogue concerning the question of the exchange of women is merely the effect of women's exclusion from the Symbolic. Or rather, their lack of narrative presence, as actants and speakers, is the logical expression of the more radical form of their silence: their presence within the Symbolic *as the site or place of the maternal*. The maternal body is overwritten and silenced by the maternal *function*—to produce children for men, and to ensure relations among men alone.

---

issue of whether Shechem rapes Dinah or not avoids a more fundamental violence against women, and so I put this question of rape to the side.

But this is the maternal as imagined by the 'son', within a male Imaginary universe. The silenced maternal body is the imagined body of the *son's* mother. Reading Genesis 34, we can see that this repressed maternal body services the fantasy of male (re)production, with Dinah metamorphosing from 'the daughter of Leah whom she bore for Jacob' (v. 1), to 'the daughter of Jacob' (vv. 3, 5, 7, 18), and also recognized as the daughter of Jacob and his sons (vv. 8, 17). In other words, corporeal maternal origins must be disavowed to allow the mirage of male productive labour, the only labour valued here. Furthermore, Genesis 34 may be read as a text that betrays all too vividly the masculine imaginary fear of the strength of the maternal line. Dinah is the daughter of Leah, the only mother given a daughter in the Jacob legend, and this is where the trouble starts.

Drawing upon the work of Luce Irigaray—in particular, her critique of exchange relations as theorized by Marx, Levi-Strauss, Saussure, and Lacan in her essay 'Women on the Market' (Irigaray 1985a: 170-91)—I will show how Genesis 34 is an exemplary narrative of all that is at stake in what she calls hom(m)o-sexual exchange. 'Hom(m)o-sexual' is Irigaray's term that defines the hidden, homosexual logic of these models of exchange, that is, the creation of relations between men. She claims that social order and the exchange relations it creates and regulates are hom(m)o-sexual, and women function merely as the conduits for relations between men and (their) meaning. This social order relies upon the repression of the maternal body and the denial of the desire of the mother. And buried beneath this precious corpse is the 'dark continent of the dark continent', the fully repressed narrative of mother–daughter love.

And so, in Genesis 34 we find that the real threat to the system is not the illegitimate or corrupted sequences of events pertaining to the exchange of a woman, beginning vividly in v. 2. It is not the breach of social codes that Shechem enacts when he 'takes' and 'shames' Dinah. This is merely the narrative *effect* of a far greater threat—woman/commodity as unbound, active and dis-abstracted subject on the move. More importantly, this feared subject is the daughter-subject of the woman who bore her. And narratively speaking, she is on the move towards women. Gen. 34.1 can therefore be read as a moment of threat on the level of form. The subsequent violent content of 34.2-31 articulates the formal threat of narrative *leakage* into a realm where different stories might have been told, perhaps in a very different way. It is the fear of women entering into the Symbolic and threatening Israelite/male identity. So, not only is Genesis 34 a story about the controlled exchange of women, but it is also a story about the need to monopolize story-telling itself.

## The Logic of Exchange

### The Abstraction of Woman's Reproductive Bodies and the Exchange of Women

Is there a particular logic at work in Genesis 34 that explains the silence of women in a story in which they play a crucial social role? In 'Women on the Market', Luce Irigaray examines various models of exchange, notably Lévi-Strauss's kinship structures maintained through the exchange of women, the exchange of commodities in Marx's theory of economic relations, the exchange of signs in Saussurian linguistics, and objects of desire in Lacanian psychoanalysis. Irigaray claims that the exchange of women, commodities, signs and desire all share a common link: they are all guaranteed by the silence of women's bodies, especially the mute maternal body (See Grosz 1989: 147). She begins with Lévi-Strauss thesis in *The Elementary Structures of Kinship* (1967) that kinship systems function because of the exchange of women. Without this exchange of women society would fall from its state of civilized grace, returning to anarchy. Women are thus objects to be exchanged by and among men.[4] Irigaray reads Levi-Strauss with a Marxist theory of commodity production (projecting 'the axis of class onto that of sex'; Grosz 1989: 147) to assert that Marx's analysis of the commodity as the elementary form of capitalist wealth in *Capital* 'can be understood as an interpretation of the status of woman in so-called patriarchal [sic] societies' (Irigaray 1985a: 172).

Like commodities, in patriarchal societies women have dual value: use value (reproducing children and labour) and exchange value. At once they are both utilitarian objects and bearers of value. Yet the exchange value of woman exceeds her use value. In this economy, when woman is exchanged her price is not determined by some bodily or physical attribute, but by the measurement against a third term beyond her physicality. This external third term (i.e. the master signifier, the Name-of-the-Father, gold, the phallus) is that which allows for the comparison between women/commodities. And so, in such societies functioning in the mode of 'semblance', where '[t]he value of symbolic and imaginary productions is superimposed upon, and even substituted for, the value of the relations of the material, natural, and corporal (re)production' (Irigaray 1985a: 171), this third term is the male phallus as gold standard. A woman's body and its natural functionality becomes thoroughly abstracted, and necessarily so. Woman as commodity has value only in her ability to create relations among men.

4. See also Rubin 1976.

In this male economy, men are the producers, exchangers, and consumers of the commodity/woman:

> ...all the systems of exchange that organise patriarchal societies and all the modalities of productive work that are recognised, valued and rewarded in these societies are men's business. The production of women, signs, commodities is always referred back to men (When a man buys a girl, he 'pays' the father or the brother, not the mother...) and they always pass from one man to another, from one group of men to another (Irigaray 1985a: 171).

This economy of 'men-only' Irigaray labels hom(m)o-sexual. Men are the exchangers, the owners, the producers of the exchangeable. In a ho(m)mo-sexual economy man's identity as social being is sustained by the exchange of women. Having no value or identity in itself, woman/commodity has only relative value, value that comes to it from outside of itself. Woman/commodity merely reflects for man his (abstract) 'labor':

> *In other words, for the commodity, there is no mirror that copies it so that it may be at once itself and its 'own' reflection.* One commodity cannot be mirrored in another, as man is mirrored in his fellow man. For when we are dealing with commodities the self-same, mirrored, is not 'its' own likeness, contains nothing of its properties, its qualities, its 'skin and hair.' The likeness here is only a measure expressing the *fabricated* character of the commodity, its trans-formation by man's (social, symbolic) 'labor.' The mirror that envelops and paralyzes the commodity specularizes, speculates (on) man's 'labor.' *Commodities, women, are a mirror of value of and for man*. In order to serve as such, they give up their bodies to men as the supporting material of specularization, of speculation. They yield to him their natural and social value as a locus of imprints, marks, and mirage of his activity (Irigaray 1985a: 176-77).

And so, Irigaray argues, beginning with the simplest relation of equivalence between commodities and the exchange of women, 'the enigma of the money form, of the phallic function, is implied' (Irigaray 1985a: 177). The value of woman lies only in her exchangeability, to the extent that 'nature' or her reproductive value has been completely abstracted as a result of its subordination to social value, in this maintaining/mirroring of male identity. Within this order, women's bodies have no value in themselves. Their bodies have only a male defined symbolic value, and this abstract value comes to the woman from beyond herself, at the expense of the materiality of her body:

> *In order to become equivalent, a commodity changes bodies.* A supernatural, metaphysical origin is substituted for its material origin. Thus its body becomes a transparent body, *pure phenomenality of value*. But this

transparence constitutes a supplement to the material opacity of the commodity (Irigaray 1985a: 179).

Women/commodities mirror and mime the need/desire for relations among men, relations that constitute 'his' very identity (including ethnic and religious identities) and her value for him.

Crucial to the construction and maintenance of this social, symbolic order is the refusal of women's bodies as valuable in and for themselves, and the refusal of women to contribute to or profit from the Symbolic order. It is the trans-formation of women's bodies into use and exchange values that institutes the Symbolic order. So, while the Symbolic order establishes and regulates symbolic exchange (Grosz 1989: 147), that order itself is founded upon the repression of the maternal body (i.e. the trans-formation of women's bodies into use and exchange values). Furthermore, that order relies upon a *'nearly pure added value'*, one that exploits a particular class of producer—women—without returning any of the benefits of the use and circulation of this Symbolic they sustain with their bodies (Irigaray 1985a: 189-90).

And the repression of the maternal body is necessary. If any part of materiality or productive nature came into play, man could no longer sustain the semblance of his own self-making. 'Society is the place where man engenders himself, where man produces himself as man, where man is born into "human," "super-natural" existence' (Irigaray 1985a: 185). Presumably man knows he is born of woman, yet so much of our cultural production bears the traces of the denial of this very fact. The structure of this denial is that of the fetishist's disavowal—'I know I am born of woman, but all the same...' Elizabeth Grosz puts it this way:

> ...the son is unable to accept the debt of life, body, nourishment and social existence he owes the mother. An entire history of Western thought is intent on substituting for this debt an image of the self-made, self-created man. One could go even further and suggest that the idea of God itself is nothing but an elaborate if unconscious strategy for alleviating man's consciousness of and guilt about this debt. As man's self-reflecting Other, God usurps women's creativity and their place as the source of the terrestial. God (and through Him, man) becomes the creator or mother of the mother.
> Born of woman's body, man devises religion, philosophy and true knowledges not simply as sublimations of his desire, but as forms of disavowal of this maternal debt (Grosz 1989: 120-21).

The repression of that body, out of which we all emerge, is crucial for man to establish himself not only as self-produced, but also as a sole producer. This repression effects both the denial of maternal origins and the appropriation of maternal corporeal power for himself.

Recently, Michelle Boulous Walker has argued that Irigaray's work on the repressed maternal body[5] provides a model of reading 'to pursue the way the masculine imaginary silences women' (Boulous Walker 1998: 2). Boulous Walker reads a number of philosophical and psychoanalytic texts and argues that within these particular Western discourses we can discern a masculine imaginary that works to silence women in quite specific ways. Like Irigaray, Boulous Walker claims that within this imaginary, it is the association of women with maternity that most effectively silences them. Her claim is that 'the maternal body occupies the site of a radical silence in the texts of Western philosophy, psychoanalytic theory, and literature' (Boulous Walker 1998: 1). I would extend Boulous Walker's textual list to include the Hebrew Bible, although for now, my text is Genesis 34. If we examine this text closely, we find certain linguistic and narratological features that draw together, as logically coextensive, the absence of narrated women's voices in a story about the problems concerning the exchange of women and their symbolic maternal status. 'Woman', as such, does not exist. She is the contained and silenced prisoner of the place of the maternal function so as to ensure the continuation of the social order she supports without recompense.

*The Economy of Sexual Exchange in Genesis 34*
In Genesis 34, the exchanging of women between two supposedly different groups is the crucial issue. According to Irigaray, models of exchange operate according to two orders: exchangers and the exchanged, each of which is homogeneous and identity-based (Grosz 1989: 147). In other words, there is a general level of identity-based equivalence between the *subjects* of exchange. So too, the objects of exchange. But Genesis 34 is about the *problem* of likeness between men-exchangers. It is a story about the difficulty of deciding who is 'us' and who is 'them', particularly if read from a 'priestly' perspective (Camp 2000: 279-322). The men of Shechem do not bear the Israelite inscription of *socio-religious* identity and order, that is circumcision.

And yet one thing is thoroughly unquestioned in Genesis 34—the *given* status of the exchange of women among men. Prior to the question of social identity as a marker for the validity of one group to exchange with

5. Boulous Walker is also interested in Michèle Le Doeuff's investigations into the modes of silencing at work in Western philosophical discourse.

another is the already established status of an *economy of sexual exchange*, a social order that is already sustained through the symbolic exchange of women by men. In other words, Genesis 34 is a story about violence enacted by one group of men upon a 'different' group, a violence that erupts around the question of with which men the Israelites should exchange their women (within their own kinship group or with those from 'outside'?). But the precondition of this very question is the already established model of sexual exchange. Men exchange women amongst themselves.

The clearest indications of the given status of the sexual economy and its hom(m)o-sexual logic of exchange are the substantive (הילדה) used by Shechem in v. 4 in place of Dinah's name and the genealogical shifts made as the story turns to the question of the exchange of Dinah. I argue that הילדה is the crucial word in Genesis 34 that signifies the silent place of the maternal body, and accounts for the silence/silencing of Leah and the daughter who will take her place as producer within this *sexual* economy. And if we chart the variations in the description of Dinah's genealogical arrangement within this narrative, we see just how this abstracting of the maternal body, and the disavowal of corporeal origins, works to guarantee male relations (albeit tense and violent ones) at the very same time that female genealogy is sundered. As the narrative progresses, Dinah moves from being the daughter of Leah (produced for Jacob), to being the daughter of Jacob alone, and even becoming the daughter of Jacob and his sons. These genealogical distortions articulate the abstracting of women's reproductive value, at the same time that the maternal line is broken. Let us look carefully at how this works.

הילדה הזאת: *'this one whose duty it is to bear for a man'*
After Shechem has seen, taken, lay, and shamed Dinah in v. 2, he falls in love with her (v. 3). And in v. 4, he goes to his father and asks him to procure Dinah for him:

> And Dinah, the daughter of Leah whom she bore [ילדה] for Jacob, went out to see into the daughters of the land. But Shechem, the son of Hamor, prince of the land, saw her and he took her and he lay her and he shamed her. And his soul/desire/self/person/appetite/emotion/passion/very being [נפש] cleaved [ותדבק] to Dinah, the daughter of Jacob. And he loved the young boy/girl [הנער][6] and he spoke unto the heart of הנער. And Shechem said to his father, 'Get for me this one whose duty it is to bear for a man [הילדה הזאת] for a wife' (Gen. 34.1-4).

6. הנער with Kethib, הנערה with Qere.

It appears that Shechem is taken with Dinah. Rapist or not, he's smitten. However, the Hebrew language has trouble telling us exactly with what he is smitten. In v. 3, after his נפש cleaves to Dinah, who is now only the daughter of Jacob (see below), we are told that he loves the young boy/girl: הנער. Consonantally, he loves a young boy, though surely he is aware of Dinah's sex by now. It is only with Qere that Dinah is given back her sex. In the Pentateuch, apart from one instance of the full feminine form נערה being used (Deut. 22.19), the masculine, singular form נער refers to either a male or female child, depending on the context. Now, clearly from the context here, הנער refers to Dinah, the young girl. However, that the Pentateuch consistently utilizes a masculine noun even when a feminine form is available (Deut. 22.19) seems somewhat Freudian to me.[7] As Irigaray argues in *Speculum of the Other Woman*, for Freud there is no distinction between the girl and boy in the early stages of sexual development (see Irigaray 1985b: 13-129, esp. 25-34; see also Irigaray 1985a: 34-67). Or, we could say Freud's 'little man' is, strictly speaking, Pentateuchal. Either way, just as Freud cannot 'see' the sexual specificity of the little girl, the young girl's sex is ignored or is invisible in the Pentateuch's הנער. Perhaps this is an unconscious slip betraying the homosexual logic of desire behind the exchange of women?[8]

Although I cannot focus on הנער in this essay, this problematic lack of sexual distinction in the Pentateuch certainly needs further analysis. Here, I want to look at another word usually translated in the same way as הנערה, that is as 'the young girl'. However, I suggest an alternative translation of הילדה. The usual translation of הילדה as 'the young girl' conceals the service that the bodies of women are providing for men. In v. 3, Dinah is twice referred to as הנער. However, when Shechem beseeches his father to go get her for him, he uses הילדה. ילדה is usually translated as 'maiden' or 'young girl'. BDB and KB both suggest 'marriageable girl' in the case of Genesis 34, because the story seems to be suggesting that she is old enough to marry. Yet, these suggested translations—'the maiden', 'the

---

7. This point is still valid even if it is to be insisted that Deut. 22.19 must be a later insertion.

8. Irigaray's term, ho(m)mo-sexual, encapsulates both the desire for men to be amongst each other and the valorisation of all the needs and desires of men only. She argues that 'all economic organization is homosexual. That of desire as well, even the desire for women'. Male homosexuality has always been reviled '[b]*ecause they openly interpret the law according to which society operates*' and thus threaten 'to shift the horizon of that law' (Irigaray 1985a: 193).

young girl' and 'the marriageable girl'—continue to conceal the functionality implicit in the verbal root, ילד, 'to bear, bring forth, beget'. Furthermore, these translations erase the tacit role woman plays in this ancient socio-economic system.

It is crucial to return to v. 1 at this point, to see in v. 4 the nominal form of the verb that seems to justify the appearance of Leah's name in a story that silences her. *And Dinah, the daughter of Leah whom she bore* (ילדה) *for Jacob, went out to see into the daughters of the land* (34.1). The appearance of Jacob's name in v. 1 ensures that Dinah is not simply the daughter of Leah, though she is syntactically and grammatically closer at this point to Leah than she is to Jacob. But the appearance of Jacob's name also ensures that we become aware of the role of women in this economy and this story. Jacob/man is the receiver of that which Leah/woman bears (ילדה). His presence as the receiver/owner in the very first verse of Genesis 34 bestows upon the female subject (Leah) and female object (Dinah) of the verb 'to bear', their very symbolic and social reason for being. Leah bore (ילדה) Dinah *for* Jacob (ליעקב).[9] Dinah is the daughter of a woman whose productive capacity is, it needs to be stated, *for* someone else. The child (male or female), *produced* for-someone-else, becomes, in the case of the girl-child, she who will one day, like her mother, *produce* for-someone-else. Dinah is produced for Jacob in v. 1, and she is anticipated by Shechem to produce for him, that is to be his producer, in v. 4 when he refers to her as הילדה הזאת.

What the verb ילדה and the noun הילדה make clear in vv. 1 and 4 is that women both produce and are produced for men. For which men they produce is here, of course, the fundamental narrative problem. And it is a problem about which no woman is given the narrative space to speak. 'Woman' is silenced most radically when the (re)productive capacity of her body is at stake. Located at the site of this mute maternal, 'woman' ensures the replication of a Symbolic and social order within which she cannot actively participate. She ensures both the repetition of a social

---

9. The inseparable preposition ל allows for the translation of either 'to' or 'for'. However, there is a subtle, yet all too important semantic distinction. To insist upon the usual translation 'whom she bore to Jacob' seems to cover over the explicit function woman serves within this male-defined economy, suggesting instead a somewhat egalitarian model of ownership. But, woman as co-producer/owner in a story about the exchange of women and livestock? In a story where women are the exchangeable and the exchanged, exchangeable and exchanged precisely for their ability to ensure the very structure of exchange itself, and to ensure the very identity of their owners/exchangers?

order that brings and keeps men amongst themselves, for good or bad, and the continuance of stories for and about them.

In this respect, הילדה is better translated as 'the one capable of bearing for a man' or 'the one whose duty it is to bear for a man' rather than 'young girl' or 'marriageable girl'. When Shechem tells his father to get 'this ילדה' for a wife, we can see the symbolic, social role of women in operation. Dinah is understood by Shechem to be his future producer, the producer of his future. All the men of the story are brought together to discuss the implications of this desire of Shechem's, an obvious problem on the social and religious levels. But not, we might add, on the level of sexual identity sustained through the exchange of women.

It seems that, in this story, both substantives used for Dinah—הילדה and הנער—unwittingly indicate the ho(m)mo-sexual logic behind the exchange of women. As such, Genesis 34 makes it quite explicit that, as Irigaray suggests, '[w]oman exists only as an occasion for mediation, transaction, transition, transference, between man and his fellow man, indeed between man and himself' (Irigaray 1985a: 193). On the surface, these two substantives suggest that women are without a sex of their own (הנער) *until they come into the service of man* (הילדה). But even then, when her body's sexual distinction becomes clearer (i.e. her body as the only body that prepares for, contains, and then expels new life), it is only in its abstract function *for man*. 'Woman' is nothing more than the maternal function. In other words, they are without a sex of their own. Dinah as הילדה is Dinah reduced to an abstraction, to the maternal function. As הילדה she becomes the mirror of male relations and the mirage of male labour. Even the violence that ensues is a perverse marker of the success of this social order that relies upon the bodies of women to maintain the privileging of all that is male.

*Genealogical Monopoly and the Mirage of Male Labour*
I have argued that הילדה signifies the maternal function in the service of men, and as such contributes to the silencing of women. Michelle Boulous Walker argues that woman is most effectively silenced in relation to maternity, in that the maternal is only a symbolic place that is spoken for rather than a place from which one speaks. In Genesis 34, ילדה designates precisely this space that is spoken and does not speak, this mute maternal space/body that is the very foundation, according to Irigaray, of Western social and Symbolic order. We can begin to understand the silence of women in this story, especially Dinah and her mother Leah. But, if הילדה imprisons woman as the silent maternal through the *repression* of the maternal body so that its abstract function for men may take precedence,

Dinah's genealogical inconsistencies in Genesis 34 show us just how crucial this repression is for man in his social setting. I now want to turn to the genealogical descriptions in Genesis 34 to show how this crucial strategy of silencing also takes place through the *denial* of maternal, corporeal origins. I stated earlier that Irigaray claims that man disavows his corporeal origins to imagine himself self made and debt-free. But such a fantasy also allows him to value only the masculine:

> ...in order to become men, they continue to consume...[the mother], draw on her resources and, at the same time, they deny her or disclaim her in their identification with and their belonging to the masculine world. They owed their existence, their body, their life and they forget or misrecognise this debt in order to set themselves up as powerful men, adults busying themselves with public affairs...[10]

We will see that the narrative expels the mother from Dinah's genealogical arrangement as the story progresses so that Dinah may be imagined as the product of all-male labour. And, at the same time as maternal origins are being denied, the mother–daughter genealogy is denied.

In Hebrew, the word for mother is אם, but it is a word that is never used in relation to Leah and Dinah. In Gen. 30.21, we are told that Leah gives birth to a daughter ('And afterwards she bore a daughter and she called her name Dinah'). In Gen. 34.1, we are again reminded that Leah and Dinah are mother and daughter. And yet, while Dinah is identified as a daughter (בת), Leah is not identified explicitly as the mother (אם) of Dinah. Actually, in Genesis אם is associated almost exclusively with sons.[11] There are two exceptions to this rule: Eve, who is 'mother of all living' (Gen. 3.20), and Rebekah's mother (Gen. 24.28, 55). In the case of the former, the gender of the word for living (חי), whether it is read as an adjective or a collective noun, is masculine. In the latter case, אמה, 'her mother', provides the only use of אם as 'mother' of a daughter. However, she is also the only אם in Genesis who is nameless. In other words, in Genesis אם generally signifies the mother–son relationship. אם is the mother of a son and not the mother of a daughter, or if she is the mother of a daughter, she must be a nameless אם.

But, Dinah is referred to as the daughter of Leah (בת־לאה). However, she is also the one born for Jacob (אשר ילדה ליעקב). The *natural* produc-

---

10. This quotation is from Irigaray's 'Etablir un généalogie de femmes' (*Maintenant* 12, 1979, 28 Mai), and is cited in Grosz 1989: 121 (her translation).

11. Gen. 2.24; 20.12; 21.21; 24.67; 27.11, 13, 14, 29; 28.2, 5, 7; 29.10; 30.14; 32.11; 43.29; 44.20.

tive capability of Leah's body is not valued in itself but only for its social function, its ability to produce for Jacob: 'And Dinah, the daughter of Leah *whom she bore for Jacob*...' Leah's position as 'mother' is here well within the logic of this social order that figures the natural creative power of women's bodies as subordinate to their social value as producer for man.¹²

And yet, Leah and Dinah are still, at this stage, genealogically visible as mother and daughter. Dinah is explicitly the daughter of Leah (בת־לאה), and not the daughter of Jacob (בת־יעקב). We can say that the genealogical tie between mother and daughter still exists, though the relative clause 'whom she bore for Jacob' (אשר ילדה ליעקב) marks the symbolic fragility of this relationship. Of course, as I argued above, this relative clause participates in the silencing of women through their imprisonment in the maternal function. Leah's genealogical relationship with Dinah is defined by her productive function for Jacob. But we can still say that, at this point in the story, the mother daughter bond is readable. We can also lament the fact that, with the abrupt interruption of the relative clause, we can see the mother–daughter bond in the process of fading in this ancient text that our society holds sacred.

But if the mother–daughter relationship is still visible in v. 1, after Shechem's actions in v. 2, Dinah's genealogical epithets manifest the expelled mother. The mother–daughter tie seems to have been broken and disgarded. She is now only known in relation to her father or her father and

---

12. Here I am in sharp disagreement with Alice Keefe who, through an intertextual reading of Genesis 34, Judges 19, and 2 Samuel 13, finds that the violated body of a woman functions as a metonym for social disruption and warfare. This, she says, 'will point towards a meaning of the community of Israel which is constituted and expressed through a language of the female body and sexuality' (Keefe 1993: 81). This means that women's sexuality is in itself not the threat to social cohesion, but is the signifier of that cohesion. It is rape that is disruptive, not female sexuality per se. She goes on to state that

> (i)f we do not assume that women were irrelevant in the process of symbolic formation in ancient Israel, either as creators of meaning or loci of value, then the possibility arises that the trope could be grounded upon a reverence for the female body as a site of the sacred power of life and that inscribed in the convention itself may be a respect for female subjectivity (Keefe 1993: 88).

That Keefe insists on female sexuality as a signifier of cohesion in a sense leads to her fantasy of the maternal body valued as *natural* producer, valued in itself, outside of the economic system in which it is a crucial, and problematic, *object*.

her brothers. She is known as her father's daughter four times after v. 1. She is בת יעקב in 34.3 and 19, when Shechem's נפש first clings to Dinah (see below) and later when we are told that Shechem has delight in her. The use of בת יעקב no doubt indicates that the narrative events that follow are in many respects the result of one man claiming another man's property for himself. And she is referred to as בת יעקב, not בת לאה, when the narrator tells us of how senselessness or folly is the result of Shechem's lying with her (34.7). The pronominal suffix (בתו, 'his daughter') is used by the narrational voice to tell of Jacob's awareness of the defilement (טמא) of Dinah. So, once Dinah has been removed from the imagined world of women amongst themselves, and thrust into the problematic world of men and their commerce, it is as *her father's* daughter that she is known and as *her father's* daughter that she is a problem. She is no longer known as her mother's daughter.

In v. 8, when Hamor speaks to Dinah's father and her brothers on behalf of his son Shechem, Dinah is the daughter of her father *and* her brothers: *But Hamor spoke with them, saying 'Shechem, my son—his very being* [נפש] *is attached* [חשקה] *to your* [m. pl.] *daughter* [בבתכם]. *I pray you, give her to him for a wife.'* Dinah now is no longer Leah's daughter, nor is she simply Jacob's daughter. She is now the daughter of her father *and* her brothers, to whom Hamor is speaking. Genealogically, the presentation of Dinah's relation to her corporeal origin has become rather unstable. She has gone from being her mother's daughter, produced for Jacob, to being Jacob's daughter without Leah, while also being the exchangeable product of an all-male group who claim her as 'daughter'. Like Eve, it seems Dinah's maternal line is now non-existent. She is the product of male (symbolic) labour and ownership.

But it also seems that another male, Shechem, has already claimed Dinah as his own. A crucial part of himself is figuratively marking Dinah as his own through attachment. The verbs used in both vv. 3 and 8— דבק, to cling or cleave ('And his נפש cleaved [ותדבק] to Dinah, the daughter of Jacob...', 34.3), and חשק, to be attached ('...Shechem, my son—his נפש is attached [חשקה] to your [m. pl.] daughter')—suggest that Shechem's נפש has already marked Dinah as his own, and it won't let go. And this cleaving and attaching serves a purpose. When Shechem's נפש cleaves and attaches itself to Dinah, she becomes a daughter without her mother. The cleaving and attaching of that נפש of his, *his* very being, renders Dinah as nothing more than the mirror of male relations. The cleaving of his נפש in v. 3 casts out the Dinah we were introduced to in

Gen. 30.21, the daughter born to Leah ('And afterwards she bore a daughter and she called her name Dinah'), and even the Dinah we meet in Gen. 34.1, 'the daughter of Leah whom she bore for Jacob'. The *cleaving* נפש casts her as the daughter of her father alone. The *attachment* of that נפש (v. 8) miraculously disavows corporeal origins, imagining her instead as the product of male labour. She is now the daughter of Jacob & Sons. In v. 17, Dinah's brothers themselves refer to her as 'our daughter' (בתנו).[13]

After v. 1, Dinah is never again referred to as בת־לאה. And, we must note, it is only after the encounter with Shechem in v. 2 that Dinah is absented and silenced. Not only is she no longer her mother's daughter, but she is no longer actively present in this story that is ostensibly about her. She is present in the narrative world of men and their socio-economic relations only as the ambiguously sexed נער (34.3², 12), as ילדה, the silent place of the symbolic maternal function, and as the daughter of man/men. So, the breaking of the maternal line in this story is crucially related to the coming together of men to discuss economic matters involving the bodies of women, without consulting the women themselves.

### 'Mother', 'Virgin', 'Prostitute'

I have mentioned a number of times that, according to Irigaray, women are the mere mediators for relations among men. In Genesis 34, these relations are hardly harmonious. In fact, the problem of exchange between different male groups ends up with hideous acts of violence on the part of the brothers of Dinah. Most readers, feminist or otherwise, build their arguments around the question of which voice is the victorious voice according to the text. Is it the exogamy-accepting, integrationist position of Dinah, Shechem, Jacob, Hamor and the Hivites, or the ethnocentric, endogamist position of Dinah's brothers (see esp. Brett 2000b)? In other words, the main question critics ask is whether the text leaves us considering the acts of Levi and Simeon to be justified in light of Shechem's 'defilement' of Dinah, or egregiously over-reactive? However, I am going to leave this question—'on whose side is the text?'—unasked in this essay, for the simple reason that I

---

13. Of course, in Hebrew the first common pronominal suffix, נו-, is inclusive. Grammatically, 'our daughter' could include Leah. And earlier, in v. 8, when Hamor is making his offer to Jacob and his sons, he calls Dinah בבתכם, 'your daughter'. The second plural pronominal suffix כם- is masculine, though this too is inclusive and could include Leah. But since no mention has been made of Leah showing up at the bargaining floor, and since all of this exchange process involves men only, we can be certain that in calling Dinah 'our daughter', the brothers are referring to themselves and their father.

think such musings continue to ignore the fundamental violence that founds this text: the murder/silencing of woman/mother and the mother–daughter relationship.

What does interest me is the reason the brothers give for their murder of the Hivite men, and their violent assault on the Hivite women and children. Jacob is unhappy at Simeon's and Levi's actions because of the harm that might come to his budding empire. But the brothers insist on the virtue of their actions, saying 'Should he treat our sister like a prostitute?' It is easy to see the brothers taking the moral high ground here (so Sternberg 1985: 472). However, it is important to see that this is more than just an issue of morality, but one of family (male) honour as well (Fewell and Gunn 1991; Bechtel 1994; Brett 2000b; Camp 2000). And yet, perhaps there is more at stake here than the brothers' and their father's shame at the loss of their valuable commodity, that is Dinah's virginity. I want to suggest that if the maternal body occupies the place of silence, ensuring relations among men, then the prostitute's body is a body that says too much. It is for this reason that Simeon and Levi call upon the figure of the prostitute to defend their actions.

Returning to Irigaray, within this order where 'woman' has no identity of her own, where her value comes from way beyond any facet of her corporeality, there are three roles assigned to and imposed upon women: mother, virgin, prostitute. All three positions share the same function. In all her forms—mother, virgin, prostitute—'woman' serves as a reflection of man's labour, as the 'mirage of his activity' (Irigaray 1985a: 177). But because woman has both natural value and social value for man, her development lies in the transition from one to the other, from natural to social value, a passage that 'never takes place simply' (Irigaray 1985a: 185). This transformation is necessary for man's appropriation and possession of nature.

I have already said quite a lot about Irigaray's analysis of what 'mother' signifies within patriarchal societies, but I will recap here. 'Mother' is that which designates the woman on the side of '(re)productive *nature*', that is the biological fact of the natural, corporeal-maternal origin of humans understood, however, within a structure of production wherein man must deny this debt (to the natural world) to enable the mirage of his own self-engenderment, his own social, symbolic production, his own *value*. The maternal body is not valued in and of itself. It is valued only through its socially supplemented value as 'producer' for man. As Irigaray points out, in the same way that man began to own and take from the land, considering this his 'work', he owns and takes from the bodies of women without acknowledging the debt (Irigaray 1985a: 185).

Interestingly, in Genesis 34, women's bodies and the land are closely connected. When Hamor makes his offer to Jacob & Sons, he brings together the socially valued matter of women's bodies and the land: 'And make marriages with us. Give your daughters to us, and our daughters take for yourselves. And with us you will dwell and the land will be before you. Dwell and move about her [וסחרוה] and be settled in her [והאחזו בה]' (34.9-10). In other words, just as we will both take from the land, which will be ours to share and through which we will build our social identity, so too, as men, we will take from the women we carefully exchange amongst ourselves. The land is spaced as feminine, as that which will receive man and provide for him.[14]

'Virgin' is pure exchange value. Within the Symbolic, 'virgin' is 'nothing but the possibility, the place, the sign of relations among men. In and of herself, she does not exist: she is a simple envelope veiling what is at stake in social exchange. In this sense, her natural body disappears into its representative function' (Irigaray 1985a: 186). And the passage from woman to mother takes place through the violation of this envelope. Once 'deflowered', woman is removed from exchange among men, taking up her status as use value for man.

Nowhere in Genesis 34 is Dinah referred to as בתולה, a 'virgin' in its usual translation. But then 'virginity' in the Hebrew Bible is tricky business.[15] However, it is generally accepted that the crime punished by Jacob's

---

14. And this, apparently, is the *virtue* of exogamy, the virtue of the anti-ethnocentric voice in this text (Brett 2000b).

15. As Mieke Bal has shown in her study of the book of Judges, 'virginity' is the convenient term for that aspect of the daughter-sister that makes her a valuable possession, valuable because exchangeable, i.e. she has not had sex with a man before (Bal 1988: esp. 41-68). But בתולה, for Bal at least, signifies not the untouched state of the female but a threatening stage (from the male point of view) in the life of the girl-woman. It is a transitional stage between virginity under the ownership of the father (נערה) and nubility under the ownership of the husband (עלמה, 'the nubile, mostly already married woman, *before her first pregnancy*' (Bal 1988: 48)). בתולה, then, suggests the status of the female as potential object of gift *because of her nubility or ripeness*, the girl on the verge of being given, and therefore almost out of the ownership of the father bound for possession by another man. We might expect the term בתולה to be present here in Genesis 34, in light of the most relevant legal text (Deut. 22.28-29) and its explicit use of the term. However, the very absence of the term in Genesis 34 may suggest that Dinah is not ready to be exchanged as far as the rules of this exchange of women go. It is not only the taking of another man's property that is

machismo sons, notably Simeon and Levi, is the theft of property (Dinah's value as exchangeable commodity). The 'shaming' of Dinah is explicitly the 'shaming' of her owners—her father and her brothers (Fewell and Gunn 1991, Bechtel 1994, Camp 2000, and Brett 2000b). In Irigarayan terms, however, the 'theft' of her virginity is the theft of the possibility of relations among men. The shame that is Jacob and his sons is the shame of the non-productive, of those with nothing to exchange with other men. It is the shame of the derelict within an order that functions through the exchange of women, whether amongst their own or outside. Is this why, in the end, the men must come together in such a brutal way? Does the tremendously overworked phallic violence (the circumcisions, the deaths by sword) on the part of at least two men signify the impotence of those whose identity as men is threatened when their 'goods' are appropriated by another, as if they themselves were women excluded from the point of exchange?

And so, in not wanting Dinah to be treated as a prostitute, the brothers are of course protecting their own interests. But according to Irigaray, the prostitute is an ambiguous figure within this social order. She is the 'woman' who is both explicitly condemned and implicitly tolerated by the social order. With the 'prostitute', the break between use and exchange is less defined. Their bodies have value only in that they have *already* been appropriated by men, and 'serve as the locus of relations—hidden ones—between men. Prostitution amounts to *usage that is exchanged*' (Irigaray 1985a: 186). Her body, like all women's bodies, is valuable not due to its own natural qualities, but because that nature has been thoroughly used up. Her body becomes then the medium through which men relate to each other, and her body contains and conceals that very desire through the façade of heterosexuality.[16]

---

against the rules (that Shechem both knows and doesn't know?), but the rendering of Dinah as available before her time of availability has arrived. In other words, she may be too young (so Keefe 1993: 89, n. 8) Perhaps Dinah has not yet reached this stage in her life; she (or rather her 'virginity') is still her father's possession, not yet in the process of being given, because not yet ready to be given. Or perhaps the absence of בתולה pre-empts the effects of Shechem's and Dinah's encounter. Dinah will never 'progress' from virgin in the possession of the father, from pure exchange value itself, to the 'mother' in the possession of the husband, as both natural and use value in the service of man.

16. Irigaray's claim here is that sexual exogamy has never taken place. That is, all exchange under this social order is sexually endogamous, based on a homosexual logic of desire for men amongst themselves.

The exchanges upon which patriarchal societies are based take place exclusively

So, on the one hand, the 'prostitute' is that figure who does not profit her father/brothers through the sale of her body, and as such she is condemned. On the other hand, the 'prostitute' is tolerated because she is well within this logic (the very site of this logic) that reduces woman to nothing more than the mediator for men, the site of their desire for all that is masculine (themselves and each other). But one aspect that Irigaray does not pursue is that, as the radical site of the logic of exchange within this system, the 'prostitute' threatens to reveal all that is at stake in legitimate exchange between men: the desire for each other. Irigaray states that one of the presuppositions of patriarchal social order is that women are constituted as '"objects" that emblematize the materialization of relations among men…' (Irigaray 1985a: 185). But unlike the virgin and the mother, the prostitute is more than just an emblem for the relations among men and their desire for each other; she is their very corporeal locale.

Irigaray claims that male homosexuality is despised precisely for this reason: '*Because they openly interpret the law according to which society operates*, they threaten in fact to shift the horizon of that law' (Irigaray 1985a: 193). What is the 'prostitute' if not homosexual relations supplemented with the body of a woman, a body valued only because it is a 'vehicle for relations among men', the radical site of their desire for each other? And both are, of course, biblical abominations. So, in treating Dinah like a prostitute, does Shechem threaten to expose the logic of both exogamous and endogamous exchange? By treating her like a prostitute, does he render her body audible? I would say yes. Like the body of the mother, the prostitute's body says nothing about itself. As a woman's body, like the maternal body, it serves a social function for men, and if it is valued at all, it is valued according to a schema that has nothing to do with it. And yet as the radical site of the logic of exchange within an ho(m)mo-sexual

---

among men. Women, signs, commodities, and currency always pass from one man to another; if it were otherwise, we are told, the social order would fall back upon incestuous and exclusively endogamous ties that would paralyze all commerce. Thus the labor force and its products, including those of mother earth, are the object of transactions among men and men alone. This means that the *very possibility of a sociocultural order requires homosexuality* as its organizing principle. Heterosexuality is nothing but the assignment of economic roles: there are producer subjects and agents of exchange (male) on the one hand, productive earth and commodities (female) on the other. Culture, at least in its patriarchal form, thus effectively prohibits any return to *red blood*, including that of the sexual arena. *In consequence, the ruling power is pretense, or sham, which still fails to recognize its own endogamies* (Irigaray 1985a: 192).

order, it is a body that not only threatens to speak, but threatens to say too much, to expose all that is at stake in exchange.

Claudia Camp (2000) has suggested that, when read from a 'priestly' perspective, the principal tension at work in the text is between the law against incest and the desire for genealogical purity best serviced by brother-sister marriage mythology. Following Irigaray, I would like to suggest that the priestly desire for genealogical purity is best serviced by the fantasy of male reproduction, a fantasy with mythological allegiance in the creation myths of Genesis itself.[17] What is really at stake in the Dinah-Shechem moment is the breakdown of the fantasy of mono- or homo-production, which is unsustainable when men do not control the exchange of women. By justifying their actions as a refusal to allow Shechem to make a *prostitute* of Dinah, Simeon and Levi (the priestly brother) are responding to the threat of a potentially audible female body, one that actually threatens to expose the fantasy/logic of their very system of social order. 'Prostitute' is that symbolic body that paradoxically says nothing and too much.

*Female Genealogy, the Silence of Women and the Control of Stories*
I began with a question: in Genesis 34.1, why is Dinah named as Leah's daughter and not Jacob's? In order to answer this question, I turned to Luce Irigaray's thesis that social order is founded upon the exchange of women and is sustained by the total abstraction of women's bodies and their capacity to bear children. Such an abstraction and denial of the value of women's bodies enables the male appropriation of maternal power so that the semblance of a self-producing social identity, one that denies any debt to nature, may be sustained. The only labour valued, the only sex valued, is masculine.

I have argued that while Genesis 34 is, as many have shown, on the surface a story about the relationship between identity and the struggle between two kinship systems (endogamous and exogamous), this very struggle takes place only on the condition that women's reproductive bodies remain silent. That is, while women remain trapped in their symbolic role as reproducer for man. 'Mother' becomes that which is spoken,

17. It is also the fantasy behind the absence of female names in the *toledot* sections of Genesis' genealogies, usually ascribed to the priestly writer P (Jay 1992: 94-111). This fantasy of the male monopoly of birthing is also behind the strange genealogical formulae where men reproduce all on their own: ילד 'to bear or bring forth', especially in the well-known *holidh* formula, benignly translated as 'begat' or 'fathered'.

and never that which speaks. It is the symbolic position for women that ensures their exclusion from participating in the symbolic in any active sense. Or as Michelle Boulous Walker puts it, maternity is 'the site of a radical silence' (Boulous Walker 1998: 1). Genesis 34 makes this necessary silence quite explicit. The construction of identity is the business of men, and it relies upon the control of women's bodies. Women appear in Genesis 34 only ever in the service of this maxim.

But what of my original problem with 34.1? Why does the story begin with the genealogical epithet בת־לאה given to Dinah, an epithet that never appears in the story again? Genealogically speaking, after 34.1 Dinah is only ever בת־יעקב, or the daughter of her brothers and her father. And what of the suggestion that Dinah is headed towards a group of women, only to be cut off from that alliance by the sexual encounter with Shechem? I have dealt with the logic of exchange behind patriarchal social order, as analysed by Irigaray, to show that Genesis 34 describes such an ho(m)mosexual economy. I have argued that the silencing of women is effected through their imprisonment in the maternal. 'Woman' occupies the site of silence through her given status as producer for man, signified here in Genesis 34 by the use of the substantive ילדה. This silence is the effect of the *repression* of the maternal body so that the *social* value of reproduction for man is the only value possible. And related to this is the silence of 'woman' through the denial of corporeal, maternal origins. Man appropriates maternal power as his own, claiming the daughter as his own production through the genealogical epithets that deny any trace of the maternal line. Furthermore, I argued that Simeon and Levi's expression of their fear that Dinah be treated as a prostitute (34.31) is an expression of fear of the *audible* feminine. 'Prostitute' is the only figure that contains the *imagined* threat of feminine speech (though of course, this is not possible) within this logic. And what 'woman-as-prostitute' threatens to expose is that which is truly at stake: the fantasy of male-only reproduction.

But in Genesis 34, it is not simply any mother's body that is denied. This maternal body has produced a daughter (Gen. 30.21). Genesis 34 makes it clear that at the same time that maternal origins are repressed and denied, so too the mother–daughter relationship or female genealogy is also repressed and denied. But why begin with that relationship at all?

And how is this related to silence? According to Irigaray, the mother–daughter tie must be severed so that woman can enter into desire for the man-father,[18] to take the place of the mother while never having a relation-

---

18. This is the famous assertion of Freud. For Irigaray's critical interpretation of

ship with her in that place, *ensuring the repetition of the social order*. Thus, Irigaray says:

> The culture, the language, the imaginary and the mythology in which we live at the moment…let's see what ground it is built on…The substratum is the woman who reproduces the social order, who is made this order's infrastructure; the whole of western culture is based upon the murder of the mother… The man-god-father killed the mother in order to take power (Irigaray 1991: 47).

When Irigaray asserts that Western culture is founded by the (forgotten) murder of the mother, she means the symbolic murder of the flesh and blood woman, the sexuate being refused access to the spheres of religion, culture, law, etc. As such, women can have no valuable identity within the Symbolic other than as the site of the maternal function. For the mother and the daughter, there is no possibility for the sharing of space together. And the consequence of this is the inability of women to have a productive relationship with each other. This thus 'prevents them from constituting any real threat to the order of western metaphysics, described by Irigaray as a metaphysics of the Same. They remain "residual", "defective men", "objects of exchange", and so on' (Whitford 1991: 79).

For this reason, the mother–daughter relationship constitutes a real threat to this social order that requires both the separation of the mother and the daughter, and their lack of subjective distinction as prisoners of the maternal site within the Symbolic:

> In our societies, the mother/daughter, daughter/mother relationship constitutes a highly explosive nucleus. Thinking it, and changing it, is equivalent to shaking the foundations of the patriarchal order (Irigaray 1991: 50).

So, to ensure the continuation of a social order that values only the masculine, at the expense of the feminine through the exploitation of natural (re)production (women, the land), it is necessary to ensure that woman remains imprisoned in her maternal function, the site of her silence. This ensures that all relationships among women—the vertical mother–daughter relationship and the horizontal axis of women-amongst-themselves—are excluded from the Symbolic and are marked by a poverty of existence that Irigaray calls *déréliction*.[19] This sundering of female genealogies enables

---

this aspect of Freud's theory of psycho-sexual development see 'The Blind Spot of an Old Dream of Symmetry', in Irigaray 1985b: 11-129.

19. As Margaret Whitford explains, this term of Irigaray's refers to the lack of symbolization available to women, but also connotes the state of being abandoned by

the maintenance of the 'maternal' as the mother of a son, the *silent* woman. Social order is ruled by the son's relation to the maternal, never the daughter's. For Irigaray, the moment the mother–daughter relationship is symbolized and valued, a social order that relies upon the exchange of women and the exploitation of their bodies begins to collapse, as 'woman' begins to exist.

We can now see that Genesis 34.1 is not merely the scene setter for Genesis 34. I suggest that whether or not Shechem rapes Dinah in v. 2, the abrupt narrative shift that Shechem's appearance enacts is a violence that needs to be read. This very sudden shift away from the possibility of women amongst themselves in v. 1, and away from the possibility of a story about them, not to mention the sundering of the mother–daughter genealogy that takes place from this point on in the story, is *the fundamental violence* of the text. Shechem's appearance in the story at this point must be read as the dismantling of female genealogy in its vertical and horizontal dimensions. It is the refusal to allow women the strength that the perpendicular can give. And, as Irigaray points out, this sundering is necessary for the continuation of a social order that privileges the masculine.

The real threat in Genesis 34 is that which undergirds the feared loss of ethnic and religious identity that is narrated here. It is the feared loss of control over the bodies of women, which itself is the imaginary loss of control over the social and the Symbolic. In this sense, we can read 34.1 as the imagined threat that this narrative must assuage. Dinah is named as the daughter of Leah precisely to enable the breaking of that line, so that she may only ever be the daughter of men and so that the mother remains the (silent) mother of the son (in this case Simeon and Levi). Furthermore, that refusal of female identity (of any symbolic value other than use value) prevents women from having a relationship with each other.

So, what if women were to have a relationship with each other, outside the controlled boundaries of a male defined social-order? Or as Irigaray, mimicking Marx, puts it, 'what if these "commodities" refused to go to "market"? What if they maintained "another" kind of commerce, among themselves?' (Irigaray 1985a: 196). In fact, Genesis 34 begins with the

---

God, or like Ariadne, 'abandoned on Naxos, left without hope, without help, without refuge' (Whitford 1991: 78). As prisoners of their symbolic mandate as 'mothers', i.e. holders of the place of the mother or the maternal function, women can only relate to each other aggressively.

possibility of women-amongst-themselves: 'And Dinah, the daughter of Leah whom she bore for Jacob, went out to see into the daughters of the land.' Had Dinah actually made it to the daughters of the land, their own stories may have been told within what could have been a different economy of exchange. It is no mere coincidence that the journey of Dinah, the mother's daughter, towards a group of women is suddenly, even violently torn away from her kind and unceremoniously dumped into the world of men. Shechem's narrated actions on or with Dinah (rape or not, it really does not matter) ensure that the story is redirected back on to the sociopolitical stage of men-amongst-themselves. This violent redirection away from the stories of women ensures that the stories of men can be told, implying that the controlling of women's bodies and the controlling of story-telling itself are inextricably related.

LOST IN PLACE: SOME PERPLEXITIES OF INTERTEXTUAL ENTANGLEMENT

Anne Taylor

I have not yet read Arthur Clarke's *2001: A Space Odyssey*, but in 2001 I did read the ancient Greek *Odyssey* attributed to Homer. In this paper I follow a tangled thread, a line of perplexed thought, from *The Odyssey* to biblical interpretation by way of some theorizing about intertextuality and the use of scriptural texts in the lectionary, a cycle of readings for liturgical use. It is very much a work in progress and all findings at this stage are tentative.

*The Odyssey* is an epic whose action and principal characters are dependent on divine intervention, especially from Athene, the deity associated with weaving (Murnaghan 1995: 61, 63, 64). And in Homeric thought, weaving implies more than making a garment (Thornton 1970: 94).

Three times the story is told of Penelope deceiving her domestically challenged suitors with the tale that she must weave a shroud for her aged father-in-law before making a decision to marry one of them. In E.V. Rieu's English translation the versions all agree on the wording of her speech and on the success of her deception for more than three years of weaving by day and unravelling her work by night, until she is betrayed by one, or more, of her maids and forced to complete the work. It is said to gleam like the sun or the moon (Homer/Rieu [1946] 1964: 39-40, 291-92, 354-55).

The context for Penelope is that her husband left their home on the island of Ithaca when their son was an infant, and now the boy is almost an adult, nearly old enough to take over the estate, the time when she should remarry. She is lost in despair, with no knowledge about the fate of her husband.

But, as Sheila Murnaghan has observed, Athene the weaver 'is able to perform both the literal handicraft and the more metaphorical devising of plots much more successfully than any mortal' (Murnaghan 1995: 64). She improves Penelope's appearance so gifts are more readily solicited from the suitors; she weaves a plot with Penelope's husband to wreak vengeance on the suitors.

Divine and human characters are woven into the epic in a progression of stories that shuttle back and forth across time, from past events to present action. A critical reader will find many loose threads and suppressed stories, but *The Odyssey*'s male-fantasy hero gets home in time to slaughter the suitors and reclaim his wife, his estate, and his ruling status on Ithaca. The epic, like the gleaming shroud, is completed.

### *Interpretive Entanglement*

Divine and human characters are also woven into biblical stories, and the work of biblical interpretation is reminiscent of Penelope's work of unravelling and reweaving, though it tends to become messy, with no guarantee of completion or shining enlightenment. We get tangled up in knotty problems, find gaps in the text, lose ourselves in semantic problems, and discover that our readings say more about ourselves than about the text. Caroline Walker Bynum's observation explains one reason for our interpretive indeterminacies:

> No one of us will ever read more than partially, from more than a particular perspective… In the inconsistencies and ironies of texts—judged as such by our standards—we learn things the past did not understand about itself. If we are humble, we learn something as well about our own capacity for self-contradiction (Bynum 1991: 23).

That we can now acknowledge our uncertainties, and the instability of our interpretations, reflects the relatively new situation of being free to question the texts in the context of secular university environments, not bound by the expectation of fixed readings according to institutional theological agendas. It is recognized that biblical scholarship since the Enlightenment has not been able to establish the historical truth of 'the Bible', and that there are no secure notions of meaning to support apparently stable traditional interpretations (The Bible and Culture Collective 1995: 1-2).

In the 1990s The Bible and Culture Collective produced *The Postmodern Bible*, arguing for a transformed biblical criticism that would take account of a cultural context changed from that which gave rise to the scientific method of modernity (The Bible and Culture Collective 1995: 2). Reader-response theories had highlighted the role of readers in making meaning from texts, in part accounting for the phenomenon of individual varieties of interpretation, often contradictory, from the same text; the text alone was not a source of determinate meaning (McKnight 1993: 197-219).

One example of contradictory interpretations is the contrast between James Barr's opinion that the writer of Genesis 1 was influenced by Deutero-Isaiah (Barr 1968: 13), and Michael Fishbane's opinion that the creation formulations in Gen. 1.1–2.4 were exegetically reinterpreted in Deutero-Isaiah to emphasize that God was alone at the time of creation (Fishbane 1985: 324-26). They discovered different chronological orders of composition, but both scholars read Genesis 1 and Deutero-Isaiah in juxtaposition. And that minimal sense of reading biblical texts in juxtaposition either with or against each other was my first understanding of the term 'intertextuality'. The effect of creating intertextual conversations among the texts was intriguing, because whenever texts are set together a new literary context is created.

Reading their discussion of poststructural criticism from this perspective, The Bible and Culture Collective's statement about intertextuality seemed appropriate to describe the intricacy of relationships among biblical narratives. They said:

> *Intertextuality*...suggests that each text is situated for each reader in an ever-changing web composed of innumerable texts. There is no extratextual reality to which texts refer or which gives texts their meaning; meaning or reference are possible only in relation to this network, as functions of intertextuality (Bible and Culture Collective 1995: 130).

It seemed appropriate, too, for the critical approach of close reading, whereby the texts are read synchronically, in isolation from any extratextual reality; Phyllis Trible's close reading of biblical texts had pioneered the way for some exciting developments in feminist biblical interpretation. In her introduction to *God and the Rhetoric of Sexuality* (1978), for example, she trailed the description of a merciful God, 'slow to anger, and abounding in mercy', from Exodus through to its use by the prophets and psalmists. Her juxtaposition of texts containing the description was intended to illustrate hermeneutics 'at work within the Bible', but although her literary criticism of that time (1970s) demonstrates intrabiblical intertextuality, it does not appear to involve a conscious evocation of intertextual theory:

> A single text appears in different versions with different functions in different contexts... What it says on one occasion it denies on another.
>
> ...hearers construe the text variously, be they a vindictive Nahum, an angry Jonah, a repentant community, a selfless worshiper [*sic*], or an obedient Moses leading a disobedient people (Trible 1978: 4-5).

*Extratextual Intertextuality?*

The Collective attributed the origin of the term 'intertextuality' to Julia Kristeva,[1] so it seemed necessary to learn something of her theory, which turned out to be more complex than theories of the interrelationships among written texts. In the 1960s Kristeva introduced to Western readers Mikhail Bakhtin's claim that history and society should be read as texts. Furthermore, she wrote, 'History and morality are written and read within the infrastructure of texts' (Kristeva 1986a: 36), presumably including history and society within that infrastructure. Which gives a different complexion to The Bible and Culture Collective's statement that 'There is no extratextual reality to which texts refer or which gives texts their meaning.' It invites the question: *should* history and society themselves be read as texts rather than as contexts *in* which, perhaps in response to which, the 'literary word' is written?

Sacvan Berkovitch appears to have suggested just that in his proposal for cultural studies to become disciplinary rather than interdisciplinary, by seeing cultural 'texts' in literary 'context' (Berkovitch 1996: 248), reversing the situation with which he introduces his argument: 'It used to be an axiom of interdisciplinary studies that the relation of the literary to the cultural is one of text to context: literature understood in the context of philosophy, theology, psychology, national history, etc.' (Berkovitch 1996: 247).

In the Collective's account of deconstruction they explain that the term 'text' is not limited to written language, and that for deconstruction '[t]ext and its related terms' are metaphors (The Bible and Culture Collective 1995: 130). Berkovitch's use of quote marks suggests that he, too, uses the term metaphorically. But the Collective's claim that there is no extratextual reality appears to collapse the metaphor.

To describe a culture as text rather than as context extends concepts of intertextuality to include the relationships of texts with their social contexts as well as with their interrelationships among other texts. For example, in

---

1. Many others also attribute the origin of the term to Kristeva (Friedman 1991: 146; van Wolde 1997: 427 and others), but Mieke Bal has attributed intertextuality directly to Mikhail Bakhtin without acknowledging Kristeva's work (Bal 1999: 64). It seems that while Bakhtin provided the theoretical foundations as indicated by Bal, Kristeva devised the term as well as her own development of the theory (Moi 1986: 34; Kristeva 1996: 189-90) also drawing on Saussure's work and influenced by Freud (Kristeva 1997: 9).

'The Bounded Text', Kristeva does distinguish between the written text and its external (extratextual) social world for the duration of her discussion of Antoine de La Sale's fifteenth-century work, *Jéhan de Saintre*. In this essay she demonstrates how the social world exists outside of the text but its voices are recorded in the text. As an example, in fourteenth- and fifteenth-century France it was common for merchants in the marketplace to shout aloud the praises and prices of their wares, and for heralds in public squares to proclaim the news of combat, in a laudatory performance genre known as *blazon*. In La Sale's courtly romance the *blazon*, which at that time functioned unambiguously to praise the Lady, is transformed to blame by the Lady's treachery.

As Kristeva says, 'the function established according to the extratextual set (Te) changes within the novelistic textual set (Tn)' (Kristeva 1980: 53): the *blazon*'s established function of praise in the social world (the extratextual set) has been transformed to blame within the world of La Sale's text (the novelistic textual set). But she frames this discussion within an understanding of culture as a text (Kristeva 1980: 36-37, 59), thereby appearing to extend (or limit) Bakhtin's assessment of the text's relationship with the extratextual world.

## *Theory's Focus: Which Text?*

In his account of the prehistory of the novel, Bakhtin turned to the unstable parodic-travestying literature of ancient Rome and found that its diverse forms constituted 'a special extra-generic or inter-generic world' united by the common purpose of providing a corrective laughter and criticism that would force 'men' [*sic*] to experience a different and contradictory reality not to be found in the straightforward genres and languages being parodied (Bakhtin 1988: 138-39). He likened this world to a huge novel in which 'any direct word and especially that of the dominant discourse is reflected as something more or less bounded, typical and characteristic of a particular era, aging, dying, ripe for change and renewal' (Bakhtin 1988: 139).

Bakhtin regarded the novel as an artistic genre (Bakhtin 1986: 269);[2]

2. As described in the glossary to *The Dialogic Imagination*,

'Artistic' genres are those that are reworked to aesthetic purpose and can therefore be re-contextualized (a sonnet, a portrait, an art song); an 'everyday genre' is a mode of expression that involves conventions (a personal letter, table talk, a chat over the back fence, throwing rice at weddings) but is of the *byt* (ordinary everyday life) and rooted in specific contexts (Holquist and Emerson 1981: 424).

Kristeva in the late 1960s, however, was attempting to resolve what she saw as a problem for semiotics:

> One of the problems for semiotics is to replace the former, rhetorical division of genres with a *typology of texts*; that is, to define the specificity of different textual arrangements by placing them within the general text (culture) of which they are a part, and which is in turn, part of them (Kristeva 1980: 36; emphasis Kristeva's).

That particular problem appears to be inherent in an extended use of the term 'text'. It seems that Bakhtin's generic novel with its direct word bounded by its changing socio-historical context, in being assimilated into Kristeva's semiotic theory becomes a novelistic textual set bounded by an extratextual set (culture) which is itself a text. The two theorists appear to be focused on different aspects of the relationship between text and social context.³

When text and context are differentiated, then analysis of the text can take account of influences from its cultural context(s) of production and reception, and Kristeva's example seems to demonstrate this. But, by treating culture as 'text' rather than context, she is obliged to create new terms to maintain the difference between the 'extratextual set (Te)' and the 'novelistic set (Tn)'. The need to differentiate 'texts' is further complicated when writer and reader are also perceived as texts, as in Kristeva's dialogical model of Subject and Addressee that determines the genre of the written narrative: 'The writer's interlocutor, then, is the writer himself [*sic*],

---

3. Sue Vice has noted Bakhtin's orientation 'towards a more traditional model of the human subject, and of the author, than critics in the poststructural era may be accustomed to' (Vice 1997: 4). But for Kristeva, in 1985 reflecting on her early work, 'I had the feeling that with his [Bakhtin's] notions of dialogism and carnival we had reached an important point in moving beyond structuralism' (Kristeva 1996: 189). Vice has also drawn attention to critics' notice of the distinction elided by an overlap in the terminology of Bakhtin and that of psychoanalyst Jacques Lacan, and its significance: Bakhtin detects an 'other' in language, Lacan in the psyche... While Bakhtin's other is social, Lacan's is psychological (Vice 1997: 4). The significance for comparing Bakhtin's approach with Kristeva's is that she attended and was influenced by Lacan's seminars in Paris (Kristeva 1997: 19). The difference of focus between Bakhtin and Kristeva, therefore, could be that shift of her attention from the sociopolitical context to the personal psyche as a source of critical interest:

> the discovery of intertextuality at a formal level leads us to an intrapsychic or psychoanalytic finding, if you will, concerning the status of the 'creator' (Kristeva 1996: 190).

but as reader of another text. The one who writes is the same as the one who reads. Since his [*sic*] interlocutor is a text, he himself [*sic*] is no more than a text re-reading itself as it rewrites itself' (Kristeva (1986a: 56).[4]

Although this suggests a writing-reading introspection withdrawn from Bakhtin's world of social communication (Vice 1997: 47; Lodge 1988: 124), her own willingness to have her work published indicates that Kristeva, too, writes as a means of communication. If writers, readers and culture are all to be 'read' as 'texts', however, there appears to be implicit a false universality that would seek to impose the grammatical rules of texts on a non-grammatical world.

Kristeva's terminology enables the relationships among a written text, its writer(s), its reader(s) and its cultural context(s) to be regarded as 'intertextual'. My terminology is more conservative, with intertextual relationships regarded as relationships among written texts, albeit affected by all of the complicating external factors that influence their production and reception. But I have no term adequate for the relationships of texts with their social contexts.

## *Theory in Progress*

In my theorizing at this stage, use of the term 'textual' to refer to written texts, is compatible with the claim that the 'textual' and the 'extra-textual' inhabit each other (Still and Worton 1993: 33) in the sense that a text is produced within, and affected by, particular socio-historical contexts where it might, in its turn, influence people's opinions and actions. The text might eventually speak to readers from other cultures, subsequent historical periods, and very different political situations. But the claim that *all* is text (Tull 2000: 61, 71)[5] suggests an attempt to impose a form of theoretical totalitarianism that confuses literal and metaphorical uses of the term. Its apparent denial of the actual existence of non-textual phenomena such as trees or non-human species of fauna, appears to exemplify yet another version of a

---

4. Kristeva's account would seem to explain the following example from Helen Regueiro Elam, who presumably also regards readers and writers as texts: 'Texts read and write one another and translate one another without regard for primacy, secondariness, or disciplinary borderlines' (Elam 1993: 1276-277).

5. Tull cites Derrida's 'There is nothing outside of the text' (1976: 158) (Tull 2000: 63), and her example of Kristeva's textualizing of Bakhtin's 'voices' (Tull 2000: 71) appears to conform with Derrida's dictum.

colonizing mentality[6] that seeks to impose grammatical structures rather than attend to the world with a non-controlling interest. Yet my response comes from a twenty-first century reading of Kristeva's 1960s to early 1970s work, and reflects that, apart from the different ideologies, my trans-Tasman reading context as an Aotearoa New Zealander in Melbourne differs from her writing context of that time as a Bulgarian in Paris.

As I understand it, intertextuality is a phenomenon of process that encompasses the interrelationships among texts, affected by their contexts of production and reception, and the ideologies present in their subtexts; yet while acknowledging the complexity of interrelationships among them, I do not want to obliterate their differences by the use of one blanket term that labels everything as text indiscriminately. Kristeva's introduction of the Bakhtinian intertextual insight that any text is the absorption and transformation of another (Kristeva 1986a: 37), suggests something of the fluidity of the process; but an important later clarification was her argument that intertextuality involves the passage from one (or several) sign-system(s) to another, in which the 'new signifying system may be produced with the same signifying material; in language, for example, the passage may be made from narrative to text. Or it may be borrowed from different signifying materials: the transposition from a carnival scene to the written text, for instance' (Kristeva 1986b: 111).

When she writes of the passage from narrative to text I assume that she is referring to the shift from oral narrative to written text, both using the same language. In which case, in both examples the shift is from temporary forms of representation to more lasting written texts, as examples of intertextuality. This is where I am perplexed.

To take up the example of the carnival scene: the translation is from a composite event of mixed media, with its sights, sounds, colour, smells, action and so on, to the representative marks of the text that will convey in words an impression of the scene to the imaginations of its audience, partly dependent on the skills of the writer(s). The combined visual and other sensual signification of the carnival interacts with its verbal presentation within the written text, but is not itself a text.

Extratextual events motivate the production of the text(s) whose reception, if there is any, will be affected by other extratextual events. But can it

---

6. In her 'What are Poets For?' seminar at Monash University, 30 May 2001, Kate Rigby mentioned 'human racism' in connection with human attitudes to the ecological environment, and I find an anthropocentric perspective implicit in those theories which seek to place textual structures onto non-texts.

be argued that the suffusion of texts with the influence of their non-textual contexts is intertextual?

In Christian churches, for example, biblical texts are read most often in liturgical contexts. The social and theological contexts of church community and church tradition combine with the ambience of the liturgical setting to affect the listening reception of the texts. Events in the wider context of the world beyond the church will have their influence, too. As with the example of the carnival scene, extratextual reality, or even fantasy, can provide the semiotic, socio-historical and personal contexts in which texts are read and written, can influence both meaning and interpretation, but of themselves are neither texts nor necessarily structured as such. Some of the variable textual dimensions that will affect the liturgy and the readings are songs, prayers, and homilies, and while because of time constraints these remain peripheral to the main focus of my argument they form a part of its contextual background.

My interest in intertextuality is particularly concerned with the effects of shifting literary contexts and translation in the progress of some verses from the Hebrew Bible to their location in a Christian lectionary. I work with *written* texts, and my current understanding of the writer-text-reader intertextual relationship is as follows:

1. The written text is a fixed form of words, marks upon a surface, set down in *particular socio-historical circumstances*. The text remains until the marks fade or are erased, or its surface disintegrates.

(I work with texts on paper or computer screen, but in the eighth century BCE, in what was then 'Gilead, a region that was reckoned to be a part of Israel', a text was written on lime-plaster in a script that resembles the Aramaic alphabet. It is thought to have been sited on the projecting part of what might have been an internal sanctuary wall, and refers to gods, but not the God of Israel. Some of the text was washed away by rain when the building was destroyed. In 1967 it was discovered at the place now known as Deir 'Alla in the Jordan Valley, thanks to an Arab named Ali; the full extent of the text is not known, but its remaining fragments were assembled and translated [Smelik 1991: 80-84]. The writing of the Deir 'Alla text occurred in circumstances different from those of the earlier epic writings on Mesopotamian clay tablets, or the later writings of biblical Wisdom literature.)

2. The writer-who-is-also-a-reader will have written with some *intention of communication*, perhaps mediated by another person's editorial

process, such as the addition of paratextual comments, titles, subheadings and so on.[7]

(Where Kristeva's writer, script and reader are all texts, my assumption is that the [non-textual] writer of texts will also be a reader. The act of writing suggests some communicative purpose, whether or not as an act of self-communication for the writer, as in the case of a shopping list, or Kristeva's suggested writing as an intrapsychic activity. Written language is the shared means of communication from writer-reader to reader, as in the process outlined by M.H. Abrams with respect to historians: the historian/writer reads and interprets texts, then presents that interpretation to the public [or other intended audience] [Abrams 1989: 238].)

3. But writers, editors and readers each have a repertoire of *'texts in the mind'* (Tull 2000: 63), anterior or contemporary written texts (Kristeva 1986a: 39), as well as individual life contexts, and *no two individuals share the same repertoire* (Tull 2000: 63).

(This follows from the assumption that the writer is also a reader. Each individual repertoire influences the person's interpretation, so that texts read previously will influence what is written, consciously or not. As a generalized example, because the eighth-century BCE writer of the text reconstructed from Deir 'Alla wrote of Balaam, the son of Beor, there has been a tendency among those familiar with the biblical Balaam story in Numbers 22–24 '…to assume that the text is speaking about a seer who lived 500 years earlier: at a time when the people of Israel were approaching the Promised Land'. And yet, if 'the story in Numbers 22–24 had not been known, Balaam would have been dated on the basis of the Deir 'Alla text to the 8th century' [Smelik 1991: 85].

And the interpreters whose shared familiarity with Numbers 22–24 influenced their interpretation will have differed individually because each will have been influenced by other literary texts as well.)

4. So, no actual reader reads exactly the way an author intends…readers miss allusions and echoes intended by authors, and hear unintended echoes and associations (Tull 2000: 63).

---

7  *Paratext* is the term coined by Gerard Genette to name the phenomenon of those 'verbal or other productions such as an author's name, a title, a preface, illustrations' that 'surround and extend [the text], precisely in order to *present* it, in the usual sense of this verb, but also in the strongest sense: to *make present*, to ensure the text's presence in the world…' (Genette 1997: 1; emphasis Genette's).

(It is unlikely that the eighth-century BCE writer was thinking in terms of the stories that became incorporated into the biblical texts. The god Shagar of the Deir 'Alla text appears to have been important, but she is unknown apart from that text [Smelik 1991: 87]), so for current researchers her name cannot resonate with the associations that would have been evoked for contemporaries of the writer.

Further, as Kristeva observed with reference to Nerval's use of symbols in his poetry, 'The essential point is precisely the polyvalence of the symbols, and the fact that we can add other connotations that perhaps even Nerval didn't recognize' [Kristeva 1996:193].)

5. When texts are placed in juxtaposition, or if the order of their contents is altered, different literary contexts are created.

(Example: The book of Ruth located in the Septuagint amidst the 'historical' books [Judges–Ruth–1 Kings] has a literary context different from its setting within the Wisdom literature of the Hebrew Bible [Proverbs–Ruth–Song of Songs].)

6. Writing emanates from an author or authors whose perspective will always be shifting in response to new information, changing circumstances and the events that are a part of life.

(Political events such as the disruption of the World Trade Organization's meeting on September 11, 2000 and the destruction of New York's World Trade Center on September 11, 2001 (both the immediate tragedy in New York and the tragic decision of the USA administration to respond with military vengeance), have repercussions that impact on the lives and imaginations of people, including writers, throughout the world. Their perspectives will shift according to their political, religious and socio-geographical locations, as well as the different stages of their reflection on those events. And personal events such as parenthood, conversation, learning from other species, encountering oppression or discovering that one is oppressive, will also affect the shifts of perspective. Writers respond to life as other people do.

In the sphere of biblical interpretation, the development of a feminist 'hermeneutics of suspicion' (Schüssler Fiorenza 1983: xxiii), together with new information from archaeological discoveries (Smelik 1991: 1-2), have challenged both the supposed historical veracity of biblical texts and the claim that they are a source of divine revelation (Schneiders 1993: 51). Interpretive writers' perspectives will shift according to their need to accept the revelatory character of scripture or their need to refute such claims.)

7. Readers' perspectives are similarly shifting.

(Texts previously read as unproblematic are read differently from the new perspective: Aware of the depth of sexism in scripture, Phyllis Bird in the 1990s cringed at her 1970s use of 'generic' masculine language [Bird 1997: 1]. Having met her birth mother, Chung Hyun Kung turned away from the theological questions of European privilege to a theology whose primary context was 'the despised women of Asia' [Chung 1993: 4-5]. Donna Matahaere-Atariki discovered the problem of needing to own both academic privilege and its limitations: 'The unequal relationship that is constructed, between the 'us' who speak and the "them" whom we represent, hampers any concerted effort to challenge those structures that historically produce the silencing of so many [Matahaere-Atariki 1998: 70].

Such readerly awareness of ideologies within a text can lead to greater awareness of readers' own shifts of ideological perspective. It can also happen that where a text gives enjoyment, then reading and rereading can lead to a greater appreciation of its qualities, the sense of an enhanced understanding that also represents changing perspectives.)

8. So the only fixed aspect of literary intertextuality is the written work.

(Interpretive change comes from readers, not the text, which remains open to (re)interpretation and revised opinions by all who make its acquaintance for as long as it remains in existence or is physically unaltered. Writers' and readers' perspectives might have changed but the text itself, an inanimate object, does not.)

*Becoming Enmeshed*

The written/published work represents a momentary nexus; as Kristeva has written, 'The literary text is a *réseau* of connections' (Kristeva 1969: 175). The word *réseau* can be translated as *network*, or *web*, or *entanglement*, so I want to keep that translation open and her idea in mind as I venture a little way into the perplexing world of biblical intertextuality. Yet there is no 'little way' through the biblical world of the text; one either breaks free, forever trailing bits of the web, or becomes enmeshed, absorbed in the endless array of interpretive possibilities.

Old Testament texts read in Christian churches will be the outcome of translations from the Hebrew Bible, perhaps by way of the Greek Septuagint and Latin Vulgate, to a vernacular language. The shifts of language have implications for interpretation, because which texts of which bibles are taken to be authoritative sources of reference? In the sixteenth century, for example, William Tyndale was burned at the stake for his English translation that later formed the basis of the 1611 Authorized Version[8] (Isaacs 1940: 155-56, 160). So if every translation involves the transposition of the text from one sign-system to another, who determines the validity of which version? Which of whose cultural nuances remain, what is lost, what is added and how do we know?

Contextual translations have also taken place: from the Jewish Hebrew Bible to the Christian Old Testament, through changes of religious perspective and changes of literary canonical context. Different theologies are suggested by the canonical order of the books, altered from the TaNaK sequence of Torah (Pentateuch), Nevi'im (Prophets), Ketuvim (Writings) to the Christian canonical orderings of Catholic and Protestant Old Testaments which also begin with the Pentateuch but end with the Prophets, read christologically.

A further major change of literary context occurs with the contexts constructed in the lectionary: a fixed cycle of readings prepared for use in Christian liturgy. When it is used on a Sunday there will be read a few verses from the Old Testament, some verses from a New Testament Epistle, and a Gospel reading. The cyclical repetition of texts ensures that gradually, if only by osmosis, congregations will become familiar with those stories told. It also ensures that in lectionary-using churches some biblical stories are not told, at least in the context of worship. Exod. 1.15-21, for example, tells of the midwives Shiphrah and Puah, who defied Pharaoh's orders to kill the Hebrews' newborn male babies, but the relevant lectionary reading omits these verses (Monday of the Fifteenth Week in Ordinary time, Year 1) (Fox 1996: 1).

Lectionary selections give much greater access to biblical texts than was available to Catholics before Vatican II (Murphy 2000: 548),[9] but the

8. According to J. Isaacs:

> In the rendering of technical terms Tindale wilfully chose tendencious and heretical words obnoxious to such orthodox Catholics as Sir Thomas More: 'congregation' instead of 'church' for *ecclesia*, 'senior' for *presbyter* (changed later to 'elder'), 'repentance' instead of 'penance', ...(Isaacs 1940: 159).

Alice Parmelee has suggested that Tyndale's notes and comments printed in the margins of the text might have alarmed church authorities more than the translations (Parmelee 1960: 151-52), and S.L. Greenspan opted for a combination of both translation and comments (Greenspan 1963: 145-46).

9. Chapter VI.22 of the Vatican II document 'Dogmatic Constitution on Divine

juxtaposition of the readings for use in liturgical settings also affects their interpretation (Vagaggini 1976: 455). Lutheran minister Gail Ramshaw has drawn attention to the way in which the superimposition of readings changes their individual reception. Her suggested simile is that of 'the transparent overlays of anatomy in a biology textbook: as each overlay is added, the entire picture alters. Each image is to be seen in relation to the others' (Ramshaw 1999: 10).

Once seen in that relationship, the effect will be carried back into the reading of those texts in their scriptural contexts.

### For Example…

Using one form of intertextual approach, a text from Deuteronomy 4 in its scriptural context will be compared with the same text in its lectionary context, where it is juxtaposed with other excerpted texts in the lectionary. The lectionaries of other denominations will also be consulted, but for now my example is from *The Roman Missal* readings for the Twenty second Sunday in Ordinary Time, Year B:

> FIRST READING
> A reading from the book of Deuteronomy (4.1-2, 6-8)
>
> *Add nothing to what I command you, keep the commandments of the Lord.*
>
> Moses said to the people: 'Now, Israel, take notice of the laws and customs that I teach you today, and observe them, that you may have life and may enter and take possession of the land that the Lord the God of your fathers is giving you. You must add nothing to what I command you, and take nothing from it, but keep the commandments of the Lord your God just as I lay them down for you. Keep them, observe them, and they will demonstrate to the peoples your wisdom and understanding. When they come to know of all these laws they will exclaim, 'No other people is as wise and prudent as this great nation'. And what great nation is there that has its gods

---

Revelation' opens with the statement: 'Easy access to sacred Scripture should be provided for all the Christian faithful.'

A footnote on the same page comments that no official document has encouraged the availability of Scripture to all since 'the early centuries of the Church' (Vatican II 1966: 125-26). As Sandra Schneiders observed, prior to Vatican II 'the average Catholic had at best a cursory and fragmentary acquaintance with the Bible' (Schneiders 1993: 31). This apparently differs from the practice of Protestant churches founded during the Reformation period, which 'took their stand on the supremacy of Holy Scripture' (Nichol 1970: 57).

> so near as the Lord our God is to us whenever we call to him? And what great nation is there that has laws and customs to match this whole Law that I put before you today?'

This is the word of the Lord.

The paratext that precedes this excerpt consists of the 'First Reading' heading that confirms the expectation that other readings will follow; advice that the reading is from the book of Deuteronomy; and an interpretive key: 'Add nothing to what I command you, keep the commandments of the Lord.' The paratext at the end of the reading affirms to a congregation that 'This is the word of the Lord', inviting their response, 'Thanks be to God.'

The interpretive key and concluding paratext contribute to the text's reception in keeping with the controlled context of worship, linking the text with its extratextual liturgical context: '[I]t is in the last analysis, the flow, pace, and overall contour of the celebration which the assembly experiences' (Johnson 1993: ix).

The use of the second person in the paratext also indicates address to a dual audience: the people addressed in the world of the text and the listening members of the worshipping congregation. The reading presents the teaching of Moses as a mediation of the commandments of God and the lectionary's sequence of paratextual interpretive keys progress from instruction to keep the commandments, to an assertion that 'the just' will live in the presence of God (Ps. 15), a further injunction to obedience (James), culminating with the pre-Gospel accusation, 'You put aside the commandments of God.' In this way the paratextual comments connect the readings.

The body of the text is identical with the text of the Jerusalem Bible translation, except for the substitution of 'the Lord' for 'Yahweh'. This is a significant alteration. Yahweh is a masculine title, allegedly God's self-designation (Exod. 3.15) as a third-person masculine form of the Hebrew verb *hyh*, 'to be'. But the first-person form of the verb, with which the biblical God refers to Godself a few verses earlier in Exodus 3, has common gender. The biblical God's supposed masculinity becomes even more pronounced with the substitution of 'Lord', reducing more nebulous verb-based perceptions of the unimaged divinity to concrete noun-based notions of hubristic human aristocracy. As Judith McKinlay has demonstrated in a study of Wisdom's progressive biblical sex-change operation (female to male), 'this gender dimension is very much a matter of ideological commitment' (McKinlay 1996: 241).

The biblical narrative context of Deut. 4.1-8 is that Moses has summarized 40 years of journeying from Egypt to a place whence, soon after his death, the Israelites will invade the land across the Jordan River. In the reading he is preparing the way for his final teachings that take up most of the book of Deuteronomy before his death; perhaps that lends some poignancy to his exhortations that the people should choose life. Yet from a 2001 perspective, the deaths caused in the name of turning away God's anger raise some difficult questions, apparently for the compilers of the lectionary as much as for other people.

## *A Gap in the Text*

The reading flows smoothly, but note that injunction to add nothing and take nothing from what is commanded, reinforced by the paratextual comment. The verses Deut. 4.3-5, presumably because of their pastoral difficulty,[10] have been omitted from the reading:

> You can see with your own eyes what Yahweh has done at Baal Peor; all the followers of the Baal of Peor have been wiped out from among you by Yahweh your God; but all of you who stayed faithful to Yahweh your God are still alive today. See, as Yahweh my God has commanded me, I teach you all the laws and customs you are to observe in the land you are to enter and make your own (Jerusalem Bible).

In their biblical context, these verses link the Deut. 4.1-8 segment to its immediately preceding and following verses: 3.29 ('So we stayed in the valley close to Beth-Peor'); and 4.9 ('But take care what you do and be on your guard. Do not forget the things your eyes have seen…').

If included they would weave the reading back to Numbers 25, that gives an account of the violence at Beth Peor, linking also to Israel's purported slaughter of the Midianites in Numbers 31; and to Ps. 106.28-31, a truncated version of the events at Beth Peor. Within the world of the text, observation of the commandments or failure to obey them is literally a matter of life and death. But whose are the commandments? These questions invite speculation about connections between the text and the unknown circumstances that motivated its production.

---

10. Concerning difficult texts, the General Introduction to *The Roman Missal* states:

> In readings for Sundays and solemnities, texts that present real difficulties are avoided for pastoral reasons.

It further states that the omission of verses that are unsuitable pastorally enables the inclusion of readings that are otherwise of spiritual value (Ch. IV, 'General Plan of the Readings for Mass', *The Roman Missal* 1981: xxx-xxxviii: xxxiv-xxxv).

Within the text, is the biblical God being used in Deut. 4.3-4 to exonerate the murderous actions of human beings? In Homer's epic, after Odysseus and his companions have slaughtered Penelope's unwanted suitors, the old servant Eurycleia begins to triumph loudly but she is rebuked by the gore-spattered hero, who attributes the deaths to 'the hand of heaven and [the suitors'] own infamy' (Homer/Rieu 1964: 338). Similarly, the biblical God's violence in sending a plague to punish the Israelites is supplemented by the human violence of Moses' supporters (Num. 25), but in this excerpt from Deuteronomy the violence is attributed solely to God.

Deuteronomy 4.5 does not appear to present the same type of pastoral difficulty: Moses asserts that he is doing as God commands in teaching the laws and customs to be observed in the land the Israelites are about to enter, both affirming the divine source of his authority and reiterating the links made in v. 1 between observation of the laws and customs and possession of the land that is to be conquered. Those verses conjointly will require a different scanning of their much longer threads. The God who created the world and all its creatures, who blessed human beings with fertility that they might fill the earth (*eretz*), is the God who chose the children of Israel especially and promised them the land (*eretz*) which they are to occupy subject to their obedience to the commandments.[11] The whole of the Pentateuch and subsequent books are caught up in the association, with promises of land, the ancestry of the Israelites, and their relationships with God and the people and gods of other nations.

The biblical God's promises are not innocent, and again there emerge questions of the relationship between the world of the text and the extratextual world, this time the circumstances of reception. Roland Boer has taken up Edward Said's argument that the Exodus cannot be separated from the violent conquest and oppression of the 'promised land', with God's demand for the annihilation of the inhabitants. Going beyond Said, Boer reasons that 'the Exodus itself may be read as an ideological justification for precisely such acts of brutality, as a discourse…that legitimates the inflicting of oppression on others…' (Boer 2001a: 90).

---

11. As an example of the effect of transition from one sign-system to another in translation, the use of *eretz*, *ge* and *terra* in Gen. 1.28 and Deut. 4.1 of Hebrew, Greek and Latin versions respectively, allows better than English versions for a closer connection between the Deuteronomic land to be entered and the blessing of the first humans who were to fill the earth in Genesis. The Alexandrian version of the Septuagint Deut. 4.1 emphasizes the link with its promise that the Israelites will be multiplied in the land, subject to their obedience to the commandments.

If such texts are in fact used to justify oppression, as they appear to have been in the history of colonization (Boer 2001a: 90; Green 1999: 274), is the biblical Israelite oppression of Palestine being used to justify the actions of the current government of Israel against Palestinians? The verses omitted from the lectionary become very uncomfortable reading and call into question the practice of assigning a normative value to any foundational texts; it was the compilers' choice to avoid, rather than confront, the difficulty.

*What's Left (Behind)*

What remains in the lectionary suggests that the biblical Israelites (and listening congregation of Christians) should observe the commandments in order to become renowned for their wisdom and understanding. The menace of God has been removed; so, too, has the reminder of the brutality of some of the biblical God's commandments. In this instance a different perception of the deity appears to have been substituted for the perception depicted in Deuteronomy 4, with different scriptural allusions.

For example, God as the 'Father of all light' (James) evokes John 1's association of light with Jesus, the light that shines in the darkness, with the Genesis 1 account of God's creation of light, and with light–dark images throughout both Old and New Testaments. But in the lectionary context, the dual audience is not being addressed as people who have witnessed the immediate destructiveness of God in their midst, nor as a people who have themselves slaughtered others since that event (Num. 31). There is a lectionary distancing of the community addressed from the godless (Ps. 15), 'the world' (James) and Jews, and a paratextual accusation that suggests the extratextual audience should engage in some self-reflection about obedience to the commandments ('You put aside the commandments of God'). It is not the graphic life and death situation of a people being taught by a leader about to die, just before they engage in a war of conquest.

The lectionary readings within their lectionary/liturgical context in their turn evoke scriptural allusions according to the 'texts in the mind' of the listeners. For example, the Deut. 4.1-8 reading in its lectionary context is conjoined with notions of the just person who lives in the presence of God, doing no wrong to family and neighbour (Ps. 15); God as the 'Father of all light', whose word tells 'his children' to come to the help of widows and orphans (James 1); external cleanliness as less important than what happens in people's hearts (Mark 7). The just person of Psalm 15 is to hold the godless in disdain, 'the world' of James is likely to contaminate the

Father God's children, and those Jews who observe that Jesus' disciples eat with unwashed hands are dismissed as hypocrites.

Any one of these notions has the potential to open out into a fuller discourse that reconnects the lectionary with biblical sources, but how far they carry back into rereadings of the excerpts within their scriptural contexts would appear to depend on the effect of the lectionary readings on the individual listener/interpeter. Tracing the changes of such interpretive possibilities is not a clear-cut process.

And reading *The Odyssey* has left me wondering. Does the analytical unravelling of a text lead to its reweaving in a form that enhances its meaning for other readers of the text? What do interpreters thread into or subtract from the text, and for whom does it matter? As I noted earlier, both the epic and the biblical stories have divine and human characters woven into their respective texts, and it seems that massacre by the divinely approved characters is acceptable, the will of the influential deity (whether as part of the action or projected into visions of a future divine judgmental wrath). Both have male-fantasy elements, and in both of them the women have stereotypical roles, either serving the interests of men or leading them astray.

Which of them is the greater fabrication?

*Appendix: Lectionary Readings*
*Twenty-Second Sunday in Ordinary Time*
*Year B*

*First Reading*
A reading from the book of Deuteronomy (4.1-2, 6-8):

> *Add nothing to what I command you, keep the commandments of the Lord.*

> Moses said to the people: 'Now, Israel, take notice of the laws and customs that I teach you today, and observe them, that you may have life and may enter and take possession of the land that the Lord the God of your fathers is giving you. You must add nothing to what I command you, and take nothing from it, but keep the commandments of the Lord your God just as I lay them down for you. Keep them, observe them, and they will demonstrate to the peoples your wisdom and understanding. When they come to know of all these laws they will exclaim, 'No other people is as wise and prudent as this great nation.' And what great nation is there that has its gods so near as the Lord our God is to us whenever we call to him? And what great nation is there that has laws and customs to match this whole Law that I put before you today?'

This is the word of the Lord.

*Responsorial Psalm* (Ps. 14.2-5. R,v.1):

> R The just will live in the presence of the Lord.

> Lord, who shall dwell on your holy mountain?
> He who walks without fault;
> He who acts with justice
> And speaks the truth from his heart. R,

> He who does no wrong to his brother,
> who casts no slur on his neighbour,
> who holds the godless in disdain,
> but honours those who fear the Lord. R,

> He who keeps his pledge, come what may;
> who takes no interest on a loan
> and accepts no bribes against the innocent.
> Such a man will stand firm for ever. R,

*Second Reading*
A reading from the letter of St James (1.17-18, 21-22, 27):

> *You must do what the word tells you.*

> It is all that is good, everything that is perfect, which is given us from above; it comes down from the father of all light; with him there is no such thing as alteration, no shadow of a change. By his own choice he made us his children by the message of the truth so that we should be a sort of first-fruits of all that he had created.
>
> Accept and submit to the word which has been planted in you and can save your souls. But you must do as the word tells you, and not just listen to it and deceive yourselves.
>
> Pure unspoilt religion, in the eyes of God our Father is this: coming to the help of orphans and widows when they need it, and keeping oneself uncontaminated by the world.

> This is the word of the Lord.

*Gospel Acclamation* (cf. Jn 6.63, 68):

> Alleluia, alleluia!
> Your words are spirit, Lord,
> and they are life:
> You have the message of eternal life.
> Alleluia!

Or

> Alleluia, alleluia!
> By his own choice the Father made us his children
> by the message of truth,
> so that we should be a sort of first-fruits
> of all that he created.
> Alleluia!

## *Gospel*
A reading from the Gospel according to Mark (7.1-8, 14-15, 21-23):

*You put aside the commandment of God to cling to human traditions.*

The Pharisees and some of the scribes who had come from Jerusalem gathered round Jesus, and they noticed that some of his disciples were eating with unclean hands, that is, without washing them. For the Pharisees, and the Jews in general, follow the tradition of the elders and never eat without washing their arms as far as the elbow; and on returning from the marketplace they never eat without first sprinkling themselves. There are also many other observances which have been handed down to them concerning the washing of cups and pots and bronze dishes. So these Pharisees and scribes asked him, 'Why do your disciples not respect the tradition of the elders but eat their food with unclean hands?' He answered, 'It was of you hypocrites that Isaiah so rightly prophesied in this passage of scripture:

This people honours me only with lip-service,
while their hearts are far from me.
The worship they offer me is worthless,
The doctrines they teach are only human regulations.

You put aside the commandment of God to cling to human traditions.'

He called the people to him again and said, 'Listen to me, all of you, and understand. Nothing that goes into a man from outside can make him unclean; it is the things that come out of a man that make him unclean. For it is from within, from men's hearts, that evil intentions emerge: fornication, theft, murder, adultery, avarice, malice, deceit, indecency, envy, slander, pride, folly. All these evil things come from within and make a man unclean.'

This is the Gospel of the Lord.

WHO'S/WHOSE SARAH?:
JOURNEYING WITH SARAH IN A CHORUS OF VOICES

Judith E. McKinlay

> Abram took his wife Sarai and his brother's son Lot, and all the possessions that they had gathered, and the persons whom they had acquired in Haran; and they set forth to go to the land of Canaan. When they had come to the land of Canaan Abram passed through the land… (Gen. 12.5-6).

For a long time I have been interested in the figure of Sarah. I follow her down the corridors of texts but when she turns and faces me (as it were) I am unsure how to read her, for her features alter at each glance. I wonder whether I am following a whole series of interchanging women, all with the name of Sarah—the Sarah of the Call, the vulnerably 'sister-ized' Sarah, the Sarah of the long-deferred promise, the Sarah of the abused Hagar. Even the very name is unstable: is this Sarai or Sarah? But I am also interested in journeyings, in the entries people make into lands that are not theirs. While Israel's entry to the land remains a mystery, it appears in many guises, told and retold as Bible odysseys, scrutinized, analysed and reappropriated by readers, as model succeeds model, paradigm after paradigm. Tales of biblical ancestors entering the land, slipping peaceably through the country side, creeping with stealth or erupting with sword, have become part of other peoples' cultural memory, and as such they mesh with other journeys, other peoples' voyagings, other ethnic entries. For biblical readers Israel's past, like so many, 'is now not a land to return to in a simple politics of memory. It has become a synchronic warehouse of cultural scenarios' (Appadurai 1990: 4, quoted in Lionnet 1995: 16). So my interest settles here on the Sarah/Sarai who entered a land which was not hers to become part of Israel's Call narrative as it is told in Genesis 12. How am I to read her in this early ancestor tale and whose Sarah has she become in the tellings and retellings that form so many different cultural scenarios spanning both time and space?

At first glance I wonder whether she has a place at all in the Call, which tradition has long been capitalized and set in high relief among biblical texts. As it is recorded in ch. 12, the call is notably delivered to Abram alone (vv. 1-3); masculine singular pronouns, at the beginning and ending of God's speech in v. 1 and continuing into v. 2, make this very clear. Through Abram will come a great nation; through Abram *all the families/ clans of the earth will be blessed*. Not until v. 5 is there mention of Sarah, here named as Sarai, and then recorded in the context of Abram's possessions. So it is both the Sarah of the text and the Sarah of the gaps that is my interest.

Should I begin by asking questions of Sarah's place in Israel's history? While I am trained to consider biblical contexts, this is a detective task in itself; Sarah has been journeying through time, running breathlessly from c. 2500–200 BCE. When I first glimpsed her, my encounter having been initiated by John Bright, she was, if not a wandering nomad, at least a wandering 'semi-nomad', travelling 'in search of seasonal pasture...in the early centuries of the second millennium BC' (Bright 1972: 94-95), although, as Bright himself admitted, no contemporary text had managed to capture this journeying in print. But soon, having left 'Ur of the Chaldeans' (Gen. 11.31), a place once her home but now, alas, an identified anachronism (Ahlström 1993: 182),[1] she was paradoxically to be met in a much later Babylon, penned there by a scribe keen to exploit an Ur/Babylon link in an effort to persuade sixth-century Judaean exiles that they were not in an alien land at all, but in the very place from which their ancestors had come, that they were among their very own kin (Habel 1995: 117-18).[2] I continue

---

1. As Ahlström (1993: 182) notes, 'the Chaldeans do not appear on the historical stage until the ninth century BCE... This phrase does not occur again in the Old Testament before Neh. 9.7, thus it may point to a late date for the origin of the Abraham narrative and for the "promise of the land".'

2. Whether the scribal pen-mover was the creator or reviser of the narrative remains an open question. Albertz (1994: 405-406), for example, suggests that 'another large-scale literary revision of the patriarchal tradition was undertaken during the exile', understanding the ancestors 'as bearers of unconditional promises which had still not gone out of date and as models by which they could orientate themselves in their own time'. Prior (1997: 219) represents the view that '[t]he fact that Abraham is referred to as an individual only in the exilic texts (Isa. 51.2; Ezek. 33.24), and that, with the exception of Josh. 12.3-4, 12, the pre-exilic parts of the Old Testament make no mention of the incidents associated with Abraham, Isaac or Jacob suggests that the stories used by the author of Genesis may be no earlier than the period of the Babylonian exile'. His suggestion (222) is that '[t]he exiled Judahites employed the patriarchal narrative of a mythical and legendary past to affirm their right to represent all Israel, making Abraham the ancestor of Jacob and the recipient of the divine promise. This

my detective journey, now following Sarah with an eye equally focused on that scribal narrator busy shaping this tale to fit his time-bound agenda,[3] to find a fresh trail leading out once again from Babylon, but this time to a diminished Yehud, reduced to a province under Persian rule.[4] Here the scribe is shaping his narrative of a family 'called' to stake a divine right to the land (Ahlström 1993: 182) on behalf of those returnees from Babylon who have arrived back in 'the land' only to find themselves embroiled in bitter land claims. Here the land *that I will show you* (Gen. 12.1), has its own particular interpretation.[5] I pause in scholarly breathlessness to consider these varying biblical scenarios. Do I choose? Which of these is most persuasive? Sarah, wife of the ancestor promised land, descendents and a dynastic 'great nation' would be welcomed by Israelites in exilic Babylon,

promise repudiated the monarchy which, in general, they judged to have failed them and vested the divine relationship with the whole people'.

3. As Yairah Amit writes, '[w]hen biblical writers sought to describe the past, they built the picture around a particular idea, or a systematic, coherent set of ideas' (1999: 34). 'The historian...wishes also to tell a story that will interest the readers and induce them to go on reading' (108). Amit quotes Alter (1981: 32): '[F]iction was the principal means which the biblical authors had at their disposal for realizing history.' It is, however, quite possible to change the context and see the story change accordingly, a difference equally dependent on the political location of the scribe as on time. For example, Michael Prior's identified exilic writer has chosen these ancestors not so much to set up an 'Us' over against 'Babylon', as an inner Israelite encouragement. This is an anti-monarchy scribe who has seen the monarchy fail, and who therefore chooses an ancestor capable of symbolizing the god/human relationship of promise vested within the whole people, rather than being uniquely channelled through the king (1997: 222). Prior notes Garbini's suggestion (1988: 77-78) that Ur and Haran were deliberately used to make connections with the Babylon of Nabonidus, and so allow the exiles to 'ingratiate themselves to their new rulers'.

4. Heard follows a body of other scholars who suggest that in contrast to the circumstances of a deported people, 'the imperially-sponsored, temple-centred culture of Yehud will have provided precisely the sort of material context' required for the production of the final form of Genesis (2001: 9). Those responsible were Yehud's 'immigrant elite' whose concerns were ethnic definition and corresponding land claims. Heard's thesis argues for a 'high degree of correspondence between the interest promoted in the books of Ezra and Nehemiah and in the book of Genesis' (2001: 22)

5. As Ahlström (1993: 846-47) notes, a promise of land 'has no function to fill for people living in the country'. While this could apply to the Babylonian exiles, he sees the argument used in the context of a contest for land rights between the returnees and the indigenous people. Brett (2000b: 5) proposes as the agenda of 'the final editors of Genesis...to undermine the theologically legitimized ethnocentrism found in the books of Ezra and Nehemiah'.

but the move to pen an origin story significantly different to that of Exodus makes equally good political sense for a scribe in Yehud; overlords cast into the sea may not have gone down too well with the Persian leadership. But I am now a suspicious reader; this is no real-life, met-in-history Sarah, but a scroll-captured character, carefully drawn to suit her writer's/writers' interest(s). I may scrutinize and analyse and make considered choices, but this will remain Sarah, the pawn of biblical storytellers.

But if texts read differently according to the suggested positioning of their scribal narrators, they also interpret differently according to the context of their readers. While the pens of scribes have been at work behind Sarah, I am now the reader in front of this text, and as I listen I hear her journeying resonating with other journeyings, for I myself am a descendent of travellers who journeyed long and hard to reach Aotearoa New Zealand, leaving the Highlands of Scotland for Nova Scotia, before moving on yet again. Norman Habel's translation of *ger* as 'immigrant' (Gen. 17.8), and his description of Gen. 11.31–12.9 as a 'migration narrative' help to key in these connections (1995: 116-19). So I recognize that I am following this story with the keen interests of a reader located in a much later (post)colonial context. Immediately parallels come to mind. For canonically positioned as Israel's—or Israel's ancestors'—first arrival in the land, this is where the Bible would have us believe it all begins for Israel, there is no space for any earlier history in Canaan, just as in my postcolonial world 'settlers' ideologies involved in nation-building have a historical starting point, which occurs at the moment of colonial conquest and the beginning of settlement...the period prior to conquest and settlement is often constructed as pre-historical' (Stasiulis and Yuval-Davis 1995: 21).[6] This is how we learnt our own history when I went to school; it began with the arrival of the first Europeans.

But journeying with Sarah may involve more than seeking parallel experiences. What motivates this study is the suspicion that she may be

---

6. My colleague Dr Margaret Eaton reminds me that this frequently coincides with the move from oral to written tradition. The use of the word 'ideologies' is apt here for the earliest written material was, for the most part, set down by writers with a mission in mind. As James Belich notes '[m]uch of the early literature on New Zealand was in fact part of two great advertising campaigns: the effort to obtain support for missionary activity and to cast its achievements in the best possible light, and the effort to attract settlers to a young and distant colony in competition with better-known fields of immigration such as North America where land was cheaper and the voyage out shorter' (1986: 327).

lurking in 'the warehouse' of my country's 'cultural scenarios'. Recently I visited an art exhibition where one of the central works was a large painting by an Australian artist, Imants Tillers, entitled Diaspora. While it was one coherent work it gained its effect through being composed as a series of connecting panels, at the centre of which, as its focus, was the large and dynamic figure of a woman. But what most caught my eye was that the panels comprised a visual intertextuality, for there, on panel after panel, were copies of familiar and influential works, setting the diasporic theme within its cultural context. So a European Mondrian and a New Zealand McCahon, from opposite ends of the world, both had a place, representing their part in the life of a diasporic Australia. In much the same way I would like to set a place for Sarah in a collage, not of paintings, but of voices who speak out of a past that is part of the cultural scenario of Pakeha history in Aotearoa New Zealand. For in countries such as mine, that have a settlement history in which missionaries and churches have played a significant role, biblical texts, either consciously or subconsciously, have been a part of the cultural scenario; they entered with those first steps off the boats that landed on our shores.

So in my proposed collage I decide to reserve places for the voices of some of the early European settler women who travelled across the world to enter the land of Aotearoa. It may simply be a matter of sharing parallel experiences with the journeying Sarah but it may also be the Bible's influence that I am hearing, with its whispers of Sarah and Abraham below or behind the settler women's words. For there is indeed a sense of call in the letter to her cousin written by Charlotte Brown on 8 April 1829, as she was about to leave London with her husband to work as CMS missionaries.

> If our Heavenly Father (as I trust He has) has indeed pointed my way He will support under every trial (Porter and Macdonald 1996: 60).

And a sense of land promise underlying Maria Richmond's journal letter to friends, written from New Plymouth, 11 November 1853:

> The wonderfulness of the change, the ease and certainty with which one traverses such wastes of water…the feeling of coming home, as it were, to a country wanting you, asking for people to enjoy and use it, with a climate to suit you, a beauty to satisfy and delight, and with such capabilities and possibilities for the future (Porter and Macdonald 1996: 90).

Certainly there is no sense of this being other people's land, in contrast to Charlotte, who had added in the same letter,

> It is true that we shall be exposed to the fury of an uncivilized people, but He in whose hands are all our ways can subdue the most savage natures and protect us as easily in New Zealand as in England.

While there is no expression of such apprehension in Genesis 12 there is a certain ambiguity in the biblical narrative; both in 11.31 and 12.5 the land to which Abram is called is named as *the land of Canaan*. Mention of Canaanites themselves comes explicitly in the context of the *'elon* of Moreh (v. 6), perhaps hinting at a place of Canaanite worship, perhaps even to Asherah with her strong tree connections. It is, however, strikingly not Asherah or any other Canaanite deity who appears, but Israel's god, Yahweh, who promises no less than the land itself. While Abram's immediate response to build an altar there and then to this god is understandable and even appropriate in the context of Yahwistic devotion, this building—and not of one altar, but of at least two (vv. 7, 8)—in someone else's religious patch would seem at the very least presumptuous, if not openly provocative. There would be, as Jantzen has pointed out, a reality in there being Canaanite symbols present, as the Canaanites are the ones holding and occupying the land, whereas 'Abram's altar corresponds only to the promise he believes himself to have heard by the oracular tree' (1993: 22). Of course, it could it be, as Norman Habel suggests, that 'YHWH is portrayed as present in the land and one with the God revealed at sacred sites within the land' (1995: 130-31). But which Israelite writer would have been so bold as to suggest that?! Certainly it conjures up a picture that one might include as an intertextual panel, of a Garden of Eden scene, where all is idyllic, where the universal god walks among the trees and no major separations between peoples have yet occurred. Yet on a surface reading, assuming with the texts that follow, that these Israelite ancestors *were* 'other' than the indigenous peoples of the land, there seems a certain naivety in their assumed right to be there, in the company of those 'others' whose land they have just entered and are looking to appropriate. Listening for the cross-cultural echo, I wonder whether this is a similar naivety to that expressed by Sarah Stephens writing to her sister, on 23 January 1842.

> As we landed we saw two of the natives squatting with their blankets, their faces much tattooed. They looked so pleasant and held out their hands to shake ours which several of us did... What has been said of them, as far as I can judge, is not one bit more than they deserve. They are a fine race of people and there is a great deal of intelligence in their countenances (Porter and Macdonald 1996: 33).

A positive comment? There is at least a whiff of patronizing cultural superiority in her *granting* them 'a great deal of intelligence'. But certainly, once in the land, there is no expression of fear or sense of danger, such as Charlotte had anticipated. So too Sarah, in the silence behind Abraham, apparently moves through the land in equal safety; no fears are expressed until the departure into Egypt. But before I pick up this puzzling disjunction, I want to add another reading, another panel to this imagined collage of voices. Recognizing that readers read gaps as well as text, I want to move out from the scholarly conversations for a while to listen to those whose art is creative imagining, which may or may not have either scholars or the faithful in mind. So I wish to add Sara Maitland's and Jenny Diski's Sarahs to my panels, for these writers, too, are journeying with Sarah.

> Once she prayed with the same zeal and faith as he does still. Then she learned that this God of his was not hers. Everything she knew of now belonged to Abraham: the sheep, the servants, the tents, herself. And his God, too. That it is not so somewhere else, far away, in the scented courts of her childhood, is little or no comfort to her. She left them proudly, she cannot return. Abraham's God does not listen to a word she says to Him (Maitland 1987: 113-14).

> Perhaps she knew all along that there could be no return, that life was lived in only one direction and memory merely tormented the discontented with its capacity to look backwards, but, as in a dream where the dreamer suspects they might be dreaming but refuses to vacate the dreamscape, Sarai allowed memory to whisper to her of the past and chose to believe it said future. Though she thought she was humouring her deluded husband by going along on his trek to nowhere as ordered by no one, she was in truth no more in touch with reality than Abram… They came to a land called Canaan. It was no different from other places they had travelled through, a mixed land of desert and wells, lush enough in parts to sustain herds, with settlements here and there but with nothing of the urban sophistication of Ur or even of Harran… It seemed to Sarai to be just another place they were passing through on their journey of promised but never-to-be-reached destination (Diski 2000: 126, 130).

These Sarahs of the gaps stand at a distance, with barely a glance at the ancient scribes. Is this the biblical Abraham's Sarah at all? But as I read Sara Maitland and Jenny Diski reading Sarah, I find myself nodding; I now recognize this woman of tormented memory and teasing dreams whom I have had such difficulty drawing out from the shadows of the biblical text. She is a woman that I can understand. But does she still keep her place in the biblical scenario? I find that it is Jenny Diski's pointer to the narrator's use of irony that provides the connecting link, for it returns me both to the biblical text and to the postcolonial lens. For while the biblical plot turns on the irony of a husband promised descendents through a wife already revealed as barren (11.30), there is an even more fundamental irony shared with the postcolonial reality, which Gelder and Jacobs explore in reference to Australia, that 'one's place is always already another's place and the issue of possession is never complete, never entirely settled...one is always (dis)possessed, in the sense that neither possession nor dispossession is a fully realizable category' (1998: 138), that 'what is "ours" is also potentially, or even always already, "theirs" ' (23). As Brett (2000b: 51) notes, this is the Genesis irony that the 'land promise is delivered in the very territory which is to be possessed by Abram's seed, at a site that was probably sacred to the original owners of the land'.

These categories of 'ours' and 'theirs' again raise those knotty questions of political division, of 'whose' land, mentioned earlier. For if, as scholars are now suggesting, Israelites and Canaanites were originally not distinct, but one people ethnically, then an Abraham and Sarah marked as outsiders, with a deity quite distinct from those of the Canaanites, would hint of their being characters in a highly political, if not polemical, text, seeking to mark out quite deliberate and particular divisions. Details such as the altar to Yahweh are then not so much a sign of naivety as of a polemical palimpsest, with the signs of a would-be erased memory of shared identity showing through. On this understanding the *'elon* of Moreh may well be the trace of an erased Asherah, to whom Abraham, and perhaps even more particularly Sarah, would not have been strangers at all. The divine name, so carefully inscribed within the overlaying text, that is responsible for the Call and that dislocating move to a distant land with its promises of a future, which the present narrator is at pains to present as the divinely legitimated past, is now the marker of a deliberate dissonance, the marker of a would-be ethnic and cultural divide. With this agenda the text is looking very different. Place this 'Israelite' Sarah on the panel, and there is again a conversation to be found with the women in that early colonial world of Aotearoa New Zealand. For while Maria Richmond and Sarah Stephens may have felt optimistic and positive about life in the 'new' land, Fanny Dillon's letter to her sister Lilly, written from Waimea, 12 October 1843, sees it differently.

> The government at Auckland is both imbecile and weak; they treat Rauparaha like an independent sovereign instead of one of the Queen's subjects and we are told not to resist him. The Maories [*sic*] are very cunning and

very treacherous and never to be depended on either for good or bad (Porter and Macdonald 1996: 109).

But such a context of alarming fearful distrust stands closer in my collage to the Egyptian episode that begins at v. 10. Here there is a narrative disjunction, a further storyline dislocation; for no sooner has Abraham made his proprietorial tour around the land of the Canaanites, than the land itself disgorges him and sends him off to Egypt, where

> ...he said to his wife Sarai, I know well that you are a woman beautiful in appearance; and when the Egyptians see you, they will say, 'This is his wife'; then they will kill me, but they will let you live. Say you are my sister, so that it may go well with me because of you (vv. 11-13).

If I had difficulty bringing Sarah into view in the first half of the chapter, that is now no longer the case. If vv. 6-9 allowed glimpses of a distant memory of a time without tension or conflict, this second narrative episode moves the reader to a world where all is suddenly thrown into separation. Sarah may have been hidden in those earlier verses, with only the gap-filling fictioning imaginers bringing her to voice, but the reader was given no reason to fear for her safety. Now with the flight to Egypt comes fear. But while Abraham, the male, may be fearful, with a fear driven by the fantasy of other men having sex with his wife, it is the woman who discovers the world to be a dangerous and risky place. The text itself protects certain ambiguities. Did Sarah survive this ordeal sexually unscathed? To be taken into Pharaoh's house is at the very least suggestive of sexual taking, of being subject to the male gaze from those not morally entitled; this is clearly a Lacanian world under the Law of the Father.

But once a space is opened up for readers drawing upon the insights of psychoanalysis and other contemporary critical approaches the conversation soon becomes multivoiced, as analysts of gender are swiftly joined by those of race and ethnicity. For current gender/race studies are pointing to the way in which 'in nationalist and racialist narratives...women often play important symbolic roles...carrying in their bodies the collective love and honour of "the nation" ' (Lutz, Phoenix and Yuval-Davis 1995: 9). It is, of course, not only the honour of Israel that Sarah is carrying in her body, it is also the hopes for the seed of the divine promise which will allow Israel to come into being. The biblical tension is now sharp. Is both the honour and the promise in jeopardy? And what of the bearer of the honour? Is there to be protection for her, or is she to suffer violation? Is such a fate even to be whispered by readers of this sacred ancestor narrative? But gender/race findings note that such issues of protection/violation for women are key themes in national narratives. While there is clearly a distinction to be made between the experiences of women who are protected and those who are violated, both moves can be recognized as being 'exploitative in that each silence women' (Lutz *et al.* 1995: 10). What is further disturbing in the Genesis narrative, if it can be assumed that up to this point she has journeyed under the protection of Abraham, is that Sarah now apparently moves from that protection to violation. For once in Egypt, Abraham's sole care is for his own protection.

The layers of interpretative possibilities that these voices are raising are resulting in adding layers of vulnerability for Sarah. She is no longer simply Sarah, wife of an ancient once-upon-a-time Abraham, if she ever was that, no longer an immigrant woman whose story resonates with and influences those of later biblically literate settler women, but an archetypal Sarah in a gendered and ethnically polarized world of women's alienation, where both protection and the risk of violation see her silenced. The analytical terms may be anachronistic but the dynamics show a disturbing fit.

At this point I stop to reflect that a silent Sarah entering Canaan, and a silenced Sarah carrying the vulnerability of Israel with her into an unwittingly violating Egypt is a disturbingly passive female origin figure, a reflection which sends me back once again to consider those early biblical writers and more particularly those early Israelite editors. If this is a later Persian era narrative, as suggested above, then this assumes the displacement of other female figures who had significant roles in earlier, but now possibly canonically later, origin accounts. Has the quick thinking Canaanite Rahab, that Deuteronomistic rescuer of Israelite spies and pivotal accomplice in Israel's entry to the land, been now replaced/displaced by this vulnerable, silent and passive Sarah, who has instead to be rescued herself by the God of plagues? Rahab may have been an unwitting player in the theological struggles occasioned by the angst of a sixth century exile and its accompanying problems of theodicy, but she stands out as a woman of initiative and cunning enterprise in marked contrast to this canonically earlier, but now probably later penned, matriarch. Ironies multiply in the contrasts. For one of the ironies of the Rahab narrative lies in the fact that a woman who was openly available for violation becomes the protected, in return for having protected the would-be Yahwistic violators of both her land and body; Sarah in contrast has moved from protection to being the exploited in a land now doubly removed from being her own.

Lay a postcolonial template over this intertextual conversation and the contrast between wife, or even sister-wife, and prostitute resonates again with colonialist discourse. As Ellen Armour writes (1999: 176-77), in the context of United States black/white polarity, 'Only (in)visibly white women enter the domestic circle where they move from daughter to wife to mother (all positions marked by the phallus)… Her desire is his desire, in many ways… The question or possibility of her *jouissance* has no place within the phallocratic economy', in contrast to African-American women who 'are constituted as nothing but desire, nothing but sexuality'. Here colour is seen as the significant boundary marker, but 'Otherness' in all its forms tends to divide women in these terms. Is this what Abram knows? That once they enter Egypt, Sarah will be seen as a woman of 'otherness' and therefore presumed not only as desirable but as desiring? And he concurs! In view of the now recognized connection between violated woman and violated land, this is a disturbing addition to an origin narrative.

But it is also possible, as suggested above, that the Genesis beginnings are to be dated later than those of Exodus, in which case Sarah's silent acquiescence also contrasts markedly with the enterprising initiatives of the women who birthed the Exodus narrative, those shrewd quick thinking midwives, and its celebrator, the daringly outspoken Miriam. But if Miriam and the midwives, together with Rahab, now lie beneath Sarah, in this historical palimpsest, I would want to keep a space where the whispers of their voices could be heard echoing in an intertextual chorus, for on closer viewing there are some notable similarities between the women in all three origin tales. In each scenario there is a problem: Genesis is promising descendents but Sarai is barren (11.30), Miriam is party to the rescue of the baby Moses, but later challenges his very god-given authority (Num. 12), while in Joshua the spies, protected by Rahab, have set out from Shittim, the very place where Israel fell sexually into the arms of the women of Moab, which resulted in the sin of worshipping the Baal of Peor, resulting in turn in the deaths of many Israelites (Num. 25.1-5). Irony has balanced irony: a barren wife setting out with the promise of descendents; a sister rescuing a brother only to attempt to displace him; spies leaving the place of prostitution for the house of a Canaanite prostitute. Above each has hovered divine displeasure, barren wombs a sign of that, as so many biblical women knew well, so too the whiteness of the scaly skin hinting of God-sent death, while mention of a prostitute resonates with echoes of other texts where metaphorical prostitution carries the full force of the sin of violation of Yahweh's covenant (Hawk 1991: 61). But as I consider this, I recognize that however much they have in common, what distinguishes Sarah in this entry narrative is her silent acquiescence. It serves well, of course, to benefit her male partner, Abraham, the very one who has placed the husband–wife partnership in jeopardy, but who, nonetheless, is restored to wealth and fortune. But by Pharaoh or by Yahweh? A rhetorical question, for 'in the context of the patriarchal history, only Yahweh has absolute power', which is able, as here, to 'subvert the misuse of power by humans' (Smith 2001: 102).

And so the final outcome of the story of ch. 12, which is the subsequent return to the land, thus reads as a second divine legitimation. If this has been the goal all along, then Sarah has indeed carried out her part of the job well. But the silencing continues; after her presence has been noted in the first verse of the next chapter (13.1), she immediately returns to her place beneath the text. In the dividing of the land, the vulnerability is no longer hers; that the narrator sees no discrepancy between Abraham's statement to Lot, '[i]s not the whole land before you?' (v. 9) and his own comment that 'at that time the Canaanites and the Perizzites lived in the land' (v. 7) returns me once again to my own colonial history, to the voices of New Zealand historians such as James Belich who writes, '[a] situation of parity with, or inferiority to, peoples like the Maori simply did not accord with British expectations. The British were not satisfied with part of the land, part of the economy, or part of the government' (Belich 1986: 304). Although apparently now uninvolved, Sarah has nonetheless played her part in the move towards this land-taking.

So where has my journey brought me? Which Sarah and whose Sarah have I been discovering? If her earliest story-tellers might have had difficulty in recognizing some of the reading companions who have journeyed with me and now occupy places in my collage of voices, so be it. Sarah the faithful matriarch is a dead matriarch if she does not journey with others. But who chooses her reading companions? If 'interested' writers and readers have been accompanying her ever since she first appeared on a scroll, is there a list of applicants to be ranked in order? Over centuries scribes, editors, scholars and creative imaginers have taken Sarah and shaped her to fit their own careful construals. I would suggest that for (post)colonial readers in Aotearoa, and Australasia, there is a need to scrutinize the Sarah of ch. 12 and read her with care, for in this canonically first entry in the ancestor cycle of origin narratives, this is a Sarah clearly enmeshed in a discourse of land claims. Musa Dube's call to examine such texts for their imperializing influence makes this an imperative (1998: 130; 2000).[7]

---

7. See Sugirtharajah (1998: 93): 'Postcolonialism is...a reading posture. It is a critical enterprise aimed at unmasking the link between idea and power, which lies behind Western theories and learning. It is a discursive resistance to imperialism,

(Post)colonial women readers need to read her carefully if she is to have a place in our lives. And yet the reading task itself is fraught with difficulty for she constantly eludes our would-be categories. She moves in ambiguity, slipping through the boundaries. For where is she in this power-laden tale? Was she a willing partner in Abram's move, or the reluctant and doubting wife as Maitland and Diski suggest? Was she Abram's Sarah or Pharaoh's in Egypt? Even a postcolonial reading ends with the uneasy question: Was she a colonizer or, in gender terms, the silently colonized? Finally, with so many companions on the reading trail is there a danger that Sarah might become unrecognizable to the point that she is no longer the Sarah of church and synagogue, and does that matter? Or is her role to remain in the midst of a chorus of voices all of whom would claim her, asserting the complexities in all reading journeyings? Perhaps the metaphor of a collage of voices serves her best, so that she stands as its pivot, giving space for all who have need of her, and allowing the challenge and critique as continuing conversation.

imperial ideologies, imperial attitudes and their continued incarnations in such wide-ranging fields as politics, economics, history and theological and biblical studies'.

GENERATIVITY AND PLACE: THE GENEALOGIES OF GENESIS 1 TO 11
AND NEGOTIATING A SENSE OF PLACE IN AUSTRALIA

## Anne Elvey

In 2001, the Centenary of Federation in Australia, an exhibition entitled '?Lost and Found: A Shared Search for Belonging', held jointly at the Immigration Museum and the Koorie Heritage Trust in Melbourne, brought Aboriginal and migrant experience into creative dialogue. In the exhibition catalogue, photographs of Neil McLeod's painting 'All They gave us for Our Land is a Blanket Once A Year' and of a ceramic work 'When the Saints Come Marching In' by Neil McLeod, Anton McMurray and Gordon Huang are presented on the same page. Where the former refers to the effective theft of Aboriginal lands by the British colonizers, the latter calls into question the influence of Christianity and the Bible on Aboriginal culture. This latter work 'shows a broken culture; depicting red owls as the traditional story-tellers, they head toward the minister on his white horse, the new culture, through the broken vessel—which represents change. They then appear pink and white transformed into Christians or half believers' (Geia 2001: 17).

The catalogue notes tell a traditional story which becomes a metaphor for the entrapment of colonization. When some boys torture an owl, the Wandjina, a powerful spirit ancestor, sends a flood to drown them, but a kangaroo rescues them. Just as they are safely inside her pouch, however, the kangaroo changes into a Boab tree and they are trapped inside forever. The notes also relate that a missionary who is told this story responds dismissively: 'You must learn the new ways and forget those old stories, learn about Jesus and the Bible' (Geia 2001: 17). In identifying the traditional story-tellers with the tortured owl and the new culture with both the dismissive missionary and the boys inflicting the torture, the artists challenge me to think about the violence of colonization as also an entrapment of the colonizer.[1]

---

1. I also refer to this exhibition and these artworks and some ideas arising from this paper in Elvey (2002).

The Boab offers an image of an entrapment that occurs when certain narratives are repressed by a kind of colonial meta-narrative, which continues I think to inform postcolonial imagination. Such an entrapment resonates with what Roland Boer (2001a: 117-19) has identified in Australian colonial experience as the imaginary of a lost Eden, an imaginary that has material effects in non-Aboriginal relationships both to Aboriginal peoples and to their lands. For Boer (2001a: 117-19) sense of place is inflected by the Edenic myth in three ways: i) lying outside the primeval goodness of creation the land is untouched by the divine; ii) the land exemplifies the curse that accompanies the loss of paradise; iii) the land is reimagined as Eden itself. In each case the inscription of the Edenic myth upon the land is part of a failure to deal with the land and its peoples on their own terms, a failure which continues to trouble contemporary Australian quests for a sense of place.[2]

The invocation of Edenic imagery in Australian colonial narratives suggests further a particular resonance between the biblical 'prehistory' set out in Genesis 1 to 11 and settler self-understanding in Australia. This link becomes explicit in Judith Wright's earlier of two novels based on her own family history, *The Generations of Men*, where she writes referring to her great-great-grandparents who migrated to Australia from England in the nineteenth century:

> Indeed, there was about their story something of the atmosphere of the Book of Genesis, and some aura, too, of supernatural descent clung to them—since it was an axiom that in Australia existed no beauty and no tradition, no art and no aristocracy, and since all things good came from a country unknown to their children and grand-children (Wright 1995: 5).

The 'country unknown' becomes for descendants, such as the child Wright imagines her grandmother May to have been, an imaginary place, even a kind of Eden, the source of 'all good things'. Ed Noort (1999: 22) writes that in Gen. 2.8 'in the east' describes 'a garden in Eden' in both spatial and temporal senses as far away and in the pre-time. It seems to me that settler narratives suggest a similar experience of distance, such that the place of emigration is not only far way but in a sort of pre-time, so that time and narrative begin with the moment of arrival in the 'new' country. But there is at the same time a prehistory situated in the 'old' country.

---

2. Peter Read (2000) brings some of these complications of a sense of place into conversation in an eclectic selection and interpretation of poetry, song and oral histories. For an articulation of the ways in which non-Aboriginal desires for a sense of place in Australia remain troubled see Read (2000: 2-3).

Now this has parallels in the Genesis narrative, and certainly in scholarly readings of the narrative of Genesis 1–11, where prehistory turns over into history around the points of Abramic migration in Genesis 11 and 12.[3] My intuition is that this movement from prehistory to history within both the Genesis and settler narratives around the trope of migration touches upon the fraught question of origins in a particular way. In what ways are migrant peoples to speak of origins when they live in the lands of the birth of others? At what point does geography overtake genealogy? When does the new land become home? What of the migrant's relationship to earlier inhabitants of the land?

Frank Crüsemann (1996: 57) addresses aspects of these questions of origin when he considers the ethical enigma posed by the necessity of a 'universal orientation to the well-being of all' in the context of the necessity for persons to establish a 'group-related…identity, which particularizes the universalistic attitude'. For Crüsemann (1996: 58-63) in Genesis, especially by way of the genealogies, 'which form something like a skeleton' of the book, the origins of humankind and the origins of Israel are interconnected through a genealogical system which exceeds the expected parameters both of ethnicity and of relationship to one's ethnic homeland.

Like Crüsemann, Mark Brett (2000b) focuses on the final text of Genesis as a product of the Persian period. Reading this as a period of Persian imperial governance, Brett listens for the resistant voices in the editing of the text. For Brett (2000b: 44, his italics), '*overt ideologies of human dominance, male dominance or primogeniture are allowed to stand, but alternative perspectives are juxtaposed in such a way as to undermine the dominant ideology*'. Brett (2000b: 5) discerns a counter-colonialist thread in a narrative deconstruction of the primacy of the first-born and the notion of the 'holy seed' which supports the 'theologically legitimised ethnocentrism found in the books of Ezra and Nehemiah'. He highlights episodes, such as Abraham's purchase of a burial ground from the Hittites in Genesis 23, where negotiation is favoured over appropriation. Brett (2000b: 93) indicates moments in Genesis 29 and 30 when '[g]eography takes precedence over genealogy' and alerts the reader to

---

3. Scholars vary on where in fact the prehistory ends and history begins. Claus Westermann (1984), for example, finishes his commentary on Genesis 1–11 with comment on verse 11.26. Walter Brueggemann (1982) takes the 'prehistory' to 11.29. In each case, history begins with the family of Terah who will migrate from their birth land. Without, however, questioning the notion of a division between prehistory and history, Naomi Steinberg (1993: 39) places this division at 11.10.

the way in which the geographical referent for the land of one's birth shifts from Ur of the Chaldeans (12.1; 24.4, 7) to Canaan (31.3, 13) as genealogy begins to be grafted into a 'new' land.

While Brett's reading of Genesis calls into question any colonizing claim to (sacred) origins, I want to take a slightly different approach to these questions of origin and place. By bringing an ecofeminist hermeneutic, which attends to the maternal and the material, to bear on the genealogies of Genesis 1–11 I want to reconsider a particular aspect of Australian genealogical narratives, which I call 'the myth of a colonial genesis'. Writing of settler societies, Daiva Stasiulis and Nira Yuval-Davis (1995: 21) state: 'Whether stressing the differences or the similarities with their mother [sic] countries, the settlers' ideologies involved in nation-building have a historical starting point, which occurs at the moment of colonial conquest and the beginning of settlement.' Taking as their point of origin the pioneer, such narratives invoke 'the myth of a colonial genesis' eliding the story of another place which is the condition of possibility of an 'origin' in this place. Rather than telling a narrative of economic and political exigencies which necessitated a migration, forced or otherwise, to this place—in which the illusion of 'being somewhere' (see White 1956: 9) must be created—the creation of this illusion slides into the illusion of a genesis in this place, which obfuscates the particular relationship to place of its first peoples.

The concatenation of feminist and postcolonial approaches to address these questions of origin, however, is not without its problems. Western feminists in particular have been challenged to acknowledge the ambiguity of their position as both colonized and colonizers (see, for example, Moreton-Robinson 2000). Not only has Western feminism often failed to be attentive to the other, but it has also been founded on the construction of other women as other than the ideal feminist (who is free, enfranchised, gainfully employed…) and on a position of relative privilege with respect to many other women and men (see, for example, Pattel-Gray 1995). One of the strengths of feminism, however, has been its self-critical stance. In recent years many Western feminists, among them biblical scholars such as Elisabeth Schüssler Fiorenza (1992: 102-32) and ecofeminist philosophers such as Val Plumwood (1993: 41-68), have sought to describe structures of hierarchical dualism so that the feminist critique of patriarchy is understood within and in parallel with a larger critique of the colonizing processes of making 'other'. For Plumwood (1993: 41-55) in particular this critique, which is attentive to the material damage to people and place that are the result of and often reinforce such colonizing processes, brings together ecological, feminist and postcolonial sensibilities.

In a certain sense the critique of patriarchal and colonialist approaches, which represent indigenous people, women, bodies, matter and nature, as irrational and subordinate others, has also lent itself to feminist approaches that are attentive to these others. Within this critical framework, I think the attentiveness of feminist theorists such as Luce Irigaray (for example, 1993: 7-21) to the feminine/maternal can intersect with a postcolonial approach by highlighting some ways in which colonialist discourses are framed by systems of phallocentric language and thought, which elide not only the maternal, but also the material more generally.[4]

At the risk of making what may appear to be an essentialist move, then, I want to focus here on what are 'matrices of origin', the necessary conditions for human being in place.[5] The notion of 'matrices of origin' is in debt to but broader than the notion of the maternal. It turns an eye and an ear to the often forgotten conditions of human being in place. These conditions include notably earth (in the particularity of land, water, air, plants and other animals) and embodiment (with emphasis on the pregnant body), but also the particular set of social, cultural, political and economic circumstances and relationships with others which shape one's being in place. The focus on 'matrices of origin' suggests an approach to the received text that looks for ways in which the pregnant body, for example, is forgotten or remembered there. Such an approach highlights the way in which this forgetting and remembering in turn shapes the text.

---

4. While Gayatri Chakravorty Spivak (1988), for example, criticizes the way in which French feminism has constructed 'the third world' as other, she later writes: 'I have come to think that in the face of patriarchal reappropriation of decolonization, isolationist nationalisms, and internalized gendering, there can be exchange between metropolitan and decolonized feminisms' (Spivak 1993: 144). In her 'revisiting' of French feminism, Spivak (1993: 146-60) gives particular attention to the maternal.

5. In relation to Derrida's (1994: 7) understanding of the gift as 'aneconomic' and Spivak's (1993: 148) description of the pregnant body as 'prepropriative', certain 'matrices of origin', such as pregnant bodies and earth, can be read as bearing the 'aneconomic' character of the gift. In the case both of pregnant bodies and earth, relationships between self and other occur within a constitutive sociality, which resists inscription as property and matter for control. Pregnant bodies and earth are spaces of an interconnectness, which in turn gives space to and in this sense 'grounds' what Derrida calls the 'impossible' and Heidegger the *Abgrund*. In this sense bodies, pregnant bodies and earth may provide a material link to the abyssal structure of the word. See Elvey (unpub.: 79-111).

At another level, the focus on 'matrices of origin' raises questions about the character of the biblical text itself. Readings, such as Brett's (2000b), look to a particular matrix of origin for the text indicated by its redaction within a Persian imperialist framework. Another reading would consider the way in which interpretation of the biblical text within an Australian context is an interpretation of a text displaced in both space and time from its matrices of origin. This paper takes a limited focus on the way in which the particular matrices of origin that are pregnant bodies and earth are represented in and shape the text of Genesis 1–11, in particular the genealogical material. It reads this text also as a displaced text, which shapes the colonial memory of non-Aboriginal Australians in particular ways. Specifically the paper considers a resonance between a forgetting and remembering of the maternal in the genealogies of Genesis 1–11 and a forgetting and remembering of the material (pre)conditions of settlement in settler genealogical narratives.

The paper is also part of a wider project to consider intersections between senses of genealogy and senses of place in both contemporary and biblical contexts.[6] The project is prompted by my observation both of the popularity of genealogical research in settler societies such as Australia and of the plethora of discourses concerning place and sense of place in Australia.[7] In what ways might these senses of genealogy and place be related? In what ways might biblical concerns with genealogy already intersect with these contemporary concerns?

---

6. In a contemporary Australian context, I am interested in both Indigenous and non-Indigenous uses of genealogical research and of family history. Contemporary Indigenous uses of genealogy are varied. Sally Morgan's now famous *My Place*, for example, tells an Aboriginal family history. Within her study among the Yarralin people, Deborah Bird Rose (2000: 74-89, 110-22) discusses the role of genealogy with a wider kinship system. Heather Goodall (1999) highlights the complex possibilities and problems for Aboriginal people using genealogical research to support claims to native title or to reconnect with family. In the current paper, however, I am principally addressing one aspect of non-Indigenous genealogical representation, namely the inscription of Australia as a site of ancestral settler origin.

7. Increasingly in Australia, for example, exhibitions are revisiting questions of origins and place. In 2001 in addition to the exhibition '?Lost and Found: A Shared Search for Belonging', to which I referred at the beginning of this paper, there was an exhibition of quilts at the Immigration Museum entitled 'Quilted Journeys: Stories of Immigration' and a touring exhibition for the Centenary of Federation entitled 'Belonging' at the State Library of Victoria.

## Genealogy, Land and the Pregnant Body in Genesis 1–11

Genealogies have been read as the 'organizing principle for the entire Bible [both Hebrew and Christian]' (Andersen 1994: 263). Moreover, within the book of Genesis, 'the genealogical framework provides the overall structure of the book' (Andersen 1994: 263). The term תולדות, which marks the beginning or the resumption of genealogical lists at 5.1; 6.9; 10.1, 32; 11.20, 27, first occurs in Gen. 2.4 where it refers to the generations of the skies and the earth. Here the description תולדות, derived from ילד, 'to bear' a child, links the first and second creation narratives as generations. The resonance of birth is already present in the first creation narrative, where the verb ברא, which links the creation of humankind in 1.27 with the creation of the heavens and the earth in 1.1, has within its range of meaning (in the niphal form at least) the nuance of birth-giving.[8]

But the use of תולדות in relation to creation has a further resonance. Brett (2000b: 31) suggests that the usage in 2.4a implies that 'the land [but more precisely in 2.4a 'the heavens and the earth when they were created' השמים והארץ בהבראם] is the parent'. Brett is careful to write 'parent' rather than mother, because his reading of the force of תולדות here does not imply an association of earth/land with the bodies of women, as will happen elsewhere in the Hebrew Bible. Indeed given the patrilineal character of the genealogical lists introduced as תולדות at 5.1 and 11.20, for example, the implication might be that the parent, whom skies and earth most closely represent, is the ancestral male.

Norman Habel (2000: 46) argues that up to the creation of humankind in 1.26-27, the earth story in Genesis 1, 'presents a beautifully unified narrative, with Earth as the primary character. The story commences with uninhabited Earth hidden beneath primordial waters and darkness. *Elohim* is also present in the darkness as a mysterious moving breath or spirit.' Over the course of the first five days and into the sixth, earth appears and is revealed 'as the centre of the cosmos and the source of life' (Habel 2000: 46). In 1.24-25, for example, there is a cooperative mutually between ארץ and אלהים. The earth's bringing forth 'living creatures of

---

8. ברא also occurs in 1.21 concerning the creation of creatures of the sea and air. In other places the verb עשה is used. As is the case in 5.1, ברא and עשה could be understood as standing in parallel. That is, ברא need not imply creation from nothing in opposition to a making from available materials implied by עשה. In the piel of ברא there is also the sense of destruction—the cutting down of trees (BDB, 135), which in Robert Pogue Harrison's (1992) terms shadows 'civilisation'.

every kind...' (1.24) stands in parallel with and occurs by way of God's making 'the wild animals of the earth of every kind...' (1.25). The generations of skies and earth registered in 2.4a summarizes a movement in which the primordial uncultivated earth of 1.2 gives rise in cooperation with God to the known earth from which comes all plant and animal life, except humans, whose creation by the divine is unmediated by earth. Habel (2000: 46) argues that '[w]ith the appearance of human beings onto the scene...power relations shift radically'. 'Humans are elevated to the side of God/celestial beings over against Earth' (Habel 2000: 47). Brett's reading of the land as parent effectively calls into question the anthropocentrism identified by Habel. But the patrilineal associations of תולדות in the subsequent genealogies suggest that the concept of generations is supported in the text by an androcentric framework within which the anthropocentrism Habel describes *can* rest comfortably.

That this 'fall' into anthropocentrism is ambiguous, however, is testament to the complexity of relationships between humans and other-than-humans in Genesis 1–11. Walter Brueggemann (1982: 11-12) identifies three ways in which relationship between human and other-than-human creation is represented here: first, all are a single undifferentiated category of creature before the creator; second, human creatures are superior to a properly subordinate non-human creation; third, at times only human creatures are represented in the text. The last is the case in particular in the genealogies where anthropocentrism coincides with androcentrism.

The ambiguity surrounding the anthropocentric use of תולדות to mark skies and earth as primordial (male?) parent also echoes in the shifting senses of ארץ in Genesis 1 to 11. Just as the later genealogies sometimes exist in more than one version, the generations of earth and heavens (2.4a) set out in 1.1–2.3 are retold in 2.4b and following, where the human (האדם) is formed from the cultivated ground (האדמה) and placed in a garden in Eden (2.7-8). Here when the situating of Eden in relation to named rivers and regions first establishes a sense of place (2.10-14), the meaning of ארץ shifts from earth as a whole, to specific lands, such as Havilah (2.11) and Cush (2.13).

Central to this shift toward the specificity of place is the way in which particular lands become representative of earth. Another key factor is the way in which human encounter with earth is related to the fertility of the ground. It is significant, then, in Genesis 2 that the sexual differentiation of humankind occurs (2.21-23) at a remove from the divine sculpting of humankind from the ground. Female humanity, and thereby a sexually differentiated humankind, is formed from the body of אדם rather than from הָאֲדָמָה. But in the series of 'punishments' of Gen. 4.14-19 both pain in childbirth and difficulty in cultivating the ground are set down in a gendered differentiation of labour, which implicitly links the (in)fertility of the birth-giving body with that of the ground. Later after a second episode of 'crime and punishment', there is a parallel between the female generation of the child Enoch and the male generation of the city of the same name (4.17). These are isolated but indicative moments within a narrative in which an intersection between women, pregnant bodies, place and land is not fully developed.

The valence of אֶרֶץ, in relation to earth, land, a particular land or the people of that land, continues to shift within Genesis 1–11. But while אֶרֶץ occurs frequently throughout the narrative sections, apart from the table of nations in Genesis 10, there is almost no mention of אֶרֶץ in the genealogical material. The double use of תּוֹלְדוֹת for the generations of earth and skies and the generations in a genealogical list, however, not only suggests that earth and skies are parent of a divinely ordered creation, but also inscribes (largely patriarchal) narratives of family or national origin as stories of sacred origin.[9] This appeal to a 'sacred' origin also occurs in Australian settler narratives. Writing of public history in Australia, Graeme Davison (2000: 85) points to the almost 'sacred' character of genealogically inspired family reunions, which frequently take as their point of meeting the 'original' place of settlement.[10] This 'sacred' character resonates in Frederick McCubbin's *The Pioneer* painted three years after Federation. Traditionally used for religious themes, the triptych form of painting implies that a sacred origin underlies this genealogy of place and nation told visually through a family narrative.

When the divine creation of humankind is recalled at the beginning of the genealogy in Genesis 5, the sacred origin of genealogy becomes explicit: 'This is the list (תּוֹלְדוֹת) of the descendants of Adam. When God created humankind, God made them in the likeness of God. Male and

---

9. In the Gospel of Luke this is encapsulated in the reading backwards of the genealogy of Jesus through Adam to God (Lk. 3.23-38).

10. In *The Ancestor Game*, Alex Miller (1992: 278) locates this attitude to family ancestry in the character of Mrs Halloran, 'a distinguished matriarch, the keeper of a thing which is of a primordial nature, a thing so sacred and extensive and complex and Biblical and reaching into the archaic origins and virtues of the Hallorans' Australian genesis'. In Miller's novel, however, Mrs Halloran's is a minor part, set within and in contrast to an ancestral narrative which moves between Australia and China interrogating the myth of a colonial genesis.

female God created them and God blessed them and named them 'Humankind' when they were created' (5.1-2).[11]

The failure to mention earth here repeats and reinforces the anthropocentrism of 1.26-27. Moreover, immediately following this in 5.3 the divine prerogative of creative self-imaging (1.27) is transferred to the male human being: '[Adam] became the father of a son in his likeness, according to his image, and named him Seth' (5.3b). In the תולדות formula and throughout the genealogy by way of a sequence of male begetting that uses the same root word ילד, there is an echo of the maternal act of birth-giving. Despite this echo, however, the material necessity of the pregnant body is elided in a genealogy from which women are almost wholly absent (but for the formulaic note that daughters as well as sons are produced by these fathers): *When A had lived x years he became the father of* (ויולד) *B. A lived y years after the birth of* (הולידו) *B and had* (ויולד) *other sons and daughters. Thus all the days of A were x+y years; and he died.* It is almost as if the father does the birth-giving here.

Within the wider narrative of Genesis 1 to 11 the material conditions of conception and birth, however, *are* registered (if only summarily) at 4.1-2, 17, 20, 22, 25; 6.4. The births to Eve of Cain and then Abel and to Cain's wife of Enoch, and later of Seth to Eve each occur after the narration of an event of separation or violence. Immediately following the expulsion of the man and his wife from the garden of Eden and the barring of the way to the tree of life, Eve conceives and bears Cain (Gen. 3.24–4.1). Just after Cain leaves the divine presence because of the curse God has put on him for his murder of Abel, Cain's unnamed wife conceives and bears Enoch (Gen. 4.16-17). After human work is separated into different occupations and another killing occurs, the no-longer-named wife of Adam conceives Seth (Gen. 4.20-25). Within the genealogy of Cain, two women, Adah and Zillah are named as bearing children to Lamech. As Günther Wittenberg (2000) argues, after the alienation of Cain from earth because of his violence, there is in the establishment of cities and city-based occupations an 'emancipation' from earth. But at this point of the narrative, these modes of separation remain interwoven with the material necessities of pregnancy and birth, material necessities that might also indicate human embeddedness in earth.

As the narrative progresses, however, the pregnant body, as emblem of human continuity and capacity for life in the face of human limitation, is

---

11. Biblical quotations are from the NRSV with the substitution of the proper noun 'God' for the masculine pronouns in the text of the NRSV.

displaced by a genre of genealogy in which a pattern of birth to the male is inscribed and in which the first-born male receives precedence (Gen. 5, 10, 11.10-32). D.J.A. Clines (1994: 294) comments that '[t]he thrust of the Genesis 5 genealogy is toward death, even though human life continues'. Richard S. Hess (1994: 66) reads the genealogies as ending in narratives of disaster. He argues, however, that unlike comparable ancient Near Eastern genealogies, which look to the past, the biblical genealogies are oriented toward the future (Hess 1994: 68). In a similar way, the final panel of McCubbin's *The Pioneer* looks forward beyond the death of the pioneer couple to a new Eden (see *The Age*, 16 August 1905, quoted in Clark and Whitelaw 1985: 149).

Like the paradisiacal city of McCubbin's painting, the genealogy of Genesis 5 is emblematic of the growth and prosperity of humankind in the face of human mortality. This genealogy emerges as a consequence of divine blessing inherent in the act of creation, and is specifically registered as תולדות after the people are reported as beginning to invoke the name of YHWH (Gen. 4.26). The genealogical form recurs (10.1-32; 11.10-32) after the narratives of the flood (6.11–9.27) and the fall of the tower of Babel (11.1-9) and suggests another mode of new beginning after loss.

It is important to remember here the complex origins and functions of the narratives and genealogies of Genesis 1–11. For example, two main types of genealogy occur, the segmented type of Genesis 4 and 10 and the linear type of Genesis 5 and 11 (Wilson 1994: 211). Both types of genealogy exhibit characteristics of depth and fluidity. In linear genealogies, depth, that is the number of generations listed, is the 'most important formal feature' (Wilson 1994: 211) and is indicative of a certain depth of memory within the tradition. Fluidity, that is the ability for genealogies to change, is reflected in differences in names or order within parallel genealogies (compare 4.18-19 and 5.18-24). Fluidity 'reflects actual or desired changes in the domestic, political, or religious ties between individuals and groups' (Wilson 1994: 212). This is evident in Genesis 4 and 5, for while the 'patrilineage from Cain to Lamech...leads to the escalation of violence', the genealogy of Genesis 5 leads to righteousness (Brett 2000b: 40). The genealogies from Cain to Lamech and from Seth to Noah represent contrasting possibilities for the future of earth (see Brett 2000b: 40).

These contrasting possibilities are expressed through the different performative effects of the two sections. For example, referring to Gevirtz (1994), Hess (1994: 11) describes the performative function of Gen. 4.23-24: 'The increasing unruliness of the couplets may be compared not only with the pride and murderous rebellion of Lamech, but also with the moral decline characteristic of the line of Cain and culminating in the judgment of the chaos of the flood'. In contrast the rhythmic patterns of ch. 5 suggest a divine orderliness carried by the patrilineage. The interruptions serve to enhance this sense of a divine order evident in the origins of the patrilineal line (5.3), in the righteousness of Enoch (5.24), and in the birth and naming of Noah (5.29).

Earth/land and place are recalled here in so far as Noah will reverse the curse on the ground (5.29; cf. 3.17 and 4.12). But this occurs against the threat of the destruction of the entire earth in the flood (6.11-13). In the flood sequence (6.1 to 9.27) where narrative and genealogy intersect (Brett 2000b: 40), the pregnant body becomes an emblem of the escalating wickedness of humankind (6.4). Since heavenly beings seem to be the agents of this wickedness (6.4), the outstanding scandal here is the divine determination to destroy earth (6.11-13) (see Gardner 2000: 117). With the ensuing flood narratives and the divine promise to refrain from a repetition of such environmental devastation, this determination is itself embedded within the genealogical note of Noah, beginning in 6.9-10 and concluding in 9.28. In a pattern of new beginnings, the genealogical form threads the text and marks the narrative as simultaneously continuous and disjunctive. Genealogy has taken over the function of the pregnant body as signifier of new beginning after separation or loss, so that in Gen. 6.4 the pregnant body itself becomes a marker not so much of new possibility but of loss. What is threatened is a loss of earth itself.

But while the righteousness of Noah and the thread of the genealogical pattern are at one level narrative assurances of hope against the threat of loss, the 'loss' of the pregnant body continues to resonate in the text. Within the narrative of Genesis 1–11, each of the occurrences of crime and punishment is followed by a 'new beginning', a renewed narrative of origins. This re-telling of origins moves from narratives of conception and birth in Genesis 4 to the institution of patrilineal lists in Genesis 5. Following the flood and in a departure, however, from the almost unrelenting linearity of the genealogies of Genesis 5 and 11, the genealogy of Genesis 10 looks much more like a family tree. Nevertheless while second, third, and even ninth sons are remembered as generators of families, languages, nations and lands (10.5, 20, 31), women continue to be erased and the material necessity of the pregnant body is no more than an echo in the repetition of the term תולדות (10.1, 32). In the summary vv. 20 and 31 this echo of the birth-giving body is lost when תולדות is replaced by בני 'sons of...' (see also 10.1, 21, 25, 32). Moreover, in the movement from one generation to the next, as Simons (1994: 244-5) notes, there is a slippage between the use of ילד (10.1, 8, 13, 15, 21, 24, 25, 26) and the use of בני (10.2, 3, 4, 6, 7, 20, 22, 23, 29, 31). While this usage reflects, I think, the horizontal spread of the genealogy here, where many sons of a father are named, the effect is also to further elide the birth-giving body.

As Crüsemann (1996) argues, however, the genealogy of Genesis 10 has another effect. The generations of Noah's sons encompass a great diversity of nations, representative of all humankind, and their 'spread abroad on the earth' after the 'global' devastation of the flood (10.32) (see Crüsemann 1996: 66). This spread—a new flood after the flood—finds its ends in a metonymy between nations, languages, families and lands (10.5, 20, 31). Two words are used in Genesis 10 to denote this spread, namely פוץ (10.18) and פרד (10.5, 32). Used in relation to the spread of the coastal peoples (10.5) and the spread of the nations (10.32), פרד has a resonance of separation or division (see Gen. 2.10; 13.9, 11, 14; 25.23; 30.40). Used for the 'spread' of the families of the Canaanites (10.18), פוץ has a resonance of being scattered, even shattered (BDB, 806-807). פוץ occurs again in the story of the tower of Babel in relation to its builders' fear of being scattered (11.4), a fear which is realized by YHWH's 'punitive' action (11.8, 9). An undercurrent of concern about diversity, which will become explicit in 11.1-9, may already be at work in the genealogical celebration of the spread of the nations in Genesis 10.

At the beginning of ch. 11, then, it is as if the potential chaos of this new flood must be contained. Against the many nations, languages, families and lands that have their ancestral roots with Noah, '[now] the whole earth had one language and the same words' (11.1). Here is the first note of a migration, a 'breaking camp' (11.2). This is a migration not of a particular family or kinship group as will occur with Terah in 11.31 and Abram in Genesis 12, but of the whole earth, representing in this instance all humankind. If the migration is read as 'from the east' rather than the alternative 'eastwards', then this recalls, I think, the expulsion from Eden. As a further narrative of 'crime and punishment', the story of the fall of the tower of Babel (11.3-9) offers an alternative origin for the diversity of human languages and nations.

This narrative of separation, loss and dispersal, which recalls the earlier losses of the Eden narrative and the flood, is followed by a return to the genealogical patterns of Genesis 5. But toward the end of the list of the generations of Shem beginning at 11.10, the genealogy changes from linear (11.10-25) to segmented (11.26-32) form. The genealogy of Terah, which begins again in 11.27, introduces Abram with his brothers Nahor and Haran. Wright (1995: 7) likens her settler ancestors to this archetypal patriarchal ancestor, who will become Abraham, a name that resonates through Judaism, Christianity and Islam.

In addition to the children of Haran and Nahor, this genealogy of Terah names two women, Sarai and Milcah, the wives of Abram and Nahor respectively (11.29). At this point, notice that Sarai is who both barren and childless interrupts the genealogy (11.30). It is as if the textual elision of the pregnant body within the genealogical form takes form in Sarai's barrenness and childlessness. Here where the genealogy of Terah overtakes the genealogy of Shem, there seems to be an end to the line of the first-born.

Immediately following the notice of Sarai's barrenness is the narration of Terah, Abram, Lot and Sarai's migration to Haran (11.31). This migration is held within the genealogy of Terah by the final stylized notice of Terah's death (Gen. 11.32). It is perhaps here that the problematic of origin finds a focus. The pattern of repeated origins, which is in debt to the material necessity of pregnant bodies and earth, is interrupted by the contingency of the corporeal. Where the genealogical pattern can include the corporeal contingency that is the death of the patriarch, because the firstborn carries the line forward toward and beyond his death, it cannot accommodate the barrenness of the matriarch. The migration is founded on this barrenness and becomes in turn a new point of origin.

Although the genealogical form will interrupt the narrative again on several occasions, it is as if at this point the migration substitutes for the birth of the first-born.[12] The migration to the intermediate place of Haran named for the third son who died in the land of his birth generates the Abramic narrative that ensues. Whereas God will mandate Abram's further migration (12.1ff.), there seems to be no catalyst for Terah's displacement other than the failure of a female body to serve as 'place' for a first-born son. It is as if, at an unacknowledged level of the text, the infertility of the matriarchal body, which could also be read as inhospitality, renders the land of Ur no longer hospitable to Terah and his family.

The notice in 11.28 that Haran died in the land of his birth (בארץ מולדתו) not only recalls the birth-giving body but also links this body with the parenting land. Nowhere else in the genealogies of Genesis 1–11 is a son listed as dying before his father. The reference to the land of his birth, also the land of his kindred, points ahead to the migrations in which others of his kindred will leave the land of their births and will die and be buried

---

12. Moreover, Sarai's barrenness will in effect reproduce in the later narrative two first-born, Ishmael and Isaac, who head competing (?) genealogies.

elsewhere. This emphasis suggests that the first generation of migrants experience migration as separating the land of their births and their kindred from the land of their deaths.[13]

The intermediate migration undertaken after notice of Sarai's barrenness is directed toward Canaan. Instead this migration ends in Haran. The naming of place after the son who has died in the land of his birth suggests I think not only a desire to keep alive the memory of the lost son, but also something about migration. Just as the genealogies forget but keep the generativity of the pregnant body, the process of migration both forgets and keeps in the place of immigration the circumstances of emigration.

### *Prehistories and Histories of Being in Place*

Suzanne Schech and Jane Haggis (2000: 232) write: 'Even eighth-generation Australians mark their origin from an arrival, so even the most continuous white lineage of belonging harks back to the fact of migrancy.' In conjunction with the imaginary of a lost Eden in all its guises, Australian genealogical narratives, such as Wright's *The Generations of Men* (1995), suggest a story of colonial genesis, which has resonances in the genealogical patterns of Genesis 4–11. Following the accounts of origins in Genesis 1–3, three modes of *new* beginning emerge in Genesis 4–11: birth-giving by way of the maternal body, patrilineal descent encapsulated in the genealogical form, and migration.

The loss of Eden in Genesis 3 and a series of episodes of crime and punishment in Genesis 4–11 are interrupted and held together by a sequence of genealogies. Not only do the genealogies offer moments of continuity with earlier narratives and genealogies, but in their separation from these earlier narratives and genealogies, they also present the repeated possibility of a new point of origin. These genealogies of fathers and sons, frequently highlighting the generation of the first-born male, re-present the origin in relative proximity to the *here and now* of the narrative. This re-presentation of the origin occurs in ways that are forgetful of the material givenness of pregnant bodies. The language of genealogy, however, recalls what the form forgets. The pregnant body, which gives way to the patrilineage and is simultaneously remembered and forgotten there, becomes an absence that prompts a migration. In turn this migration is held within the

---

13. In the later Genesis narratives the referent for land of birth and kindred shifts from the land of Abram's birth (24.7) to the land of birth of his grandson, Jacob (31.13), presumably from Ur of the Chaldeans to Canaan.

genealogical form. In the Australian colonial context, migration itself is forgotten and settlement becomes the focus. A certain transformation of the land accompanies colonial settlement and the imaginary of settlement as 'genesis' is underwritten by a forgetting of its material conditions: What occasioned migration? Who was displaced is the process?

Let me summarize the argument of this section with the following table:

Patterns in Genesis 1–11

1.1 a birthgiving (God gives birth to the heavens and the earth)
1.1-2.3 First Creation Account
2.4 These are the generations (תולדות) of the heavens and the earth when they were created.
2.5-25 Second Creation Account
3.1-24 Expulsion from the Primeval Garden
4.1-2 two birthgivings (Eve conceives and gives birth to Cain and Abel)
4.3-16 Murder of Abel & Curse of Cain
4.17 a birthgiving (Cain's wife conceives and gives birth to Enoch)
4.17-22 first genealogy from Cain to Lamech's children, including…
4.20, 22 two birthgivings (Adah bears Jabal; Zilhah bears Tubal-cain)
4.23-24 Lamech's Revenge
4.25 a birthgiving (Adam's wife gives birth to and names Seth)
4.26 male descent and the first invocation of the name of YHWH
5.1-2 This is the list (תולדת) of the descendants of Adam.
5.3-32 Genealogy from Adam to Noah and Noah's sons Shem, Ham and Japheth.
6.1-8 Wickedness of Humankind & Divine Favour on Noah
6.9 These are the descendants (תולדת) of Noah.
6.9-10 Brief return to genealogy of Noah.
6.11–9.27 Flood, Covenant & Related Noah Narratives
9.28 Completion of genealogy of Noah.
10.1a These are the descendants (תולדת) of Noah's sons.
10.1-32 Genealogy of Noah's sons, Shem, Ham, and Japheth: Table of the Nations.
10.32 These are the families of Noah's sons according to their genealogies (לתולדתם) in their nations; and from these the nations spread abroad on the earth after the flood…
11.1-9 From One Language to Many: Tower of Babel
11.10 These are the descendants (תולדת) of Shem.
11.10-26 Genealogy from Shem to sons of Terah: Abram, Nahor and Haran.
11.27 These are the descendants (תולדת) of Terah.
11.27-30 Genealogy of Terah (including death of Haran in the land of his birth בארץ מולדתו 11.28)
11.30 Notice that Sarai is barren.
11.31 Migration from Ur of the Chaldeans to Haran.
11.32 Completion of genealogy of Terah.

The absence of the maternal in the genealogies of Genesis 5–11 has a parallel in the forgetting of the material conditions of migration in the imaginary of a colonial genesis in Australia. It is not simply the linguistic coincidence of the terms *mater/materia/matrix* but more particularly the elision in each instance of certain material conditions for being in place. The significance of these elisions is not in the first place textual; rather it is found in material effects for women, indigenous peoples, lands and earth. Such effects are indicated by the foreshadowing of a divine determination to destroy earth (Gen. 6.4) and by the recollection of the violence toward pregnant bodies of invading armies (2 Kgs 8.12; 15.16; Amos 1.13). They resonate in the redactors' resistance to Persian imperialism as well as in the work of Indigenous and migrant artists in the exhibition '?Lost and Found: A Shared Search for Belonging'.

In the context of Aboriginal and migrant experience of settlement/invasion in Australia, some of these artists have characterized a Christian minister as saying: 'You must learn the new ways and forget those old stories...' (Geia 2001: 17). When the site and moment of settlement are inscribed as a space/time of origin in place and a beginning of colonial history, two 'matrices of origin' are relegated to prehistory: the 'old stories' of Indigenous peoples and the 'old country' of the migrants. But just as the pregnant body, which in the life of the Western individual inhabits a kind of psychic prehistory, is remembered as well as forgotten in the patrilineal genealogies that overtake it, the history of settlement is haunted by the dual 'prehistories' of migration and colonisation.

The long genealogy from Adam to Terah and his sons, threading the narrative from Genesis 5–11, links history with prehistory. The move from prehistory to history around the trope of migration stands beside an interweaving of prehistory and history through genealogy itself. Similarly while the appeal to a memory of colonial genesis remains, within Australian writing the complexity of the theme of genealogy is being addressed by writers such as Alex Miller (1992) and Kim Scott (1999).[14] As a critical response to her earlier narrative, Wright's *The Cry for the Dead* (1981), is deliberately attentive to the 'prehistories' of settler being-in-place: the

---

14. In his novel *Benang*, Nyoongar writer Kim Scott (1999) brilliantly deconstructs non-Aboriginal desires to find in their ancestry 'the first white man born' in a particular Western Australian town or region by taking this phrase to represent the failed desire of eugenicists, such as the character Ernest Solomon Scat and the 'Protector of Aborigines', A.O. Neville, to create 'the first white man born' of Aboriginal descent. See also Scott 2001.

political and economic exigencies of relationship to the 'other place' of emigration and the interwoven narratives of Aboriginal displacement. In Genesis 11 Haran, who dies in the land of his birth, becomes a figure of kinship and place left behind in the displacement that is emigration but carried into the place of immigration that now bears his name. As person and place, Haran suggests one aspect of the complexity of relationships to people and place embedded in the migrant sense of being-in-place. Haran's link to the land of his birth also recalls a debt to the materiality of pregnant bodies and earth that is ambiguously held in the formulation of biblical תולדות.

SANCTUARY AND WOMB:
HENRI LEFEBVRE AND THE PRODUCTION OF ANCIENT SPACE

Roland Boer

Henri Lefebvre, Marxist philosopher and social scientist, one-time member of the French Communist Party, parent of numerous offspring, director of the Institut de Sociologie Urbaine in Paris (Nanterre), intellectual inspiration for May '68 in France (at the tender age of sixty-seven), author of no less than sixty-six books, remains one of the under-translated giants of the great tradition of French intellectual life from the 1930s to the 1980s.

I undertake here a rather specific task, which is to engage in a critical discussion with Lefebvre's *The Production of Space* (1991a) in order to consider the construction, or, as Lefebvre insisted, the production of space in the ancient world, specifically in this case the Bible. The book was the final product of an intense investigation, as David Harvey points out in the Afterword, into urbanization and the question of space between 1968 and 1974, the year the book first appeared in French, after a number of others from the same project.

*Various Spaces*

Before I plunge into the stream of his work, I need to make some comments about method. Lefebvre operates with a few crucial moves, strategies that are distinctive marks of his dialectical Marxism.[1] To begin with, he constantly seeks to link the abstract realm of theory with the concrete reality of praxis, speaking of the connections needed between mental and social space, describing in detail features such as urban traffic and human dwellings and then moving into theoretical discussions of habitus, flows and so on. But there is also the retrospective–prospective dialectical habit he assumes, running back, sometimes to his favored Greece and Rome, to

---

1. For this reason I prefer Lefebvre over the non-Marxist although valuable developments of his work in Edward Soja (1996) and James Flanagan (1996, 1999, 2001).

pick up a certain topic and trace it through to the contemporary situation, only to cast a view into the future.

Dialectical thinking, Hegelian or dialectical Marxism, has been a characteristic feature of Western Marxism, and one finds it in operation, and explored, in the work of the Frankfurt School, especially that of Theodor Adorno, and those closely connected with the school, such as Walter Benjamin and Ernst Bloch. It is also central to the methods of others, like Georg Lukács, Fredric Jameson and, of course, Henri Lefebvre. The dialectic has not necessarily been restricted to Western Marxism (although that term, a product of the Cold War, is now falling by the wayside); for dialectical thinking, termed dialectical materialism, was also central to the intellectual endeavor of the old Eastern European communist countries. The taint of Stalin always meant that many Western Marxists trod warily, seeking out less mechanical and deterministic forms of the dialectic. A few have indeed sought out a non-dialectical Marxism, among them Louis Althusser and Gilles Deleuze, whose thinking may indeed provide one of the ways forward for a post-Cold War Marxism.

Another may be from Lefebvre, whose Marxism runs to the left of the French Communist Party, from which he was expelled in 1957 after a thirty year membership. Calling his dialectic a 'dialectical materialism' as well, but finding the Stalinist line of the French Communist Party too restrictive and stifling, Lefebvre developed a Marxism profoundly touched by situationism and surrealism, but also with a deep sensitivity for human living. He wanted to take up what he felt was Marx's unfinished project in so many ways: he saw that work less as a fixed body of texts to be exegeted with the reverence accorded sacred texts and more as the beginning of a much larger program of intellectual and practical work. The introduction of the question of space is but one of the ways in which Lefebvre undertook to expand Marx. (For instance, he argued that the tendency to reduce society to questions of economics and politics in both Marxism and liberalism was incredibly restrictive: the issue of space was one of the ways of shifting away from such a fixation.)

Less a process that, like Hegel, called for *Aufhebung*, a supersession that kicks the whole problem, the impossible contradiction or antinomy, onto another level in which the problem in question suddenly becomes a much smaller issue in a wider context, Lefebvre's dialectic is one that plays with the opposition or contradiction in question. Toying with it, looking at it from myriad perspectives, and inevitably favoring the lesser term of the opposition in order to move through the whole problem, Lefebvre kept his dialectic open and running. At times he picks up the threefold dimension of a more conventional dialectic, speaking of, for instance, energy, space and time, or of truth, beauty and rhythm, or, as I have already suggested, economics, politics and space. They might be analyzed separately, in conflictual pairs, or on an entirely different tack (see 1986: 42), bringing in an item from elsewhere with which to raise questions about one of the terms under discussion. He does this effectively in *Critique of Everyday Life* (1991b: 141, 145-47, 226), where he connects the notion of the quotidian with religion, especially the popular, half-conscious practices of religion (for Lefebvre, traditional French Catholicism). One distinctive feature of Lefebvre's dialectic is that it produces a profound destabilization of the received notions concerning particular terms and their relationships, which is distinctly reminiscent of the practices of a certain poststructuralism that arose at the time Lefebvre was himself doing his most influential work.

A dialectical reading of the construction of space in the ancient Near East might run in a number of directions, seeking out the play and flow between rural and urban, contrasting the production of space in seats of religious and political power and that of the peasants, or tracing the interaction between the crucial commerce of the sacred and that of space, or contrasting texts from the MT and the LXX in order to read for their different productions of space. In fact, I have found, due to a spasmodic practice of what might be called spatial reading over the last decade or so, that many of the texts of the Hebrew Bible, my specific focus of expertise, give over to spatial analysis.

A distinct form of Lefebvre's dialectic appears in his discussion of space. It is perhaps best to refer to Lefebvre here on the conceptual triad that recurs time and again in the book:

1. *Spatial practice*, embracing production and reproduction, and the particular locations and spatial sets characteristic of each social formation. Spatial practice ensures continuity and some degree of cohesion. In terms of social space, and of each member of a given society's relationship to that space, this cohesion implies a guaranteed level of *competence* and a specific level of *performance*. This is space perceived (*perçu*) in the common sense mode.

2. *Representations of space* (*représentations de l'espace*): the discourses on space, the realms of analysis, design and planning, which are tied to the relations of production and to the 'order' which those relations impose, and hence to knowledge, to signs, to codes, and to 'frontal' relations. In other words, the conception of space (*l'espace conçu*).

3. *Spaces of representation* (*espaces de la représentation*): the deeper presuppositions behind plans and definitions. Coded, recoded and decoded, these spaces embody complex symbolisms, linked to the clandestine or underground side of social life, as also to art. It provides partially concealed criticism of social orders and the categories of social thought, and may happen through bodies, aesthetics, gender and so on. As the third part of a dialectic it offers, as lived space (*l'espace vécu*), as historical sediments or glimpses of the new, utopian possibilities of a new spatialization of social life (see Lefebvre 1974; 1991a: 33, 245; Shields 1999: 160-70).

As ever, Lefebvre's descriptions leave one simultaneously puzzled and illuminated. There are in fact a number of other terms used in relation to space that I want to touch upon in a moment—social space, absolute space, abstract space, contradictory space, mental space, natural space and so on—but the above distinctions are in fact crucial, not only for Lefebvre but also for my reading of some Hebrew texts that will appear in the next parts.

In order to make sense of these three central categories of his spatial dialectic, there is some philosophical legwork to be done. Although it seems like a commonplace now, the idea that certain givens of human experience are social and economic constructions rather than immovable and eternal, natural, objects, was an argument that still needed some work in the early 1970s. The constructionism that now reigns across the humanities and social sciences owes a large debt to the work of Marx and Marxists like Lefebvre, so that it has become possible to see how bodies, genders, sexualities, apart from the more common targets of religion and the family, are constructed in certain ways in certain social formations. But in Lefebvre there is a crucial difference that I want to emphasize. He speaks not of the 'construction' but of the 'production' (*la production*) of space. In the first point of his spatial dialectic, production is closely tied in with reproduction, the perpetuation of the means of production in question.

More than a linguistic quibble is at issue here, for 'production' evokes the crucial Marxist category of mode of production, into which I need to diverge for a moment or two. For Marx and Engels (and I draw here from *The German Ideology* (Marx and Engels 1976)), human beings both produce and are produced: they are produced by the conditions in which they live but they also produce those very same conditions. The production of the means of subsistence through the organization of physical resources affects their social and cultural life, but it also acts to remake the material life of the people in question. That is, their very being and nature as human beings is produced by their production of subsistence in relation to nature.

In other words, for Marx mode of production is the way human beings produce their means of subsistence in relation with nature and the existing mode of production. It is the means required for the production of the necessary and luxury items of human existence. Marx identified two dimensions: the forces or means of production, which designates human interaction with nature in terms of raw materials, technical knowledge and the uses of labor; and the relations of production, which refers to the patterns of human interaction and allocation of labor.

At this point we find some of the terms in the first two categories of Lefebvre's spatial dialectic—(means of) production in spatial practice and relations of production in the representation of spaces. Indeed, the ultimate category for any Marxist criticism worthy of the name is mode of production, a notion simultaneously abstract and concrete, since it deals directly with the understanding of history.

Let me provide a few examples that will return in some form in my discussion of the biblical texts. In capitalism, the great focus of Lefebvre's work, the means of production involve industrial (a euphemism for capitalism is sometimes the 'industrial revolution') and now electronic or cybernetic technologies, the extraction of minerals, the massive farming process of agribusiness, unequal wages and the mobilization of masses of low-paid workers, especially women, children and workers in the 'Third World'. The social relations of production involve the fundamental distinction between bourgeoisie and working class, which is now thoroughly globalized. The ideologies of such a mode would include liberalism and the oppositional Marxism. Its culture is marked by the growth of popular and media culture over against high culture, as well as the all-pervasive presence of commodification. Its politics involves the rise of the nation-state and democracy, and a legal system whose prime focus is the protection of private property, whether that be the individual person or non-human objects. Along with commodities, money and capital itself, Lefebvre argues that a particular form of space has also been produced: the city, as successor to the medieval town, has become the center for finance, government, human and social living. In relation to this the rural has been transformed into an area for the capital production of food and other raw materials, supplying the cities from whom it expects its money; and human dwellings have been produced in terms of the bourgeois family, 'boxes for living in' on private lots.

Or, at the other end of the scale, the so-called Asiatic mode of production has as its means of production the various techniques for widespread hand-tooled agriculture with domesticated animals. Any new developments in technology are directed towards agriculture (improved quality of implement metal, or irrigation, and so on). The relations of production involve a multitude of small landholders that pay tribute to various layers of a significant bureaucracy, at a local, 'national' and imperial level. At the top of the bureaucracy is the imperial center—Babylon, Egypt, Asshur, Beijing, etc.—where the tribute is lavished upon a standing army (used to ensure the regular payment of tribute and increase the empire), buildings of imperial government and religion and the relatively large number of officials required to keep the system running. Culturally and ideologically religion or the sacred was the central language for expressing political, philosophical, juridical, political and other matters (except that it is a little anachronistic to put it this way). The production of space in the Asiatic mode of production depended upon the layering of tribute payments enforced upon the peasants: very few centers of bureaucracy (the ancient 'city') towards which all tribute was directed, and then the subservience of even these spaces to a larger center, of which the smaller centers seem like various points on the spokes of a wheel. The spatial practice was then focused upon the flows towards and away from the centers, and this was inextricably tied up with the religious centralization in the places of power and the destination of tribute. If the language and ways of thinking could operate only in the sacred, then the spatial direction always looked towards the point of tribute payment. Domestic space was then ordered in terms of the need to maintain such a system, and the family unit was a much larger affair focused on ensuring that there was produce to survive and pay tribute: many generations, as many children as possible, single-room dwellings in which humans and animals all spent the night, if not a good part of the day as well.

With these kinds of descriptions, bare though they are, one gets a sense of the difference between modes of production—something Marxist criticism is able to highlight. Of course, the problem with any approach that seeks to periodize history according to one pattern or another is how to account for longer patterns, the carry through of one item into other modes of production, whether they are sacred texts or the status of the peasant. So, in Marxism a growing awareness has arisen of many overlaps, foldbacks and glimpses of new forms found at any one moment, but the assumption is that one mode of production will end up being dominant

This is basic Marxist theory, but it provides the background necessary to understand Lefebvre's insistence on the 'production' of space. One of the results of a shift to 'construction' over against 'production' in the more recent development of the idea is that 'construction' conjures up the notion of social construction, the social context that constructs the individual, bodies, genders and so on. What are lost in the transition are both the specific historical dimensions of a Marxist theory of modes of production, and its connection with economics, politics, ideology and so on.

I have also been speaking, albeit somewhat briefly, of the whole issue of the spatial practice that is produced in different modes of production. But Lefebvre points out that a mode of production needs to perpetuate itself, to reproduce itself, a process carried out at all levels from the macro-economic (the investment of capital and the deployment of finance capital), to class (the reproduction of the labor power of the working class) to the personal (a point close to home for Lefebvre and his many offspring from a series of partners). Indeed, the reproduction of modes of production is a distinct way of introducing the sexual into the most fundamental of Marxist categories, for Marxism has not been noted for its ability to deal with Eros in a positive fashion: the ability to do so has usually been imported. Lefebvre shifts gear and argues that production and reproduction cannot be separated, taking a tip from the traditional Marxist notion that the basic means of production (technology and resources) also include the numbers, patterns and distribution of human population. But in order to think about this adequately one needs to think about sex, and not just the processes of breeding, but the libido itself.

Yet, the spatial practice of which Lefebvre speaks, and the space that is produced, refers primarily to social space, the space created by humans in their interaction with nature, each other and former modes of production. Social space appears in relation to, and over against, physical or natural space, the space of a nature in which human beings increasingly have the upper hand. Since capitalism is now rampant, Lefebvre, while admitting that natural space remains the point of departure for considerations of space and the social process, argues that social space under capitalism now has nature at its mercy: everyone wants to preserve nature, yet everything now seeks to undermine such a desire. Natural space for Lefebvre disappears rapidly over the horizon, for the very 'nature' upon which we now look has been produced by human beings (see 1991a: 30-31).

But there is one final distinction of the categories of space listed above that I have not explored: that between frontal and hidden, the overt and the covert relations of production. For this is the key to his distinction—an odd one on first reading—between the representations of space and spaces of representation. Not only does each mode of production produce specific types of social space (as well as all sorts of other forms from other modes that are subsumed as subvariants), but it also has a specific type of relations of production (the organization of human resources in terms of class, division of labor, and so on). But the issue here is how those relations of production operate spatially. In order to trace this, Lefebvre invokes all the complexity of his dialectical materialism. Under capitalism, he identifies three types of interaction between reproduction and the social relations of production: biological reproduction, the reproduction of labor power and the reproduction of the social relations of production. Each of these three interacting layers is displayed symbolically, simultaneously exhibited and displaced, that is, concealed. Such a symbolic system works with relations of production that are both out there and not, in the forefront and clandestine, explicit and repressed. The former, overt type appears in the forms of monuments, public art, and buildings, especially those of state and business; this is the realm of the representation of space, the frontal, obvious node of the relations of production. The more covert and clandestine version, the shadowy realm of spaces of representation, is interested in what is hidden, closed over, spaces that represent in wayward and diverse fashions.

Lefebvre's oft-repeated example is one he in fact loathed—the bourgeois family home. The overt dimension of the house, facing the street (and do not all detached houses have to face the street?), is its sitting room or formal lounge room, where considerable expense is outlaid: lounges and tables and exquisite chairs, with expensive curtains and pieces of art either on the walls or standing. The public realm of the bourgeois house is one of decor, money and repression. Perhaps the only other room allowed such visual presence is the formal dining room, usually leading off from the lounge room. But there is another realm of such 'boxes for living in' that marks a whole series of repressions: the preparation of food takes place out of sight, as do toilet functions, both evacuating and washing. If these are relegated to the back of the house, the most hidden is sex itself, restricted to night time in the parents' bedroom, with a locked door and when the children are asleep, or, if older, out of the house.

To return once more to the distinctions between spatial practice, representation of space and space of representation, it seems to me that any application of such categories must recognize that the distinction Lefebvre makes between biological reproduction, the reproduction of labor power, and the reproduction of the social relations of production is one that applies to capitalism. As he notes, 'it should be pointed out that in precapitalist societies the two interlocking levels of biological reproduction and socio-economic production together constituted social reproduction—that is to say, the reproduction of society as it perpetuated itself generation after generation, conflict, feud, strife, crisis and war notwithstanding' (1991a: 32). All the same, the powerful distinction between the representation of space and space of representation remains in place, since the lack of distinction between reproduction and production applies directly to the realm of social practice. The notion of covert and overt, of hidden and clear, comes of course from the Marxist perception of class conflict as crucial to historical processes. And it is not for nothing that Lefebvre locates the opposition in the realm of relations of production, where class and class conflict operate in Marxist thought. The frontal class, the one of monuments and impressive buildings and the clear marks of power, stands over against that class which is repressed, beaten down and exploited. Lefebvre's innovation is to widen this to the symbolic field of relations of production, of class relations.

And since it is a symbolic field that is his primary concern, it seems to me that such an approach may be taken up in the reading and interpretation of texts as well. While spatial practice in the ancient world may be more difficult to trace in the texts that derive from it, the representation of space and space of representation are far more amenable to the consideration of texts, including texts from the Hebrew Bible.

There is one final issue before I turn to the Hebrew Bible. A substantial portion of *The Production of Space* seeks to refashion Marxist periodization in terms of space. This is a grand plan that involves a prior commitment to periodization as a viable way of considering history itself. Of course, if one is, like Lefebvre, persuaded by the power of Marxism and Marxist analysis, then historical periodization is an issue and a problematic that needs some thinking. And if space and its production are inescapably tied to mode of production, as I have argued above, then there will necessarily be different types of space for different modes of production. What is interesting about all of this is that the substantial part of *The Production of Space* is given over precisely to such a periodization; Shields, in his advocatory study of Lefebvre (1999) remains unimpressed by the larger system-building dimensions of Lefebvre's Marxism—to which he remained committed throughout his life—preferring the freer, playful, erotic and lived radicalism of this indefatigable writer. For me, however (and this may be symptomatic of a much larger dimension of my physical and intellectual life), the sheer imagination and ability to sustain thought in this way is one of the most impressive dimensions of Lefebvre's work. So, in the following table I have outlined in the first two columns the received Marxist periodization of history in terms of modes of production and what might be called the cultural dominant—a particular way in which culture, and in fact the superstructure as a whole, might be characterized. In the third column I have lined up the various productions of space as Lefebvre follows them through in the bulk of his book.

*Modes of Production and Space*

| Mode of Production | Cultural Dominant | Space |
|---|---|---|
| Hunting and gathering, agriculture and husbandry (tribal society, primitive communism or the horde) | magic and mythic narrative | absolute space (nature) |
| Neolithic agriculture (the gens or hierarchical kinship societies) | kinship | absolute space |
| Asiatic mode of production ('oriental despotism' and divine kings) | religion or the sacred | sacred space |
| Ancient or classical mode of production (the polis or oligarichal slave-holding society) | 'politics' in terms of citizenship of the city-state | historical space (political states, Greek city-states, Roman empire) |
| Feudalism | relations of personal domination | sacred space |
| Early capitalism (classical and monopoly forms) | commodity reification | abstract space (politico-economic space) |
| Late capitalism | commodity reification | contradictory space (global capital vs. localized meaning) |
| Communism | original forms of collective and communal association | differential space (future space revaluing difference and lived experience) |

What I have done here is take the periodization of space in Lefebvre's work, linked it with Shields's discussion and tabulation (1999: 170-72), and then fine-tuned a number of aspects where I think that Shields misses the point somewhat. I find it odd, for instance, for him to argue that such a periodization is linear rather than dialectical, for Lefebvre himself argues that each of the types of space is contained, albeit in subordinate or hidden forms, in each of the modes of production. Further, each mode of production and of space cannot exist without dialectical connections to those forms around it, especially the ones that precede and follow. Finally, in periodizing space Lefebvre carries out the grandest dialectical move with space and time themselves, the inescapable categories (thanks to Kant) of thinking in the modern, capitalist world.

I need to close my theoretical section with a closer look at the realms of absolute space and sacred space, for they are relevant to the biblical material I want to visit next.

The original moment is the space of nature itself, absolute space, pure space. In this context the first social space of the tribe inscribes itself, specifically the semi-nomadic tribe of a hunter-gatherer society, with its seasonal paths, temporary camps and border zones. Whether hunting for game, engaged in limited agriculture or even in the first farming settlements, absolute space dominates. The production of space is here analogical, conceiving of the camp, settlement or village—that is, human society—in terms of a mythic body, with the layout of such settlements narrativized in mythic and magical narrative. There is a distinct anthropomorphism in the representation of space, the settlement and its environment, with settlement and its outside understood in terms of the body and its beyond.

Sacred space, that which follows absolute space temporally and logically in Lefebvre's schema, is produced with the emergence of the city-state, which he finds in the ancient Near East, traditional Asian societies such as that of China, and also the early stages of the Greek world. Rome and its empire comprises a new stage, that of historical space. In other words, over against the more conventional division that begins with Greece and the reliance of such a mode of production on slave labor—a system whereby the very economic and social, let alone the cultural, possibilities of the Greek and Roman worlds are enabled by the labor of slaves—over against this characterization, he posits the emergence of the city-state and then of the Roman imperial system as the points of transition. This is a larger argument that I don't need to pursue here, but it is symptomatic of Lefebvre, for whom the city was a vital dimension of his lived experience, as well as much of his writing and research, that the emergence of the first cities should be central.

But this is not capitalism (for which he reserves his most sustained analysis and critique): in the new city-state the sacred and the political are inseparable. The location of palace and temple in the one location, side by side and often connected as one building, marks the possibility of the city-state. The sacred city—Babylon, Beijing, Egyptian cities of the Pharaohs, Jerusalem itself—supersedes the village and the semi-nomadic tribe to constitute the new, central sacred space. Despot, city and the gods are inseparable: the despot is, in many cases, god, a descendent of a god, or in a relationship much closer than any other citizen; the city is where the god-despot dwells. In exacting tribute, such cities dominate the rural regions surrounding them, pushing back nature, the realm of absolute space, through the technologies of political, economic and sacred power. This form of the city mutates into the Greek *polis* and even dimensions of the Roman *urbs*, in which the sacred space of the city, as *imago mundi*, is set over against the barbarian outside, that realm beyond the power of the city-state.

Ironically, in light of my own particular use of Lefebvre, he is at his weakest with these early productions of space. His energy was of course directed to capitalism and its emergence and dissolution, but the realm of absolute space, although suggestive, is too much shot through with European, especially French, conceptions of the primitive and pre-historic. He is on better ground with sacred space and the emergence of the city-state, although, as some have argued, it is very much gendered in terms of heterosexual binary, with the realm of the city-state characterized as active and masculine and the outside as passive and feminine. Apart from the fascinating and vast program of Deleuze and Guattari in *A Thousand Plateaus* (1987), especially the notion of the *urstaat*, what is sorely needed for this kind of work is a detailed consideration of earlier modes of production and their construction of space.

My use of Lefebvre, then, while bouncing off this spatial schema, is more interested in reading for the production of space, specifically in terms of the threefold dialectic of spatial practice, the representations of space and the space of representation.

### *Biblical Spaces*

> How much can we really learn, for instance, confined as we are to Western conceptual tools, about the Asiatic mode of production, its space, its towns, or the relationship it embodies between town and country? (Lefebvre 1991a: 31-32).

The texts I might discuss are legion, but I restrict myself to one, namely 1 Samuel 1–2. Here we have a rather inconspicuous text that touches more with Lefebvre's lifelong concern with the quotidian, everyday lived life. I should make it clear that whereas Lefebvre assumes the representational function of texts, from architecture through human bodies to written texts themselves, the kind of representation he works with is not of the sort that is second nature to most biblical scholars, namely, the specific history of a people or a period, the acts of states, groups of people or individuals from day to day and year to year. Historical research remains focused on locating texts in such a history and reading them for reference to it. In this respect the energy now directed at the Second Temple period, arguing for very late dates, works with the same set of assumptions; it is only the period that has changed.

So, while the referential function of a text like 1 Samuel 1–2 can tell us little about any figures such as Samuel or Eli, or the events surrounding them, or even the moves of story-tellers and scribes who may have told or penned such a story at an indeterminate later period, it can tell us something about the production of space, of broader economic and cultural patterns in a much larger time frame that beggars any effort at more specific dating.

Since 1 Samuel 1–2 is a written text, it speaks, according to Lefebvre's schema, of the representations of space and spaces of representation: that is, as a text it functions in some representational way. It can then speak only in a secondary manner about spatial practice; or rather, there is a spatial practice of the text that refers to the spatial practice of whatever social formation it comes from. As far as the representation of space is concerned—the 'frontal' discourse of space, the logic, ideology and conceptual depictions of space in relation to modes of production—we need to begin with the last verses of Judges, which may be read as an introduction to this text: 'And the people of Israel departed from there at that time, every one to his tribe and family, and they went out from there every one to his inheritance. In those days there was no king in Israel; every one did what was right in his own eyes' (Judg. 21.24-25). Following the suggestion of David Jobling, I read these verses as not so much a condemnation of the chaos just depicted, a conclusion to the story of the Benjaminites, but rather as the possibility of a desirable state of affairs, without a king to rule over them and exact tribute and so on. In this case, the verses set up the spatial possibilities of 1 Samuel 1–2.

So there is a man from his own inheritance—Ramathaim-zophim of the hills of Ephraim—and from his own tribe and family—Elkanah the son of Jeroham, son of Elihu, son of Tohu, son of Zuph, and Ephraimite (1 Sam. 1.1). The representation of space here is a dispersed pattern of living, each person living in a particular geographical and tribal place, what Lefebvre would designate as a *habitus*. The issue is one of the relations of production, specifically the distribution of human beings and their relations to each other in the production of what is required for human existence. The naming of the two women of Elkanah, Hannah and Peninah, is part of the same logic, as is the crucial statement, 'And Peninah had children, but Hannah had no children' (1 Sam. 1.2). The problem as it unfolds in this story is the barrenness of Hannah, which, as the story makes clear, is distinctly *her* problem, since Peninah had sex with the same man as she. This touches on the question of the reproduction of the means of production, as well the spaces of representation, to which I will turn in a moment. But what we have here is an economic unit, given that families of whatever shape are at basis economic units in particular modes of production. David Jobling, following Norman Gottwald, has argued that under the monarchy we find what may be termed a 'tributary' mode of production, a revised form of Marx's famous Asiatic mode of production. Prior to this, under the ideal of judgeship that appears in Judges and 1 Samuel, he prefers, following Marshall Sahlins (1974), the notion of a 'household' or 'familial' mode of production, that is somewhat more egalitarian in terms of sexual difference than what follows under monarchy, to Gottwald's 'communitarian' mode of production (Gottwald 1999). He also makes explicit use of Karl Wittfogel's *Oriental Despotism* (1963) to argue that the 'transition from a more egalitarian to a tributary mode is typically accompanied by shifts from female-based to male-based patterns of kinship and social organization, from a low-level agriculture dominated by women to an intensive agriculture organized by men, and from the extended family to the nuclear family' (Jobling 1998: 146). Apart from the reactionary nature of Wittfogel's argument (it is directed against the Soviet Union) and the technologism (changes in mode of production have to do with uses of water and irrigation), what lies behind it is the fantasy of Bachofen (1967) and Lewis Henry Morgan (1985), with their arguments for a prior matriarchy before patriarchy took over. Jobling's is more gentle version, but it still assumes such a background. As will become clear in what follows, such a position is difficult to sustain.

But let me stay with the representations of space: the immediate narrative event is the annual journey to worship and sacrifice at the sanctuary at Shiloh. This journey, the path taken from a small space in the hills of Ephraim to Shiloh, is one of those flows of which Lefebvre speaks time and again, open to what he also calls 'rhythm analysis' (see Lefebvre 1996: 219-40). The annual journey frames the story itself, determining its rhythm: at the end of this particular trip, 'they rose early in the morning and worshipped before Yahweh; then they went back to their house at Ramah' (1 Sam. 1.19). But then, after conception and birth, the family, minus Hannah and Samuel, travel to Shiloh again (1 Sam. 1.21). Eventually Hannah goes up after weaning the child in order to dedicate him to the shrine (1 Sam. 1.24), they return home (1 Sam. 2.11), and then return year by year with a robe for Samuel which Hannah makes for him and gives to him at the time of yearly sacrifice (1 Sam. 2.19) The annual journey to the major shrine of course indicates the importance of the shrine itself, with its priestly family, Eli, Hophni and Phinehas. In contrast to Ramah (רמה), the shrine, the place of worship, no matter how modest or grand, is a key representation of space, a frontal dimension which orders the lives of the smaller economic units of the extended families and tribes. The spatial pattern is like a wheel with unequal spokes leading in all directions from the center, or perhaps like an asterisk with lines leading out and coming into the point at the middle, the sanctuary. What we have here, then, is the production of sacred space and its organization of the social and economic patterns of human life.

The spatial patterns of the sanctuary itself, while not laid out explicitly as in so many places (the tabernacle of Moses, Solomon's temple, Ezekiel's temple plans and so on), appear as well. Eli, semi-retired (Hophni and Phinehas are the priests—1 Sam. 1.3), sits 'on the seat beside the door post of the temple of Yahweh' (1 Sam. 1.9), able to observe Hannah praying. The line of sight is important here as well, for, apart from suggestions of voyeurism, Eli commands the sanctuary with his sight, although his insight itself is lacking with regard to Hannah.

What of the spaces of representation—the clandestine or underground side of social life, the sediments of lived space, of gender relations and family patterns, and the possibilities of something new? The annual journey to Shiloh moves from Ramah (רמה) and back again. Ramah emerges as one of these of spaces of representation, from which Hannah, Peninah, Elkanah and then Samuel emerge. Elsewhere in 1 Samuel (7.17; 8.4; 15.34; 16.13; 19.18-23; 20.1; 25.1; 28.3) it is the exclusive domain of Samuel (see Fokkelman 1993: 7). The journey itself is occasion for rivalry between Hannah and Peninah, for the latter taunts Hannah over her barrenness. Peninah provokes and irritates, so Hannah responds with weeping and refusal to eat. An ineffectual Elkanah, who 'loves' Hannah, can only ask questions restricted to the space of representation—weeping, eating, her heart and her barren womb (1 Sam. 1.8).

It is these kinds of family dynamics that have led Carol Meyers to argue for the importance of the public/private divide in this and other stories. The curious turn of the Meyers' argument is to search for the active presence of women in the biblical narratives, a presence screened by the effects of theological and male dominance in biblical studies, in terms of the domestic or private sphere: thus, Hannah's sacrifice in 1 Sam. 1.24 becomes a private ritual, an aspect of 'family religion' (Meyers 1994: 101) that is more apparent in the MT. The catch here is not only the problematic public/private distinction that it assumes but also that any attribution of female agency in ritual remains in the private sphere—hardly a gain in an assumed world of public male dominance. It seems to me that Lefebvre's distinction between spaces of representation and representations of space are much more subtle and workable, for the whole public/private distinction is tied too closely with capitalism itself.

Thus, apart from the family dynamics, the bodies of the women function as the major spaces of representation, specifically their wombs (רחם), the matrix of the story (for which Ramah, רמה, as a veiled pun, itself becomes a cipher). It is as though the wombs are set over against the sanctuary, the other pole around which this story oscillates. Both hidden, and foregrounded, Peninah's fertile womb contrasts with Hannah's barren womb. It is the cause of their conflict, a marker of her economic superfluity (Elkanah gives her but one portion), and the focus of her prayer in the sanctuary. Her vow—to dedicate the son born as a Nazirite to Yahweh at the shrine—focuses again on her womb, for she seeks Yahweh to open her womb in reverse to the divine closure (1 Sam. 1.6). Then it is time, after the blessing pronounced by Eli, for Elkanah's seed to find its way into her womb, where a son is conceived and born (1 Sam. 1.19-20). Hannah's body is now the location of sex and impregnation, and it remains fecund, particularly after the dedication of Samuel and the annual blessing from Eli (2 Sam. 2.20-21). I will return in a moment to the pattern whereby various males—Eli, Elkanah and Yahweh—all ensure Hannah's fertility.

Hannah's body works in one other way in this text, apart from empty womb, source of anguish, and then blessing, divine visitation and sex. I refer here to Eli's singular lack of perception: he observes her mouth and her lips moving. This is the realm of representations of space, for Eli, the priest in the sanctuary of Yahweh, is in that realm. It is also, for Lefebvre, the zone of perception, space that is perceived. Spatial practice breaks in here, percieved space, for Eli perceives her lips and her mouth, but that is all, given his spatial role in the story, all that he can perceive. She, however, speaks in her heart, but her voice is not heard. The very use of heart in this sense, very different from the observed heart of medicine, or (to avoid too much anachronism), an open dead body, is in the realm of the symbolic and the mythic. The heart as lived is very different from the heart as thought and perceived. Desire, Hannah's desire, her anxiety and vexation (1 Sam. 1.16), and mythification appear here. The contrast between Eli and Hannah could not be sharper in terms of space: the one comes from the representation of space, the other from the space of representation.

Eli sees her mouth and lips, but does not hear her voice. Hannah's heart acts as a metaphor for her womb, but her womb cannot be mentioned directly. In a perceptive *tour de force*, Eli concludes she is drunk. In response to Eli's rebuke, she admits not to pouring drink into her body, but pouring out her nephesh to God (1 Sam. 1.15). Yet, even though her womb draws the prayer from her, she reveals to Eli none of the content of her prayer. Other parts of her bodily self, internal and external, have been revealed, but not her womb and its vexations. The spaces of representation in this case are not as myopic as Eli, for in the realm of the shrine, the external and frontal representation of space, it is not possible for her womb to be mentioned, seen or referred to. It is a realm both crucial to yet suppressed by the overt structure of space in this text. Hannah's womb remains unspoken and unperceived within the sanctuary, since sanctuary and womb are at odds with each other in spatial terms. If we pick up Lefebvre again, we find that in the production of sacred space, the realm of nature and of women's bodies is suppressed and removed from the domain of shrine, temple and also city. But this space, what he calls absolute space, does not disappear; rather, it retreats into the interior, into the enclosed spaces of caves, nooks and crannies, alleyways and of course bodies. The womb becomes a prime site for such an investment of alternative space, outside the bodies of males, of sanctuaries and cities, it yet remains crucial to the pattern of sacred commerce: hence the roles of Eli, Elkanah and God in relation to her womb. So here, it seems, we find the intersection of absolute space and sacred space, an overlap that Lefebvre himself was keen on locating.

Is there a utopian possibility in these spaces of representation, specifically with Hannah's womb and the way that it is the focus of the story? If we follow the work of Butler (1993), Grosz (1995) or Blum and Nast (1996), as well as Lefebvre, then bodies, especially female bodies, spatially exceed our representations and images, twisting away from patriarchal signs and controls. It would appear, on one reading at least, that the militant anthem of 1 Sam. 2.1-10 fits the bill. It celebrates the strengthening, by God, of the weak and lowly, the bringing down of mighty kings, powerful, proud and arrogant men. The hungry, feeble and barren find food, strength and pregnancy (see especially Jobling 1998: 166-68). And barely a critic who wishes to oppose more conventional commentaries can resist, especially when locked into a severely limiting analysis of the characters themselves, the argument that the narrative gives (limited) range to Hannah's agency: Meyers speaks of the 'validity and autonomy' of her actions (Meyers 1994: 102); Amit of Hannah's 'delicacy', 'virtue' and 'sensitivity' in protest, when one is more sympathetic to Hannah's perspective rather than, as with a legion of male commentators, to Elkanah's (Amit 1994: 75); Klein (1994) of her move from being the victim of mimetic desire to a social redeemer who refuses such a logic; and Jobling for a deliberate strategy of recuperating Hannah's initiative for an ecclesial context in which such women are few and far between (Jobling 1998: 131-42). For Jobling, however, Hannah's initiative seeks to forestall the arrival of kingship and restore the traditional order of judgeship (which is, for Jobling, at least a little more egalitarian), although the irony is that it is precisely Samuel who becomes king-maker and ends the older order.

Only Klein and Jobling recognize that despite Hannah's initiative, she is finally coopted back into the larger (mythic) logic of the narrative (Klein 1994: 92; Jobling 1998: 165). My argument is a little more dialectical: Hannah's agency cannot be gainsaid. However, it is not so much that she is coopted, reluctantly, back into the narrative: it is through her agency, her initiative, that she becomes a key to the deeper logic of the system itself. And a major signal of that logic is the interactive of space, for here we find the dominant mode asserting itself time and again.

What of Lefebvre's final category? Spatial practice appears at certain points that reflect an economy of the sacred, a sacred commerce in which issues of production and reproduction can only be perceived in terms of the sacred. So it is that Peninah taunts Hannah on the annual journey to Shiloh, specifically after the allocation of portions to each member of the extended family, for Hannah would be given only one portion (1 Sam. 1.4, see also 7). Why not at other times, in this story? At this moment the role of the divine in reproduction is highlighted: on the journey, or rather at Shiloh, after the sacrifice, sacred commerce comes to the fore.

In order to maintain a mode of production it is necessary to reproduce labor power, that is, human beings. In different modes of production this may happen in different ways. For instance, in slave-holding societies the slaves who do the work for the system to keep functioning are acquired through conquest, systems of debt, as well as children of slaves. However, in most cases human reproduction plays some role, especially in those where tribe or gens plays a fundamental role in the relations of production. The reproduction of large families, often polygamous, is crucial for the mode of production to sustain itself. So it is with this story, although with a few twists.

Firstly, there is the curious pattern of reproduction that seems to follow another rhythm from that of sex itself. In order for Hannah to conceive, she first goes to Shiloh, prays at the shrine, receives a blessing from Eli, is remembered (1 Sam. 1.19) or visited (2 Sam. 2.21) by God and then has sex with Elkanah. It seems as though she needs three men for the whole process to work (1 Sam. 1.20; 2 Sam. 2.21). As far as the rhythm of the story is concerned, it is only after the annual sacrifice and vow that the correct combination comes together for conception. This odd pattern is reinforced by the obverse, when she does not go (1 Sam. 1.22), promising to do so when she has weaned the child. Then, when Hannah brings Samuel to dedicate him at the shrine, there is no pregnancy either, for there is no blessing, visitation, or sex in the story at that moment.

It seems that the story has the making of a sacred commerce, a divine economy in which the system requires the activity of God to keep it running. But there is another feature that at first seems to undermine all this: is the dedication of Samuel as a Nazirite, to live and work at the temple, not an undermining of the need for labor power in the unit of the extended family? Would it not fit the logic of the system better if he were to grow up in the family and take his share of the workload? In the end, I would suggest, Hannah has the system at heart, for in dedicating the child to Yahweh at the shrine she ensures that the sacred commerce will continue. Not only does she fulfill her vow (1 Sam. 1.11)—necessary to avoid a divine curse—but she ensures that the role of the shrine and its priesthood in the production of sacred space is maintained. This is the reason, in a spatial analysis, why the sons of Eli, as well as Eli himself, must appear worthless and corrupt in the story (2 Sam. 2.12-17, 22-36). Their sin is so great for it is a sin against God rather than other people (2 Sam. 2.25). Samuel, therefore, is their designated replacement, and Hannah thereby performs a crucial function for the maintenance of this particular production of space and its mode of production (the Asiatic mode of production). Her boy, the product of her womb, must go to the shrine in order to underwrite its continuance at the hub of the spokes. Hannah is crucial to the story, as Meyers among others argues on the basis of the frequency of her name, her role in naming Samuel and her use of dialogue (Meyers 1994: 96-100), but this is only because she is central to the ideological economy of the narrative.

Do even the spaces of representation fall victim to the spatial practice of a particular mode of production? Does Hannah's womb also, despite the utopian glimpse it provides, reinforce the system as a whole? It would seem so, except for one detail: it all takes place at Shiloh, not Jerusalem.

Here I make a dialectical move, characteristic of Lefebvre and other Marxists indebted to him such as Fredric Jameson, taking the discussion to another level and widening out the problem in a whole new way. What difference does Shiloh make? A whole lot, it seems to me.

The story is curious in the context of the larger scale into which it falls, especially if we keep Noth's construction of a 'Deuteronomistic History' in mind (1991).[2] I want to pick up but one piece of this proposal, namely the centrality of the construction of the first temple by Solomon in the structure of the work. One of Noth's arguments was that the work exhibited an over-riding structure into which the ethereal author, creatively named the 'deuteronomistic historian', fitted the bits and pieces cobbled together for the history itself. At the center of this planned work, and at the middle point of the chronology, Solomon begins building the temple (see 1 Kings 6.1). But not only is the temple central in a chronological sense; it also functions as the only place for legitimate worship of Yahweh. The other places, especially the high places, but also the other shrines and minor places for worship are therefore illegal, not to be tolerated. And this applies even to those with some apparent pedigree, such as Bethel, Dan, and of course, Shiloh. So, a continual pattern becomes apparent in the 'Deuteronomistic History', in which worship must be carried out in Jerusalem, at the temple, and nowhere else, and yet alternative worship continues. The various shrines and high places become contested zones, the subject of polemic and theological condemnation.[3]

Spatially, such a conflict is crucial on a number of levels. The split between Rehoboam and Jeroboam is read in terms of the legitimacy or otherwise of the sanctuaries *to which people travel for sacrifice and worship*. Jeroboam, in order to stop the people going to Jerusalem, sets up worship in Bethel and Dan so that the people may go there, so that the hubs are now located within the territory of Israel and not Judah (1 Kgs 12.25-33). This becomes a leitmotif for the rest of Kings, any condemnation now connected with the proverbial sins of Jeroboam. The contest closes with Josiah's destruction of the sanctuary at Bethel (2 Kgs 23.15-20). Indeed,

---

2. I write 'construction' advisedly, for, as I argue in *Novel Histories*, the 'deuteronomistic history' is produced in the space between the biblical text and Noth's critical work. He read Deuteronomy–Kings as though it were the 'deuteronomistic history', and in order to construct it as such he saw it as a historical novel. See Boer 1997, esp 13-14, 77-103.

3. This is where I disagree with Fokkelman's suggestion that Gibeah, Shiloh, Bethel and Bethlehem are all part of the same central zone around Jerusalem (1993: 1-2). Rather, they form the outposts of Jerusalem itself.

Josiah's reform, with its long list of items destroyed, abolished, annihilated and ground into dust, embodies such a spatial contest in intricate detail, for the danger exhibited there is that if such a pattern of religious observance were allowed to go unchecked, it would infect the temple in Jerusalem as well.

Finally, there is not unexpectedly a theological glue to all of this that runs through from beginning to end. The basic theological bifurcation of this 'history' is between obedience and disobedience: following the laws and wishes of Yahweh will lead to blessings, understood in terms of land, long life, wealth and offspring; falling away, worshiping other gods, and thereby disobeying Yahweh's commandments, which appear strategically at the beginning in Deuteronomy, will mean early death, misfortune, and ultimately, the spatial punishment of dispossession from the land, which is of course the punishment, according to this story, for continued apostasy.

So, in the broader context there is a spatial dynamic at work that lifts the whole consideration of Shiloh to a new dialectical level. If Shiloh falls into the category of one of these shrines, a hub of sacred space outside Jerusalem, then it is, as a whole, part of the spaces of representation. If sacred space seeks to control worship and economics in the central city and temple —and for Lefebvre sacred space relies not so much on the shrine alone as on the sacred city—then Shiloh is in another place, namely that of suppressed spaces, of the elements of an older spatial organization that has now succumbed to the new order. Along with the various high places, grottoes, trees and so on, it is now a space of representation, on par with domestic patterns and bodies themselves. What this means is that whereas in the story of 1 Samuel 1–2 Hannah's womb, the major space of representation in the text of 1 Samuel 1–2, acts as one pole over against the sanctuary of Shiloh, in the larger context, her womb and the sanctuary fold into one space. The spatial logic of this is that the very possibility of a story about her womb can only take place in a narratively marginal, suppressed space such as that of Shiloh. Were it set in the Jerusalem of Solomon's temple, then it would have faced a narrative fate comparable to the suggestion of Solomon that the baby fought over by the two sex workers in 1 Kgs 3.16-28 be cut in two.

Also, the sheer absence of descriptions, plans and designs of the shrine at Shiloh marks it off as less a representation of space than as a space of representation. All I was able to glean from the text was the centrality of Shiloh for the annual journey of the family to worship. By contrast, the issue of plans, building programs, sources of finance, interior design, and so on is inseparable from the consideration of the temple in Jerusalem.

Thus, 1 Kgs 5.15 (ET 5.1)–7.38, is concerned with various facets of the building of the temple, roughly a third of the total textual space given over to Solomon's reign (1 Kgs 3–11), let alone the dedication in the long ch. 8. Chronicles pumps this up even further, with 2 Chron. 1.18 (ET 2.1)–4.22 devoted to temple construction, and then a further slab of text, three chapters (2 Chron. 5–7), given over to the dedication of the temple. This is not all, for further temple plans appear in Ezekiel 40–48, and a good section of Ezra and Nehemiah is given over to the story of the rebuilding of the temple and then the city of Jerusalem itself. Various prophets (Haggai, Isaiah, Jeremiah, Ezekiel) agonize over the temple, the book of Psalms sings its praises and hopes for the future rest there (the Maccabees). Finally, the only other stretch of text with as much detail about the construction of a sanctuary is of course that of the tabernacle. The detailed instructions of Yahweh, down to the fineries of interior design, curtain material and clothes for the priests, are passed on to Moses over forty days and nights on Mt Sinai itself (Exod. 25–30), and then replicated in the description of its construction (Exod. 35–40). This is no less a representation of space than the temple in Jerusalem, and the two are linked through the wayward track of the ark of the covenant, which makes its way finally into the temple in Jerusalem.

The fleeting description of Shiloh pales by comparison to the inordinate attention given to temple and tabernacle. Boring stretches of text to be sure, but interesting precisely because of their boredom and tedium, particularly in terms of space. Let me return, however, to the tension I noted earlier between the central sacred space of Jerusalem and its temple which is so characteristic of the Asiatic mode of production. In the same way that worshipers and their acts of worship flow to the temple, so also their tribute flows into the city and the ruling class that feeds on the surplus product extracted from the peasants. Should we read the narrative presence of alternative, submerged and repressed spaces as sites of resistance, as places where older types of space remain and also from where new possibilities might arise, especially if they are connected with patterns of bodies that we find there as well? On one level it seems as though this is indeed possible, but I want to make another point here: It is not so much that we should side with one or the other as a better space, but that the contradiction between the two is part of the very production of space for such a socio-economic system. That is, the centripetal site for sacred observance, with its temple and palace, the site for political and economic power that is simultaneously religious, cannot exist without the centrifugal spaces of alternative sites for worship, and so also political and economic activity. Jerusalem cannot exist without Shiloh, and vice versa, for this is the dialectical logic of such a production of space. It is therefore a mistake to argue for either the correctness of the henotheistic/monotheistic ideology of certain dimensions of the text or for the viability of widespread polytheism. Both exist within this particular mode of production as necessary counterparts to each other.

Thus far I have read 1 Samuel 1–2 at two levels—the immediate one of the story centered on Shiloh and then a larger one of the relation between Shiloh and comparable places with Jerusalem. But there is another, wider, level that reinforces my argument (but which cannot be argued at length here), for if we look at the larger context we find that for most of its existence Jerusalem found itself in tension with stronger imperial centers, whether of the Egyptians, Babylonians, Assyrians, Persians, Greeks or Romans. On this level, Jerusalem becomes an outside rim on a much vaster wheel, perpetually oscillating between subservience to larger imperial centers and limited independence. On this level too, then, the fundamental contradiction of the Asiatic mode of production cannot be avoided, namely the centrifugal force of the periphery and the centripetal force of the center. Such a pattern perpetually replicates itself on a range of scales.

## It's Lonely at the Top:
## Patriarchal Models, Homophobic Vilification and the Heterosexual Household in Luther's Commentaries

### Michael Carden

In this essay I will be exploring the heterosexual utopics in Martin Luther's commentary on Genesis 12–19.[1] In particular, I want to explore how homophobia, as evidenced in his use of Sodom and Gomorrah to vilify opponents, is a crucial element in constructing a portrait of the idealized heterosexual household so central to Luther's social vision. His commentary on these chapters is quite extensive so I will only focus on a small sample of episodes today. I should also point out that I am not 'blaming' Luther for the heterosexual structures of contemporary Western societies, however, I see Luther as a representative of a broader social process, both in his day and in ours, which is illuminated by and reflected in his text. To this end, in my reading of Luther I will also make occasional comparisons to two medieval texts.[2] The first, Peter Damian's *Book of Gomorrah*, is as Mark Jordan (1997) points out, the eleventh-century birth text for the word/concept of sodomy (Latin *sodomia*). The second, the Middle English poem *Cleanness*,[3] is a secular text that, through 'its linkage of homophobic wrath and paradisal heterosexual pleasure' (Keiser, 1997: 3) in its re-telling of the events of Genesis 18 and 19, anticipates some of Luther's discursive moves.

At the outset, I wish to observe that reading Luther is, for me, a rather complex and disturbingly engaging experience. I am raised Roman Catholic and still feel strong connections to a Catholic identity. At the same time,

---

1. I am using the Pelikan and Lehmann (1955–) English translation series of Luther's *Works* (LW), in particular volumes 2 and 3 translated by George Schick. Citations will be by volume and page number.

2. This paper is drawn from a much more extensive analysis of Medieval and Reformation Christian texts on Sodom that forms part of my PhD dissertation.

3. I will be citing this text by line number using the Gollancz edition translated by Brewer (1974).

I am marginalized in that tradition and am one of many who are highly critical of the current Pope and of the whole Papal, Vatican and hierarchical structure. If I have a Catholic identity it is one of reforming or radical Catholic, especially concerning questions of sexuality, gender and hierarchy. So when I read Luther, I find points of connection and almost fellowship but also of disconnection, disenchantment and radical disagreement. Reading Luther, I become very much a radical Catholic queerboy who applauds every time Martin trashes the Pope but is appalled much more frequently by Luther's political ideology and his prejudices, only one of which is his homophobia. Reading Luther, therefore, is an experience for me of consciously reading from multiple reader positions at the one time.

Luther's commentary on the story of Sodom and Gomorrah is a very complex site of contestation, as are indeed all his writings. He is highly conversant with both medieval and patristic exegesis and displays awareness of rabbinic exegesis although his knowledge of the last appears to be derived from Nicholas of Lyra. He is not reluctant to argue against other exegetes and he vigorously puts forward his own interpretation. However, Luther is not only arguing points of exegesis and theology. In challenging Rome, he is taking a political stance and he is conscious that reform demands a new social order. Luther is an advocate for a tripartite understanding of social power and authority—the authority of the Word (the Church), of government and of household. As an advocate for a new Reformed German polity and church, Luther's commentary illustrates Dollimore's point that 'we must understand a much longer history wherein homophobia intersects with, for instance, misogyny, xenophobia, and racism' (Dollimore, 1991: 29). To which list I would add anti-semitism and class. While I will not be able to give adequate treatment today to questions of anti-semitism, as will be seen, class issues are crucial in Luther's text in a way that I have not seen in texts prior to the Reformation, with the exception of the poem, *Cleanness*.[4]

It is in this framework that Luther consistently holds up Lot as a worthy model. However, for Luther, models will have some flaws or failures. Luther is opposed to any doctrine of good works as a source of justification. So, while he has his heroes in the biblical narratives, he is quite adamant that 'even the greatest saints were human beings who could fall into sins and often fell horribly; but when they were saved and later on were

4. Furthermore Luther is not only taking aim at Rome and its German supporters but also at his opponents among the more radical Reformation movements with their own social and political visions.

endowed with various gifts, this is entirely the result of God's mercy, who calls us by His Word and does not cast us aside' (LW, 2.249). Luther is also writing for congregations who are composed of people who were, like him, raised in the Roman church and so it is again appropriate that his role models are flawed. By way of illustration, in his commentary on the calling of Abraham (Gen. 12) Luther argues vehemently against rabbinic traditions of Abraham as a defender of monotheism that instead, prior to his call, Abraham was an idolater. His fundamental point in this argument is that with Abraham:

> …it is something far greater and more difficult that he allows himself to be convinced that the religion in which he was reared by his parents was ungodly and contrary to the will of God. It is our experience too that it is by far the most difficult of all tasks to win those who were brought up in the papistic religion, even though it is manifestly ungodly and blasphemous. Yes, even we ourselves who renounced the doctrine of the pope long ago, still have to struggle often and hard to overcome this wretchedness (LW, 2.251).

In this passage, Luther's Abraham, and his Lot, graphically illustrate Paul Hallam's observation that 'the more I read the commentaries, the more they all seem like autobiographies, albeit disguised' (1993: 84).[5]

In what follows I will discuss four sections of Luther's commentary on Genesis 12–19. The first two sections—Genesis 12–17, Luther's treatment of Abraham, Sarah, Lot and their respective households, and Gen. 18.1-15, the meal at Mamre—are outside Sodom but lie under the anticipatory shadow of the events there in Genesis 19. The final two sections—Gen. 19.4-11, the siege of Lot's house, and Gen. 19.12-14, the angels and Lot's sons-in-law—deal with the crisis that leads to Sodom's doom and who is saved from Lot's household. In each of these sections, Luther uses the biblical narrative to sketch his portrait of the ideal erotic, familial and social order. In each of these sections, too, Luther's use of the narrative to vilify his opponents reveals the fundamentally homophobic nature of his erotic project. I will explore the ways this homophobia exposes the moral flaws and unsustainability of Luther's erotic project of compulsory patriarchal

---

5. As a queer man, this passage from Luther caused me to reflect on the process of coming out. It is not simply a matter of declaring I'm gay/lesbian/bisexual/transgender. It is an ongoing process of attending to a whole range of issues such as internalized homophobia, misogyny, etc. The experience that Luther describes for himself and his followers coming out of Rome is oddly similar to my own experiences coming out of homophobia and heterosexualism.

heterosexuality and of its descendant, the compulsory patriarchal and heterosexual erotic systems, dominant today in Western industrial societies.

### 1. *Genesis 12–17: The Road to Sodom*

For Luther, Abraham is called out of idolatry just as he and his congregations have been called out of Papistry. But this analogy is not the only one that Luther makes at the beginning of the Abraham narrative. The reader next meets Sarah. While Abraham is presented as a model of Faith, Sarah is a different type of model, that of the Wife. Her 'womanly heart' is 'moved by the Holy Spirit' so that she follows 'God when He called' and accompanies Abraham (LW, 2.252). Luther paints a picture of Sarah being pressured by her relatives to abandon her husband but the 'godly wife bravely disregarded the flatteries, entreaties, and threats, and followed her husband' (2.252). Not only Sarah, but also 'the household servants…were far better and more obedient than they are nowadays, and they were unwilling to desert the head of the household' (2.252). Here in these paragraphs Luther begins to map on the Abraham narratives an idealized hierarchical and heterosexual order. The household is one of the three divinely established points of authority, the others being church and state. Abraham's household represents all three because he is both a founder of a nation and a preacher of the Word. The household of Abraham is Luther's utopian vision of a godly society. Obedient servants represent the compliant subordination of the sanctified hierarchy of class. Sarah's obedience represents the compliant subordination to the sanctified domination of men over women. This domination reflects the sanctified heterosexual nature of this godly society.

Almost immediately Luther presents a counter-society, that of the Catholic monastery. Luther contrasts Abraham and Sarah to monks saying that no monk can compare to the 'monk Abraham' who leaves everything to follow 'God when He calls him into exile' (2.252). Abraham also has 'godly Sarah as his companion in this monastic state' (2.252). This 'monastic' state of Abraham and Sarah is, of course, a contradiction to the world of the monastery because Abraham and Sarah are husband and wife. Luther is presenting the patriarchal and heterosexual household as the place for the genuine godly life and denying the claims of the cloister. In Luther's commentary, the cloister is identified with Rome. If Rome is the anti-society and anti-church, then the cloister is the anti-household. As Luther approaches the gates of the anti-society, Sodom, the cloister as a same-sex environment will become a site for explicit homophobic vilification of

Rome. Indeed, in his commentary on Genesis 12, Luther compares monks to the apples of Sodom. The apples were outwardly 'most beautiful, but if one opens them, they are full of ashes and a vile odor' and likewise, 'the hypocritical obedience of the monks is combined with contempt for God and true religion' (LW, 2.269).

Against the suspect homosocial world of the cloister, Luther offers his own vision of heteronormatively appropriate male-male bonding in the relationship of Lot and Abraham. Lot is Abraham's companion and is attached to him 'like a proselyte' by the deity (LW, 2.275). Luther even compares the relationship of Abraham and Lot to that of Naomi and Ruth 'who was a daughter of Lot' (LW, 2.276).[6] Abraham is a high priest and his household 'the true and holy church' (LW, 2.280). Lot is also head of a household because he has a wife, daughters and servants but, as Abraham's nephew, he is subordinate to his uncle. But this is a different type of hierarchy than that of husband and wife. Lot is Abraham's 'faithful friend… brother'[7] and, as such, 'a great boon and a precious treasure' (LW, 2.335). With Lot, Abraham can 'converse about religion' and from him 'hear words of comfort' (2.335). Something, Abraham can't do with Sarah, apparently, because Luther makes these comments to express Abraham's loss when he and Lot have to part. Abraham is head of his household and Sarah is subordinate to him. While Lot is also subordinate to Abraham, unlike Sarah, he is male and a head of a household. Class parity is essential for homosocial relationships because, as will become apparent, Luther has a low opinion of lower classes such as servants.

Lot and Abraham separate because of the strife between their herdsmen. Luther portrays it thus:

> Nobody should doubt that both masters often tried to put an end to it. But their efforts were in vain. The servants remain stubborn; and once they begin to hate, they do not permit that hatred to be sated or blotted out… If the mutual hatred of the domestics is such that it cannot be dispelled, it eventually spreads to the masters and affects them; for on the master rests the obligation to defend his people against the violent acts of others (LW, 2.336).

The separation is therefore a worthy act and is not to be counted against either Lot or Abraham but rather is a sign of their nobility and good exer-

---

6. I cannot resist highlighting the irony of this comparison.

7. That the relationship between Abraham and Lot is an 'outstanding example of brotherly love' (LW, 2.372) is revealed for Luther in Genesis 14 when Abraham rescues Lot from captivity.

cise of authority. In taking the initiative to suggest the separation and giving Lot the choice of land rather than directing him, Abraham models, for Luther, a godly authority. The whole relationship between Abraham and Lot is understood by Luther as a mentoring relationship. Through the separation, Lot assumes his full role as household head. As Lot makes his way to the Cities of the Plain, Luther reads into his journeying the following intent of the Holy Spirit who:

> ...gives a description of Lot's management of his household, which has no appearance of sanctity; and yet these very works in connection with the household are more desirable than all the works of all the monks and nuns... Lot's wife milks the cows, the servants carry the hay and lead them to water. God praises these works and Scripture calls them works of the righteous (LW, 2.349).

Needless to say there is no such portrait of domesticity in Genesis 13.11-12. Once more, as well, Luther sets up the godliness of the heterosexual household in contrast to the homosocial and highly suspect anti-household of the convent/monastery. There is an implicit homosexual panic in Luther's portrayal of Abraham and Lot. They are uncle and nephew and they are both married heads of households and therefore their relationship can model 'the law of love and unity' (LW, 2.336) because no suspicion of homosexuality can attach to them. Not so those same sex households of the Roman anti-society, the monastery and the convent.

## 2. *Genesis 18.1-15: A Meal at Mamre*

In his account of the events at Mamre, Luther maintains two primary themes —hospitality and a utopian vision of the heterosexual household and the role of the woman or wife in that utopia. The two are not unconnected in that Abraham's hospitable household at Mamre serves as a counter to the ungodly and inhospitable anti-society of Sodom in the following chapter. Luther uses notions of worthy guesthood and hospitality to further contrast the godly household and society from its antitheses—Rome in Luther's day and Sodom in the biblical narrative. So while Abraham 'is receiving the Lord Himself' in the appearance of 'naked, hungry...exiles' (LW, 3.178), such travellers are not to be confused with

> ...those vagrants of whom there has been a very great supply under the papacy, who either out of wantonness and flippancy or because of hope in their own righteousness went into exile of their own accord without being compelled to do so by persecution... The devil, too, has his beggars; but

whenever these have nothing they nevertheless have enough and have it in abundance, as we see in the case of the monks and the idle vagrants (LW, 3.179-80).

The monks are the creatures of Rome and Luther reminds his audience that:

> The papists are like the people of Sodom, about whom the next chapter will speak…they…oppress the poor, rage against the unfortunate churches, shed blood, carry off possessions, proscribe and drive into exile. These monstrous sins and this more than inhuman cruelty…they employ against the ministers of the Word, against the heads of households (LW, 3.181).

By drawing attention to the events of Genesis 19, Luther uses the binary of Mamre and Sodom to reinforce the image of Rome as an anti-society not only in conflict with the reformed congregations but also against the household, which for Luther is always heterosexual and patriarchal.[8]

These patriarchal and heterosexual qualities are reinforced in a paean to Sarah as model of the good wife. Luther delivers this in response to the verse saying that Sarah was 'in the tent' (Gen. 18.9). For Luther these few words are a lesson from the Holy Spirit 'about the virtues of a saintly and praiseworthy housewife' (LW, 3.200). Sarah makes a strong contrast to the majority of women who too readily succumb to the 'well known… weakness or inborn levity' of their sex (LW, 3.200). Luther complains of these women that they 'are commonly in the habit of gadding and inquiring about everything with disgraceful curiosity' and 'stand idle at the door and look either for something to see or for fresh rumors' (LW, 3.200). In contrast, Sarah:

> …tends to her own affairs and does not offend by being curious but, like a tortoise, remains in her little shell and does not take the time required to get a brief look at the guests she has and at what kind of guests they are. This modesty or restraint surpasses all the acts of worship and all the works of the nuns, and these words, 'Sarah is in the tent', should be inscribed on the veils of all matrons (LW, 3: 201).

---

8. Luther recognizes that the practice of hospitality is a central virtue in the biblical texts and that it is a crucial theme in the Mamre narrative. But he also stresses the pragmatic benefits of hospitality. He does so here by describing Abraham's response to the sight of the three men:

> Abraham thought that these three men had been driven from their homes because of their confession of the Word, and he saw that there would be no room for them in Sodom or in the neighbouring places. Therefore he receives them and believes that in their persons he is receiving God, as his words prove since he calls them (*adonai*) (LW, 3: 187).

The words, 'Sarah is in the tent', are to be the chains by which women are bound to silent, withdrawn submission to the male patriarchs in their households. The contrast with nuns underlines the heterosexual nature of the patriarchal household and, further on, Luther asks, 'What virgin or widow could compare to her (Sarah)?' (LW, 3.202), thus reinforcing the distinction between wife and celibate. The convent is an all-female household and a woman, the abbess or mother superior, heads it. As such it stands in opposition to the male-headed patriarchal household which, according to Luther, is instituted by the deity. Citing Gen. 1.27, on the creation of humans male and female, Luther argues that 'through marriage a church is brought into existence for God and that a hideous disease of the flesh is healed and the road is blocked to sin, lest it ensnare us, surely these facts also bestow grand praise on marriage' (LW, 3.202). For many people this somewhat positive evaluation of marriage and condemnation of celibacy might appeal, especially considering the erotophobic presuppositions and arguments used to promote celibacy in Roman Catholic discourse. However, Luther's vision of marriage and the lay household thus instituted offers little by way of a liberating alternative. It could be argued that a celibate woman in the female household of the convent would have more autonomy and self-determination than Luther's model housewife, silently subordinate to her husband. Furthermore, the reference to marriage healing a 'hideous disease of the flesh' would demonstrate an erotophobia in Luther's own thought as well. Sexuality in Luther's household would therefore be little compensation and one could wonder if a celibate life might not be preferable for women. Indeed, does celibacy mean a male-free sexuality in an all-female environment? Considering Luther's equation of Rome with Sodom and papists with Sodomites, I wonder if there is not a more conscious or deliberate homophobia and/or homosexual panic animating Luther's advocacy of the heterosexual household against the Roman anti-type of convent and monastery. Elsewhere, Luther condemns celibacy as 'filthy and polluted in various ways' and it's practitioners as people who 'revel in ease and abundance, and for this reason…cannot be otherwise than insane with lust' (LW, 3.210). This statement recalls for me medieval notions of *luxuria* and how it is epitomized by the Sodomites (see Jordan 1997).

Of course, I accept that the convent and the monastery form part of a rigid hierarchy within the Roman church, however Luther's household is no less hierarchical. The primordial hierarchy of husband over wife forms the base for a cluster of hierarchies of age and class. In the household:

...faithful parents bring up their children properly and accustom them to a godly conduct, and...through strict discipline they keep the domestics at their duty...we...know what are truly good works, namely to obey our superiors, to honour our parents, to manage our domestics, and to render the ordinary services which the need of the brethren demands (LW, 3.203).

The hierarchy of the cloister and therefore of Rome is an inverted travesty, mimicking the genuine and divinely instituted hierarchies of gender, class and age that have their basis in the heteronormative household.

### 3. *Genesis 19.4-11: The Siege of Lot's House*

Luther's commentary here is highly charged and overflowing with his personal and political issues. For it is in these verses that the monstrous evil of Sodom is revealed, throwing a stark contrast to Luther's utopian vision. However this passage is not so malleable to Luther's dualistic political vision because Lot, the godly protagonist, here does not easily conform to Luther's own ideology. It is only by employing a heightened homosexual panic that Luther can negotiate the moral and ideological conflicts involved in this passage. Homosexual panic, indeed, necessitates the discipline of the closet to police the erotic and maintain Luther's godly and heteronormative society.

As with his medieval predecessors, Luther must grapple with the problem of revealing that sin that must not be named amongst Christians. The big problem is that by naming or identifying this sin such exposure might cause people to experiment with it. Luther is quite open that he does not 'enjoy dealing with this passage, because so far the ears of the Germans are innocent of and uncontaminated by this monstrous depravity' (LW, 3.251). In Luther's mind, same sex desire is alien to the Germans. He tries to set up a picture of an innocently heterosexual German people but he then admits that this 'depravity' has, on occasion, crept into Germany secretly and in a small way through ungodly soldiers and lewd merchants. Lest any German be tempted to taste such pleasures Luther immediately invokes the spectre of the despised Other or enemy Outsider. Same sex desire marks the anti-society epitomized by Sodom and, for Luther, now incarnate in Rome. Thus he delivers a savage condemnation of the Carthusian monks who 'deserve to be hated because they were the first to bring this terrible pollution into Germany...from Italy' (LW, 3.252). I have not found in texts prior to Luther's text such a clear association of same sex desire with the alien Other or Outsider. He then goes on to say that 'of course' the Carthusians 'were trained and educated in such a praiseworthy manner at Rome' (LW, 3.252). The equating of same sex desire with the Opponent, the Enemy, is an attempt at both removing any possible temptation on the part of Luther's audience while continuing his polemic of homophobic vilification of his enemies.

Same sex desire represents the subversion of all the categories of the natural including the natural hierarchies of class. Therefore Luther is horrified that the text states that all the men of Sodom, young and old, besieged Lot's house and is especially shocked that the leading citizens were involved. After all, they had wives, children and domestics 'and they should have ruled these and accustomed them to discipline and modesty' (LW, 3.253). Even the old men were there, 'among whom sexual desire is dead or who…would have been able to check the frenzy of the rest' through their age and influence (LW, 3.253). Same sex desire thus undermines established order and authority including those hierarchies of age. Apparently reinvigorating the elderly, same sex desire leads them to forget their proper age based authority and decorum, returning to an adolescent state whereby they are subject to desire.[9] Luther then argues that there must have been a feast day in Sodom and the people had been whipped up into a frenzy by banqueting and drinking. So images of frenzy and riotousness are compounded with homoeroticism.[10] These images conform to medieval notions of *luxuria* and so Luther here attempts to establish same sex desire as something that arises from a surfeit of pleasure and comfort. However the image of chaos also enables Luther to contrast against it his own utopian image of the godly, heterosexual society, which is constructed around the godly, and hence heterosexual, household of Lot.

---

9. I can't help but reflect that Luther's image of age as a non-libidinous state sits rather incongruously in the larger narrative of the elderly Abraham and Sarah achieving procreative sexual intimacy in their old age.

10. The *Cleanness* poet presents Sodom as an inverted world of compulsory 'homosexuality' and similarly uses the language of class to portray it. The society of Sodom is ruled by lower types who cannot understand the homosocial, aristocratic, courtly ethos that the poet presents as part of heterosexual eros and which is epitomized by Lot. So, while, in his politeness or courtesy (*hendelayk*), Lot addresses the mob as 'noble friends' (*frende f so fre*) and 'gallant gentlemen' (*iolyf gentylmen*) (861, 864), the poet refers to the Sodomites as *wreche f* (851), *knave f* (855) and *harlote f* (860), all of which words strike me as highlighting the lower class or non-aristocratic (if not anti-aristocratic) character of the Sodomites.

> But what shall we suppose was going on in the mind of Lot... He alone feared God, and in his house he maintained discipline and chastity to the utmost of his ability, while the others indulged freely and without shame in adultery, fornication, effeminacy, and even incest to such an extent that these were not regarded as sins but as some pastime, just as today among the nobility and lower classes of Germany fornication is regarded as a pastime (LW, 3.254).

The heterosexual society is ordered, disciplined and chaste as is the heterosexual individual as modelled by Lot. Germany, by relaxing its discipline over fornication, is in danger of ending up another Sodom. Luther buttresses this warning by pointing to his contemporary Sodom, Rome. He attacks the conduct he witnessed among the cardinals at Rome who consorted publicly with women. They, and Rome itself, are equated with Sodom and its people, although the great horror of the Sodomites was that they were desiring 'what is altogether contrary to nature' (LW, 3.255).

Those cardinals in Rome also resemble the Sodomites because they commit their 'unspeakable infamies...not in secrecy or in privacy but openly' (LW, 3.254). Luther is here invoking the spectre of the closet. He compares the Roman prelates to those 'decent' sinners who 'keep their sin secret and blush with shame', whereas the cardinals and the Sodomites both 'regard sins as praiseworthy morals and suppose that they can be practiced with commendation' (LW, 3.254).[11] The Sodomites have abolished the closet and that is why they are destroyed. He says:

> The heinous conduct of the people of Sodom is extraordinary inasmuch as they departed from the natural passion and longing of the male for the female, which was implanted into nature by God, and desired what is altogether contrary to nature... Moses emphasizes this sin very much... It is not in the house that they utter such unspeakable words; but they are standing outside in the open, and by authority of the officers of the state they publicly demand that the two angels be brought out. Therefore this was not a sin of such a kind that they desired it to be secret and to remain hidden; it is clear that it was an open practice of which no one was ashamed (LW, 3.255).

Sodom is the anti-society. This status is marked by its open embrace of same sex desire as normative. Same sex desire is a disease—Luther

---

11   The medieval monk, Peter Damian, invents the closet in his *Book of Gomorrah* so as to generate homosexual panic with the fantasy of a secret society of Sodomite clergy that he will expose. However Luther invokes the closet in quite opposite circumstances. For Luther the closet is not a site of monstrous conspiracy but, instead, desirable as it is a place of secrecy and shame.

employs, in this chapter, metaphors of illness and therapy—and must be contained if not eradicated. Luther's godly and ordered heterosexual society depends on the discipline of the closet. This discipline is not only social but personal. The heterosexual (person/society) suppresses and contains same sex desire by the erotic ascesis of patriarchal heteronormativity. In this way the godly society is built and maintained. Luther seems to accept that there will be some lapses from this compulsory heterosexuality. However, as long as the regime of shame that is the closet is maintained, these lapses pose no threat. The closet is not the location of Sodomite conspiracy, as per Peter Damian.[12] For Luther, outside of the disciplined hierarchy of the heterosexual household all homosocial relationships become suspect, containing the possibility of being households of Sodom. While Peter Damian's homosexual panic is the tool for paranoid pogroms hunting out the aliens within, Luther establishes homosexual panic as a mechanism of personal policing of the limits of the erotic, of containing or suppressing the alien within. He concludes:

> if you do away with the marriage bond and permit promiscuous passions, the laws and all decency go to ruin together with discipline. But when these are destroyed, no government remains; only beastliness and savagery are left. Therefore as an example for others the Lord was compelled to inflict punishment and to check the madness that was raging beyond measure (LW, 3.257).

Same sex desire is kept in check by the heterosexual household and its discipline of the closet, and these are the foundations of the godly society. When these are taken away, society collapses into beastliness, savagery and genocide.

In discussing Lot's offer of his daughters to the mob, Luther relies on homosexual panic to exonerate him. He stresses the frenzied nature of the mob. The Sodomites are a 'raving people' whose lust has led them into 'incorrigible madness' and 'utterly incurable sin' (LW, 3.256). Against this madness, Luther contrasts Lot, the godly exemplar. Lot is portrayed as calm, courteous, employing 'soft words' to deliver a 'godly and friendly admonition' to the mob (LW, 3.256). However, the problem remains that Lot's offer itself is 'a great disgrace', exposing 'his daughters—and betrothed daughters at that—to prostitution, and not to simple prostitution

---

12. Damian's closet reflects the homosexual panic inherent in the homosocial world of cloister and convent. For Luther, these sites are not merely homosocial but intrinsically homosexual. They are the households of Sodom loudly proclaiming their sin for they are the households of Rome, Luther's current incarnation of Sodom.

but to adultery, yes, even to death' (LW, 3.257-58). Even in translation, Luther's terminology is noteworthy here. Even though he is aware that violence is also involved, even to death, he uses language that implies responsibility and choice on the part of Lot's daughters. Of course, in reality they are pawns and bargaining chips in a proposed exchange. But how does this proposed exchange conform to Luther's utopic vision of Lot as heterosexual exemplar?

To answer this question Luther revisits the arguments put by both Augustine and Lyra, informing his audience that both found that Lot had sinned in making this offer.[13]

Luther disagrees with both and, without any supporting arguments, simply declares:

> I excuse Lot and think that he adopted this plan without sinning. He did not plan to expose his daughters to danger, for he knew that they were not desired by the frenzied men; but he hoped that this would be a way to soften their wrath. Therefore this speech should be regarded as hyperbole (LW, 3.259).

The heterosexual household, as a godly household, is disciplined and hierarchical. It serves as the foundation for the godly society, which is a disciplined and hierarchical society. Same sex desire represents a broader sexual chaos and Lot, as heterosexual exemplar, cannot be seen to be surrendering to such chaos. Instead, the offer of his daughters is an attempt by Lot to shock the Sodomites out of their frenzy. Nevertheless, Luther recognizes that his position is not unproblematic and cites comparably strange actions of other biblical heroes as a context for Lot. He concludes that the behaviour of biblical figures such as Abraham and Lot should not be used to justify present day immorality. These deeds of the 'saints' are not examples or models and should be understood as 'miracles, on the basis of

---

13. Luther agrees with both his predecessors that the problem appears to be whether, in Lot's situation, it is right to employ a lesser evil to avert a greater one. In this moral balancing act Luther is, of course, in no doubt that when the 'respectability either of his guests or his daughters had to be put in peril, the sin against his daughters seemed less grave; for the other sin was against nature' (LW, 3.258). So homosexual panic serves to maintain the patriarchal hierarchy that prioritizes male over female. Luther gives a brief outline of the arguments of Augustine and Lyra and then informs his audience that both found that Lot sinned in making this offer. For Augustine, the sin is surrendering to 'perturbation of spirit' whereas for Lyra the sin is in making the offer (LW, 3.259). However, Lyra counts the 'perturbation of spirit' as mitigating circumstances, for what would otherwise be a mortal sin.

which surely nobody should make a rule or a law' (LW, 3.260). Nor should the saints be condemned for these deeds because 'we do not see the heart' (LW, 3.260). Luther's concern is Lot's authority and good standing revealing a deeper moral problem of his heterosexual utopics. The issue is the apparent handover, by Lot, of his daughters to the sexual chaos/desires of the mob. What is not at issue is Lot's power and authority over his daughters but how it appears to be exercised. Luther's heterosexual exemplar remains a benevolent dictator. A benevolent dictator is probably better than a malevolent one but remains a dictator for all that.

### 4. *Genesis 19.12-14: The Angels Revealed, Lot's Sons-in-Law*

That this dictatorship is not only one based on gender and age but also on class is now revealed in this section. Class issues predominate in Luther's interpretation here. Initially he worries about the whereabouts of Lot's herdsmen, cattle and domestics. Lot separates from Abraham because of strife between his servants and those of Abraham. However, in Genesis 19, there is no mention of Lot's servants. Luther considers the possibility that the herdsmen were outside the city with the cattle, but discounts it. He also rejects the idea that Lot sold his cattle and dismissed all the servants. The importance of this question emerges when Luther states that, therefore, the servants are still in Lot's household. If this be so, then it follows that the servants did not come forward to assist Lot against the mob and nor do they subsequently join their master in his flight from the city. Luther finds it 'exceedingly shocking that even the servants in Lot's house were against their master' (LW, 3.267). It is an example of 'extraordinary wickedness' that Lot was unable to keep 'a single herdsman or a single maidservant in their calling' (LW, 3.267). Sodom is the anti-society and its influence can be subversive of even the godliest household. Luther employs the dynamics of class to illustrate this subversion.[14] The pernicious influence of Sodom has caused Lot's domestics to abandon their master. Luther even tries to put himself in the mind of a servant. He argues that they were intimidated by the behaviour of the mob and, furthermore, thought Lot was partly to blame because the world sees 'the saints' as being 'foolish' and doing 'many foolish things' (LW, 3.267). The servants stayed behind in Sodom

---

14. In contrast, the *Cleanness* poet illustrates these subversive influences on the heterosexual household through the dynamics of gender. Despite her husband's clear instructions to the contrary, Lot's wife deliberately assaults her angelic guests by putting salt in their food (820-27).

because, even though Lot preached to them about the coming destruction, they spurned him for his apparent gullibility. Luther reflects, 'This idea pleases me more; and the examples show that domestics are usually wont to conduct themselves in this manner, especially in dangers, which reveal who are true friends and who are false' (LW, 3.267).

Servants cannot be heads of households and therefore cannot be true friends.[15] True friendship can only exist amongst the heads of households. They are the models and enforcers of the heterosexual regime and only their homosocial bonds are above suspicion. As the servants in Lot's household become possessed by Sodom's spirit of rebellion and no longer submit to the godly hierarchy of class, so too, servants are shown to be suspect subjects in personal relationships. They are more than liable to be false friends and, as they are not household heads, false heterosexuals. The discipline of homosexual panic and the closet thus becomes employed to maintain the hierarchy of class by preventing inter-class bonding, homosocial or otherwise.

Luther then turns to Lot's sons-in-law and uses them to cast suspicion even on peer homosocial relationships. At issue is why they do not believe Lot's warnings and reject him. Luther begins by speculating that they attended the previous day's feast in the city and, therefore, 'are suffering the effects of their intoxication' (LW, 3.268). Consequently, infected with Sodom's malaise, they mock their father-in-law when he warns them of impending doom. The surface question that bothers Luther is how Lot could give his daughters to such men, but the deeper issue is how could these men be in Lot's company to begin with. Luther's answer is:

> Lot had a little church in which he taught and propagated the true knowledge of God. Undoubtedly his sons-in-law were also in this church. For this reason Lot thought that they were pious and saintly… But they were hypocrites; they feigned godliness for a time, but now they revealed their true character (LW, 3.269).[16]

The sons-in-law pretend to be believers, they profess 'godliness'. But now, in the crisis generated by the Sodomites' assault, they drop the mask and reveal their true character. It could be said that they open wide the closet door because godliness, for Luther, is always equated with het-

---

15. I can only reflect that Luther does not consider that servants or domestics are liable to be in his audience or, if they are, they are not paying attention to what he has to say.

16. And once again Luther appropriates Jewish history as church history.

erosexuality or what we would call heterosexuality. Sodom is the antisociety and exposure to it has not only suborned the hierarchies of class but the whole discipline of the closet begins to unravel, as well. What is also implicit in this unravelling is that even the homosocial bonds amongst godly peers are dangerous and must be treated with care. The discipline of the closet means that you can never know if that godliness is real or sham. I keep thinking that Luther's utopics can best be summed up in the phrase 'it's lonely at the top'.

REDIRECTING THE DIRECTION OF TRAVEL: DISCERNING SIGNS OF
A NEO-INDIGENOUS SOUTHERN AFRICAN BIBLICAL HERMENEUTICS[1]

Gerald West

*Introduction*

When I travel to Kenya, in East Africa, and participate in a symposium of East African theologians and biblical scholars,[2] I envy them. I envy their intense engagement with each other and other African scholars, and I envy the absence of almost any dialogue with the scholarly discourses of Europe, Britain and the United States of America, even those fashionable figures that inhabit the margins of these imperial powers. There are few footnotes to Michel Foucault, but many to John Mbiti; Kwesi Dickson is a constant dialogue partner, but not Jacques Derrida; Julia Kristeva is almost entirely absent, but Mercy Amba Oduyoye and Musimbi Kanyoro are ever present.[3] I envy them their Africanness, their dependency on African accents.

When it comes time for me to present my paper there I feel somewhat embarrassed, underprepared for this forum. And yet they revel in my rendition of the African-imperial contestation that constitutes so much of my scholarship. They like my more single-minded concentration on the Bible and enjoy my focus on this significant text in our contexts, but immediately process my offering in terms that are more integrated and whole.

---

1. This essay is based on a paper that was presented at the 2001, A Bible Odyssey: Redirecting the Direction of Travel Conference in Melbourne, Australia in June/July 2001 under the title 'Redirecting the direction of travel: African biblical interpretation post-2001 (and other "post-s")'. I acknowledge the financial support of the National Research Foundation and the University of Natal Research Fund in enabling me to attend this conference and in funding the research that is reflected on in this essay.

2. I have added 'and biblical scholars'. The symposium makes no such distinction, and the absence of a separation between these categories is itself a marker of African scholarship.

3. I do not want to romanticize the absence of recent Western texts; their absence owes as much to the scarcity of current Western academic library resources in Africa as it is does to a desire to engage with things African.

They are warm in their praise and their critical contributions, and eager for copies of my paper. Their response, I know, is more than African hospitality; they really do embrace me as an African colleague, my whiteness and scholarly leanings mattering less than I imagine.

But their warmth worries me, remembering as I do the warmth with which Africans throughout the continent welcomed and received white explorers, travellers, missionaries and their colonial cousins. The white abuse of this welcome and reception haunts me. The damage done by white bodies, their ways of seeing and being and the goods they brought with them, have wreaked a terrible toll. So in addition to bearing and betraying my whiteness, I have begun to suspect and interrogate the goods that I bear as a biblical scholar. Watches, telescopes, mirrors, ploughs, wagons, journals, letters, guns and Bibles all played parts in the imperial drama, and were accomplices in the act of colonization. What about the categories, concepts and tools that I bring in my biblical scholarship, partial products of the imperial dream? Are they, too, damaged and damaging goods?

These questions prompt me to travel in another direction, literally and metaphorically. So I travel south to the conference that kindled this essay, to be with those from 'the colonies' and the margins of empire with whom I feel some kinship, hoping to hone interpretative tools for the struggles we are engaged in, relentlessly inspecting and suspecting the tools we carry. I also travel deeper into Africa and Africanness, further than my forebears ever ventured, redirecting the direction of travel, an unsettled settler. In so travelling I also track back in time and place to the precise moment, in a particular case, when Africans welcomed traders, explorers, adventurers and missionaries into their midst, and I observe what they may have made of them and the objects they bore, especially the Bible. From this place I fast-forward to examine some of the ways in which ordinary African Bible 'readers' constitute African biblical scholarship, finally travelling to and exploring potential sites that may contain traces of the remains of an indigenous African hermeneutic.

### *The Bible as* Bola

Following the death of Dr van der Kemp, 'that valuable man who [pioneered and] superintended the African missions' on behalf of the London Missionary Society (Campbell 1815: v):

the Directors thought it expedient to request one of their own body, the Rev. John Campbell, to visit the country, personally to inspect the different settlements, and to establish such regulations, in concurrence with Mr. Read and the other missionaries [already in Southern Africa], as might be most conducive to the attainment of the great end proposed—the conversion of the heathen, keeping in view at the same time the promotion of their civilization (Campbell 1815: vi).

John Campbell, a director of the London Missionary Society, had been commissioned and sent to the Cape in 1812 in order 'to survey the progress and prospects of mission work in the interior' (Comaroff and Comaroff 1991: 178). Campbell made his way from mission post to mission post in the Colony. When he came to Klaarwater, which was then some distance north of the boundary of the Cape Colony—though the boundary was to follow him some years later (in 1825) almost as far as Klaarwater—he heard that Chief Mothibi of the Tlhaping people, a hundred miles further to the north, had expressed some interest in receiving missionaries (Comaroff and Comaroff 1991:178). With barely a pause in Klaarwater, spending no more than a week there, Campbell and his party set off for Dithakong ('Lattakoo'), then the capital of Chief Mothibi, on 15 June 1813.

Though not the first whites or missionaries to make this trek, theirs is the first sustained visit and during this visit there is the first documented engagement with the Bible by the Tlhaping.[4] We pick up the missionary trail and tale as they arrive on the outskirts of Dithakong in the afternoon of 24 June 1813. Having crested a hill, 'Lattakoo came all at once into view, lying in a valley between hills, stretching about three or four miles from E. to W' (Campbell 1815: 180). As they descended the hill towards 'the African city', they were 'rather surprised that no person was to be seen in any direction, except two or three boys', and the absence of an overt presence continued even as the wagons wound their way between the houses, save for a lone man who 'made signs' for them to follow him. The stillness continued, 'as if the town had been forsaken of its inhabitants',

---

4.  I am of course aware that I am here relying on missionary documentation and therefore on missionary narrative constructions of such encounters, but socially engaged biblical scholars (and anthropologists [see Comaroff and Comaroff 1991: xi, 171, 189]) have become adept at 'reading against the grain', particularly in contexts like South Africa where, Itumeleng Mosala reminds us, 'the appropriation of works and events is always a contradictory process embodying in some form a "struggle"' (Mosala 1989: 32).

until they came 'opposite to the King's house', at which point they 'were conducted' into the Chief's circular court (*kgotla*), 'a square, formed by bushes and branches of trees laid one above another, in which', for this space was not forsaken, 'several hundreds of people assembled together, and a number of tall men with spears, draw[n] up in military order on the north side of the square'. And then the silence was broken! 'In a few minutes the square was filled with men, women, and children, who poured in from all quarters, to the number of a thousand or more. The noise from so many tongues, bawling with all their might, was rather confounding, after being so long accustomed to the stillness of the wilderness' (Campbell 1815: 180). All was not as it had seemed to the missionaries!

Signed upon and conducted into a dense symbolic space (Comaroff 1985: 54-60; Landau 1995: xvii, 20-25)[5] not of their choosing or understanding, Campbell and company become the objects of Tswana scrutiny. With a feeling of being 'completely in their power', Campbell confesses in a letter written some days later, 'They narrowly inspected us, made remarks upon us, and without ceremony touched us...'[6] The Tlhaping 'see', 'feasting their eyes', they 'examine' and they 'touch'.[7] Having been momentarily 'separated', and having 'lost sight of each other in the crowd', the missionaries soon gathered themselves, though they 'could hardly find out each other', and devised 'a scheme, which after a while answered our purpose; we drew up the waggons [*sic*] in the form of a square, and placed our tent in the centre' (Campbell 1815: 180).[8] Being led into a round 'square' not of their own making, they construct a square which they (only partially) control.[9] From this site of some control they plot and execute 'the real object' of their visit, which they explain in the following terms to the nine local leaders, representing Chief Mothibi in his absence from the city, who gather in their tent 'a little after sun-set' (Campbell 1815: 181):

5. The 'square' would have been round (see Burchell 1824 [repr. 1967]: 370, and references above); that it is described as 'a square' demonstrates both some recognition of the political space into which they had been brought and the desire to re-vision what they found (see Comaroff and Comaroff 1991: 182-83; Comaroff and Comaroff 1997: 287-93).

6. J. Campbell, Klaarwater, 26 July 1813 [CWM. Africa. South Africa. Incoming correspondence. Box 5-2-D].

7. J. Campbell, Klaarwater, 26 July 1813 [CWM. Africa. South Africa. Incoming correspondence. Box 5-2-D].

8. This would not be the last laager to be formed by successive sets of settlers.

9. Campbell never quite copes with the way in which local people, mainly the leadership, just walk into 'our tent' (Campbell 1815: 181, 184).

> Through three interpreters, viz. in the Dutch, Coranna, and Bootchuana languages, I informed them that I had come from a remote country, beyond the sun, where the true God, who made all things, was known—that the people of that country had long ago sent some of their brethren to Klaar Water, and other parts of Africa, to tell them many things which they did not know, in order to do them good, and make them better and happier—…[that] I had come to Lattakoo to inquire if they were willing to receive teachers—that if they were willing, then teachers should be sent to live among them (Campbell 1815: 182).

The leadership reply that they cannot/may not give an answer until Mothibi returns, after which there is an informal, it would appear, exchange of gifts: tobacco and milk (Campbell 1815: 182). A number of observations, interactions and transactions are recorded over the next few days as Campbell (impatiently) waits for the arrival of Mothibi. But in the evening of 27 June, when the uncle of the Chief, 'Munaneets', comes to their tent with an interpreter, there was 'much interesting conversation', during which the Bible is explicitly designated in discourse. Two days earlier, on the first morning after their arrival (the 25 June) Campbell and his party hold worship in their kitchen—a house in 'the square, used by them for some public purpose' but assigned to the missionaries as their kitchen—which is attended by 'some of the people' (Campbell 1815: 181). It is hard to imagine the Bible not being present and not being used as either an unopened sacred object or an opened text during this time of worship. Similarly, during worship in the afternoon of 27 June, at which '[a]bout forty of the men sat round us very quietly during the whole time' (Campbell 1815: 191), the Bible too must have been present. But the first explicit reference to the Bible in this narrative, where it is separated out from the normal practice and patterns of the missionaries, is in this discussion with the Chief's uncle.

In their constant quest for information and opportunities to provide information, scrutinizing as they are scrutinized, the missionaries 'enquired of him their reason for practising circumcision' (Campbell 1815: 191). It is not clear what prompts this question, but quite possibly what appear to be a series of ritual activities each day involving women, perhaps the initiation of young women (Campbell, 1815: 185 86, 188, 191, 194-95; Comaroff 1985: 114-18), may, by association, have generated a question to do with male initiation (see Comaroff 1985: 85-115). The Chief's uncle replies that 'it came to them from father to son'. Sensing, no doubt, an opportunity 'to instruct', the missionaries persevere, asking 'Do you not know why your fathers did it?' To which the Chief's uncle and his companions answer, 'No.' Immediately the missionaries respond, Campbell reports, saying: 'We told them that *our book* informed us how it began in the world, and gave them the names of Abraham, Ishmael, and Isaac, as the first persons who were circumcised' (Campbell 1815: 191-92, my emphasis).

The illocutionary intent of this information is clearly to establish an earlier, and therefore superior, claim of origin. Origins were becoming increasingly important to the emerging modernity of missionary England, and so the Bible was seen as particularly potent, containing as it did 'the Origin' of all origins.[10] However, what impressed the Chief's uncle and his colleagues was not this claim to an all-encompassing origin, but the naming of the missionaries' ancestors, Abraham, Ishmael and Isaac, which is why 'This appeared to them very interesting information, and they all tried to repeat the names we had mentioned, over and over again, looking to us for correction, if they pronounced any of them wrong. Munaneets, and the others who joined the company, appeared anxious to have them fixed on their memories' (Campbell 1815: 192). The book—the Bible—appeared, from the perspective of the Tlhaping, to contain the names of the missionary ancestors, and perhaps, if they picked up the intent of the missionaries' proclamation, the ancestors of even their own ancestors. This was, indeed, interesting, and potentially powerful, information. The missionary attempt to subsume the Tlhaping's oral account of circumcision under their textual, biblical account may have marked the Bible, in the eyes of the Tlhaping, as a site worth watching, and perhaps even occupying; or it may have demonstrated the dangers of this strange object of power.

Impressed, but probably also a little perplexed by this intense interest in the names of Abraham, Ishmael and Isaac, the missionaries persist, asking next 'if they knew any thing of the origin of mankind, or when they came'. The people reply, 'saying they came from some country beyond them, pointing to the N. which is the direction in which Judea lies.[11] That two

10. The English were, of course, about to have their views on origins thoroughly shaken and stirred by an English explorer and naturalist, Charles Darwin (Darwin 1963); the beginnings of this paradigm shift (in the Kuhnian sense [Kuhn 1970]) can be detected in the missionary message during the 1800s.

11. This is a puzzling reference; could it mean biblical Judaea, and if so, might the missionaries have here 'seen' confirmed the origin of all peoples, even these 'sons of Ham', from this distant land in and of the Bible? That Campbell thought in such categories is evident from a letter to Mr David Langton dated 27 July 1813, in which Campbell apologizes for not having written sooner, saying that he has 'written much from this land of Ham'. Campbell then goes on to present him with an account of his

men came out of the water; the one rich, having plenty of cattle, the other poor, having only dogs. One lived by oxen, the other by hunting. One of them fell, and the mark of his foot is on a rock to this day'. With no apparent attempt to probe this African origin story in more detail, but with a clear indication of its (and their circumcision story's) inadequacy, the missionaries immediately 'endeavoured to explain to them how knowledge, conveyed by means of books, was more certain than that conveyed by memory from father to son' (Campbell 1815: 192). The Chief's uncle, 'Munaneets', is quick to realize the source of this 'knowledge', knowing long before Michel Foucault theorized it, the articulations of power and knowledge on each other;[12] for he asks 'if they should be taught to understand books'. The use of the modal 'should' perhaps conveys, as it often does in English, a sense of asking permission; Campbell's reconstruction and representation of this dialogue (via three other languages!) may accurately capture a concern on the part of the Chief's uncle that, given the evident power of the book(s), so openly exhibited by the missionaries, they, the Tlhaping, may not be granted access to the book(s).[13] That the missionaries and the Chief's representatives have in mind 'the Book', in particular, is clear from the missionaries' answer: 'We answered they

---

visit to Dithakong (J. Campbell, Klaar Water, 27 July 1813 [CWM. Africa. South Africa. Incoming correspondence. Box 5-2-D]).

12. I use the terms 'power' and 'knowledge' in close conjunction here and the term 'power/knowledge' a little later deliberately, realizing the hardworking hyphen (in the French *pouvoir-savoir*) and slash (in the English) bear a heavy load of theory. Accepting Foucault's invitation 'to see what we can make of' his fragments of analysis (79), my use is intended to allude to this theory, especially to the fragmentary nature of Foucault's theory (79), to the implicit contrast of 'idle knowledge' (79) with local forms of knowledge and criticism, subjugated knowledges (81-82), and their emergence as sites of contestation and struggle over against 'the tyranny of globalising discourses' (83) and their appropriation as genealogies which wage war on the effects of power of dominant discourses (84), whether scientific (Foucault's focus) or other forms of dominating discourse. In particular, my use picks up on Foucault's analysis of the articulation of each on the other, namely, that 'the exercise of power itself creates and causes to emerge new objects of knowledge and accumulates new bodies of information', that the 'exercise of power perpetually creates knowledge and, conversely, knowledge constantly induces effects of power', and that it 'is not possible for power to be exercised without knowledge, It is impossible for knowledge not to engender power' (52) (Foucault 1980).

13. William J. Burchell's earlier stay among the Tlhaping, and his more secretive employment of text generally and the Bible specifically, may have contributed to this question (see Burchell 1824 [repr. 1967]: 391).

would; and when the person we should send (provided Mateebe consented), had learned their language, he would change the Bible from our language into theirs' (Campbell 1815: 192).

One of the local participants was clearly worried about this portent of outside instruction, including perhaps the presence of the Bible as a new (outside) site and source of power/knowledge, though the latter is less clear, for during the conversation, Campbell reports, 'an old man who is averse to our sending teachers, asked how we made candles, pointing to that which was on our table. He also said', Campbell continues, 'he did not need instruction from any one, for the dice [*bola* ?] which hung from his neck informed him of every thing which happened at a distance; and added, if they were to attend to instructions, they would have no time to hunt or to do any thing' (Campbell 1815: 193). This fascinating transaction, re-presenting a complex exchange, seems to suggest a profound grasp by this 'old man'—possibly an *ngaka* (an indigenous doctor/diviner/healer), given that he is wearing a 'dice', one of the elements among the bones, shells and other materials making up the *ditaola* used in divining[14]—of the danger of non-indigenous instruction. The context of the discussion, and the centrality of the Bible in the discussion, if not also centrally positioned on the table in the meeting space,[15] makes it likely that he assumes that the missionaries' book(s) are their equivalent of his 'dice'. My conjecture finds some support from Robert Moffat's account of an incident in which he writes, concerning the same people, 'My books puzzled them.' 'They asked if they were my "Bola", prognosticating dice' (see Comaroff and Comaroff 1997: 345; Moffat 1842 [repr. 1969]: 384).

Whether his aversion to 'instruction' is an aversion to both the source (the Book) and the interpreter (the missionaries) of the source is not clear, but it is an important question that in some ways sits at the centre of my study. We must not assume that this 'old man' shares the assumption of the missionaries that the book and its instruction are one and the same thing. His concern that 'if they were to attend to instructions, they would have no time to hunt or to do any thing', may reflect rumours of the time schedules and modes of production of established mission station church

---

14. I am grateful to Mogapi Motsomaesi and Mantso 'Smadz' Matsepe for elucidating and helping me to interpret elements of this encounter. For a more detailed discussion of the 'bones' used by Tswana diviners and of Tswana divination see Schapera and Comaroff (1991: 57-58).

15. Some days later during a visit from Mothibi's senior wife, Mmahutu, the Bible is clearly positioned on the table in the missionaries' tent.

and school routines to the south (Comaroff and Comaroff 1997),[16] in which case the focus of his aversion is the instruction regime rather than the source of power/knowledge itself, the Book. But I may be imagining a fissure where there is none, for this insightful 'old man' may be making a simpler point; by pointing to the candles, and asking how missionaries made them, he may be demonstrating an important difference between knowledge that he and his people would find useful—how to make candles—and knowledge that is potentially damaging and dangerous—instruction about what happens 'at a distance', such as circumcision, ancestors and origins. The book, the source of the latter, but not, it would seem from his analysis, of the former, is as much a problem as the instruction.

I pause here, having located potential incipient signs of an indigenous hermeneutic in this very early site of encounter. Biblical interpretation among this southern African people begins with the Bible as *bola*, an object of power, whether for good or ill, with the Tlhaping uncertain as to which of these will predominate. But what has brought me to this place, eavesdropping among the Tlhaping—to the Bible as *bola*? As I have indicated in my introduction, I have been brought here by a dis-ease with the tools, categories and concepts that I carry in my biblical scholar's bag. I am uncertain and uneasy about the present state of African biblical scholarship, the site to which I now turn, sharing something of my dialogue with South African black theology, in particular, and African theology and biblical studies, in general.

## African Biblical Scholarship

Having used the term 'African biblical scholarship', I must hasten to my first reflection on this phrase. I make haste because I want to acknowledge that I am chastened by my colleague Tinyiko Maluleke's critique of my use of the term 'African biblical scholarship' (see Maluleke 2000: 94-95; West 1997). Maluleke is right,

> there cannot and should not be such a thing as 'African Biblical Scholarship' if this is envisaged in terms akin to that produced by western-type training. Both African Christians and African Christian theologians have not been able to relate in any exclusive way to the Bible—as a singular collection of texts—in the way that both the historical critical and latter day sociological hermeneutics have done. Except for a small minority, very few

---

16. This entire volume of the Comaroff's might be described as a detailed study of such routines and regimes.

Black and African Biblical scholars have been able to do discipline-specific textual biblical studies (94-95).

Maluleke goes on to suggest that like ordinary African Christians, African biblical scholars' relationship to the Bible has been as 'part of a larger package of resources and legacies which include stories, preaching and language mannerisms, songs, choruses, ecclesiologies, theodicies, catechism manuals and a range of rituals and rites' (95). We must not be misled, says Maluleke, by the overt presence of the Bible among African Christians; while it is 'one of the few 'tangible' things' in African Christianity, 'The Bible', insists Maluleke, 'has been appropriated and continues to be appropriated as part of a larger package of resources' (95). And 'African biblical scholars' cannot escape this reality; indeed they are examples of this reality.

> Most, if not all African 'biblical' scholars operate as philosophers, missiologists and quasi-systematic theologians (e.g. Dickson, Mbiti and Fashole-Luke). Indeed, it seems that the more Mbiti insisted on the centrality of the Bible in African Theology, the more of a philosopher, missiologist and systematic theologian he became (95).

So I use the term 'African biblical scholarship' cautiously and carefully, accepting much of what Maluleke has to say on this matter. Elsewhere I have chartered some of the contours of 'African biblical scholarship' (Ukpong *et al.* 2002; West 2000b) and together with Musa Dube provided a glimpse of 'African biblical scholars' at work (West and Dube 2000). In this essay I take my reflections further, attempting to tease out and understand more clearly the forms of engagement between African scholars and the Bible. More specifically, Maluleke's insistence on 'African biblical scholarship' as something quite different from 'that produced by western-type training' requires probing. What, I continue to ask in this essay, are some of the distinctive features of 'African biblical scholarship'?

As I have argued at some length in the references cited above, 'African biblical scholarship' is indelibly marked by the missionary–colonial encounter and by its close association with ordinary African 'readers' (whether literate or not) of the Bible. While both of these deserve more careful attention than they have received, this essay will focus on the latter.[17]

---

17. A recent volume of *Semeia* (88) goes some way to elaborating the former (Boer 2002).

## Exegeting 'Inclusive'

In an article which argues that inclusivity is a key characteristic of African women's biblical scholarship, Teresa Okure, a Nigerian biblical scholar, states that African women's biblical scholarship 'is inclusive of scholars and nonscholars' (Okure 1993: 77). Though she does not elaborate, I will offer an exegesis of this phrase, attempting to delineate more carefully in what ways ordinary African 'nonscholars' are constitutive of African biblical scholarship (see also West 2000b).

Okure is not alone in making this claim, and the claim is not restricted to an African *women's* approach. The inclusion of ordinary African 'readers' of the Bible in African biblical scholarship is acknowledged, whether implicitly or explicitly, by most African biblical scholars. But quite what this inclusion includes is not clear. I do not think that this is merely a nostalgic or romantic yearning for a lost naivete, as it is in Western literary biblical scholarship, where the scholarly reader imagines his or her scholarly self in this 'ordinary' role. We are misled if we imagine that the advent of reader-response criticism has created a place for ordinary 'readers' of the Bible within Western forms of biblical scholarship. Surely, we might ask, ordinary 'readers' are invited to join the discipline of biblical studies among the plethora of 'readers' already clogging the corridors of the academy? We have 'mock', 'informed', 'competent', 'implied', 'model', 'average' and 'super', 'strong', 'mistaking/mistaken', 'deconstructing', 'perverse', 'feasting', 'subjective', 'transactive', 'validating', 'amazing/amazing', 'resisting' and many more readers. However, as Tim Long notes, 'while very different, all have one important feature in common: none *actually exists*. All are textual constructs, "fictive" readers' (Long 1996: 86-87). So no sooner has the invitation to 'the real reader' been extended than it becomes clear, on examining the fine print on the invitation, that only already trained readers need come, now in their new guise as 'real readers'. Real, real readers—ordinary, untrained, non-scholar 'readers'—are still not welcome. Stephen Moore, in his analysis of reader-response criticism, concurs: biblical studies as a discipline has no place for real readers. 'For biblical studies the moral is plain: criticism is an institution to which "real" readers need not apply.' Real readers of the Bible are really repressed readers (S. Moore 1989a: 90; see also S. Moore 1989b: 106); they are disabled by the disguised academic reader.

Make no mistake, African biblical scholars always re-present the contribution of ordinary African 'readers' of the Bible when it comes to public forums; I am not minimizing this representation. Ordinary African 'readers' of the Bible, most of whom are from poor and marginalized communities, seldom appear on public platforms. But their presence may partially constitute African biblical scholarship in other moments.

But before I come to the first of the ways in which ordinary African 'readers' of the Bible are included in African biblical scholarship, I do not want to allow the opportunity presented by the penultimate sentence in the paragraph above to pass. While dialogue with ordinary African 'readers' of the Bible is an important part of African biblical scholarship, it must be acknowledged that much of the dialogue that African biblical studies participates in in their scholarly capacity is with other scholars. The reading community of other scholars is a crucial component of all scholarship, including African biblical scholarship. However, as my opening account indicates, there is something of a tension among African biblical scholars, including myself, as to an appropriate hierarchy of scholarly communities. Many of us have been trained in the academies of the West, and much of our reading matter continues to come from this site of biblical interpretation. Dialogue with other African scholars outside of our particular countries is difficult, and while African biblical scholarly materials are reasonably plentiful (LeMarquand 2000a), distribution within Africa is also difficult. Part of the problem is, of course, money (Holter 1998). Travel within Africa is expensive, finding foreign currency to buy books from another African country is often impossible, and establishing regular African academic conferences usually requires funding from outside of the continent. But money is not the only problem. Some of us African biblical scholars have been bewitched by the West, and Western scholarship has become our preferred dialogue partner.

There is now, I think, a shift taking place. With the liberation of South Africa in 1994 the continent has in significant senses been restored to wholeness. New energies are coursing through the continent. We are rediscovering each other, and this is a tremendous boon to biblical scholarship in Africa. As both Justin Ukpong and I have argued (Ukpong 2000a; West 2000b), the liberation of South Africa has provided an impetus for sustained dialogue between the two major paradigms of African biblical scholarship —the inculturation and the liberation paradigms.[18] A necessary by-product

---

18. The momentum has been such that even the most resistant Western-based strains of African biblical scholarship—white (mainly Afrikaner) South African biblical scholarship and African Bible translator scholarship—have been partially coopted.

of this recovery is the recognition that we must privilege and prioritize dialogue among ourselves. We must find ways, notwithstanding the very real money matters in our way, to work together, to read and distribute each others' work, to use African-written texts in our teaching, to establish regional and continental conferences, to replenish our libraries with African resources (while maintaining and building up resources from the more traditional sources), and to publish together.

Having said this, I am not sure that other scholars, even African others, ought to be our primary dialogue partners. Moving African scholars up in our hierarchies of discourse, above Western scholars, is certainly an important step in redefining our discipline post colonization. Saturating oneself in the discourse of African colleagues changes things, hence my introductory narrative. But is it enough to keep the discourse among scholars, even African scholars? I think not; and I am not alone, as I have indicated. There is a general sense that African biblical and theological scholarship ought to be and is indeed inclusive of non-scholars—ordinary African users of the Bible.

The most minimal sense in which ordinary African Bible 'readers' might be said to be a part of African biblical scholarship is as receptors of Bible scholarship. This is not as trite as it sounds. Designing one's biblical scholarship in such a way that it can be consumed by ordinary people is no small feat and takes considerable dedication and skill. While there are those, both African and others, who see their scholarship in this way, Okure is alluding to a form of engagement that is more mutual. Ordinary 'readers' of the Bible do not simply consume the product, they partially constitute both the process and the product.

A second way in which ordinary African Bible users might be said to be included in African biblical studies is as informers for biblical scholarship. In his discussion of 'cultural exegesis', Daniel Smith-Christopher delineates an area where 'ordinary readers', in my sense of the term, might having something to contribute to biblical scholarship. He notes that Latin American liberation theologians 'have long talked about an "exegesis of the poor"' (Smith-Christopher 1995: 15). He then comments that what Latin American liberation theologians 'normally mean to suggest [by this phrase] is that the poor have a unique insight into the Bible…because their socio-economic circumstances are in some ways similar to the circumstances of those who drafted the Bible, or those spoken about in large sections of the Bible' (15). But, he continues, most liberation theologians who use this and similar phrases turn out to be talking 'about the use of the

Bible for contemporary life and faith', what he calls 'applied theology or *applications* of the biblical message' (15).[19]

Because Smith-Christopher belongs to the dominant paradigm within biblical scholarship, which believes that what biblical scholarship is really about is what the text *meant*, he wants to ask whether it is in fact true that the poor understand the Bible better than the rich (15). While he accepts that a given text may be *understood* differently in different contexts, he wants to ask questions of 'accuracy of understanding' (16). What exactly is he asking here? Lying behind his conception of biblical scholarship is the sort of distinction found in the work of E.D. Hirsch between 'meaning' and 'significance' (alluded to in Smith-Christopher's discussion), a distinction that has a long (and contested) history (see Fowl 1990: 383). Biblical scholarship, for Smith-Christopher and the majority of the guild, is about '*historical* meaning' (17). So, this being the case, 'what we [Smith-Christopher and those who share his interpretive interests] would like to know from the liberation theologians is whether the poor Brazilian peasants who read the Bible can give any insights into what the text means *for others besides themselves*, let alone whether their observations can actually guide a process of rethinking historical-critical reconstructions of past events' (16). *That* is the question he is interested in and which what he calls 'cultural exegesis' is interested in. In other words, 'Can the native American elder, the Indian or African student or scholar, give all of us new ideas about what the text *historically meant*?' (16).

The tone of Smith-Christopher's discussion may perhaps suggest that he answers this question in the negative—that only properly trained mainstream biblical scholars can do this kind of thing. But we should not be misled by Smith-Christopher's tone; he is, in fact, quite open to the contribution of ordinary readers. Ordinary readers are contributors to what Smith-Christopher calls 'cultural exegesis'. Cultural exegesis, in his use of the term, is not about various forms of sociological or anthropological analysis (12), and has little to do with the cultural studies movement (see Segovia 1995: 29-30). While comparative forms of sociological and anthropological analysis are close relatives of cultural exegesis, cultural exegesis

---

19. Although his analysis of liberation theologies is not particularly nuanced, Smith-Christopher does capture some of the significant aspects of liberation theologies. Liberation theologies do choose the poor as their primary interlocutors (Frostin 1988: 7-8). They are more interested in what the text means than in what it meant. For the poor and those who read with them the Bible is not so much about what happened as about what happens.

'asks another question' (Smith-Christopher 1995: 13). For example, whereas Robert Wilson has used ethnographic data on Siberian shamans in his comparative analysis of biblical Hebrew prophets (Wilson 1980), cultural exegesis 'would want to know what Siberian shamans would *themselves* say upon reading some passages from Jeremiah or Amos. Would a shaman see something that Wilson (or any other European-American biblical scholar) has missed?' (13). Wilson is, according to Smith-Christopher, doing 'a kind of "second hand" cultural exegesis'; while he is using ethnographic data to shape the questions he puts to the text, this cultural data comes from published sources and 'not from first hand experience' (13).

Clearly, then, the ordinary reader does have something to contribute to cultural exegesis. The ordinary reader can enable biblical scholars to see something they might have missed concerning what the text historically meant.[20] Smith-Christopher admits the ordinary reader, albeit as a consultant, to the very heart of the dominant paradigm—the sacred territory of what the text really historically meant.[21]

While there is no doubt that ordinary African 'readers' of the Bible have furnished massive amounts of information of potential value to the biblical studies enterprise, this is a by-product of something more profound. Ordinary Africans are more than merely informants for African biblical scholarship. Okure is saying something more than this; ordinary indigenous African 'readers' of the Bible—most of whom are black, poor and marginalized—are *constitutive* of African biblical scholarship in some sense. A third way, then, in which ordinary African users of the Bible might be said to be included in African biblical scholarship is to make them and their contexts 'the subject of interpretation of the bible' (Ukpong 2000a: 23). The biblical text is read for a particular people in a particular context, but it is not read on behalf of them, it is read with them. Here ordinary African 'readers' are integral to the scholar's work. Biblical interpretation is done as a collaborative act between scholars and non-scholars in which 'the resources of the people's culture and historical life experience are used as complementary to conventional critical tools of biblical exegesis' (23).

20. One could make a similar argument with respect to literary modes of reading.
21. David Tombs' study of how the sexual abuse of Latin American citizens by the military might shed light on the possible sexual abuse of Jesus during his detention is another, and particularly illuminating, example of how the experiences of peoples in the present might serve the predominant concerns of biblical scholars (see Tombs 1999).

'The goal of interpretation is the actualization of the theological meaning of the text in today's context so as to forge integration between faith and life, and engender commitment to personal and societal transformation' (24).

There is no doubt that the 'African socio-cultural context' is the subject of much African biblical scholarship, and that the African socio-cultural context saturates the forms of engagement between the African biblical scholar and ordinary African users of the Bible in his/her community. Included within the African socio-cultural context are both the particulars of specific African contexts, determined by careful phenomenological, socio-anthropological, historical, social and religious analysis (Ukpong 1995: 11-12), and general significant features that characterize the African worldview: a unitary view of reality; a divine origin of the universe and an integral connectedness between God, humanity and the cosmos; a sense of community in which people are because they are in relation to other people; and an emphasis on the concrete and pragmatic. Though not exhaustive, these features are common to most, if not all, African worldviews (Ukpong 1995: 8-9).

This third way, then, makes the ordinary African 'reader' and her/his context the subject of interpretation; the biblical scholar serves the community with his/her scholarship. In Ukpong's analysis, however, the emphasis is different with respect to what each of the partners brings to the collaborative interpretative process. Ordinary 'readers' bring their reality and biblical scholars bring their interpretative tools. This division of labour may characterize much of African biblical scholarship, but the boundaries are not always this clear. Ukpong himself mentions the important presence of 'popular approaches to the Bible' (Ukpong 1996) and commenting on my work makes it clear that the ordinary African context provides both 'the critical resources for biblical interpretation and the subject of interpretation' (Ukpong 2000a: 23).

So, both Ukpong and I include not only the socio-cultural context of ordinary African 'readers' as definitive of our (and African) scholarship, but also their 'critical resources'. This then is the fourth and (for now) final way in which ordinary African Bible users might be said to constitute African biblical scholarship—through their interpretative resources. But while we can and do characterize the African socio-cultural context we still have some way to go in properly characterizing non-scholarly African critical interpretative resources. To put it differently, ordinary African 'readers' of the Bible partially constitute African biblical scholarship in the ways reflected on above, but what does this include by way of their dealings with the Bible as *text*? Their questions and experiences clearly do make a significant contribution, but what about their interpretative strategies with respect to text, the scholar's domain of training and expertise?

In my own work I have stressed that we ought to allow the interpretative interests and strategies of ordinary African 'readers' to constitute African biblical scholarship. I am using the phrase 'interpretative interests' here in the way that it is used by Stephen Fowl (Fowl 1990). Briefly, Fowl suggests that instead of talking about the 'meaning' of a text, we explicate 'meaning' in terms of interpretative interests; interpretative interests being those dimensions of text that particular biblical scholars privilege as the location of 'meaning', whether this be in the text itself (literary, structuralist, etc.), behind the text (historical-critical, socio-historical, etc.) or in-front-of-the-text (symbolic, metaphorical, etc.) (see West 1995: 131-73). What, then, are the interpretative interests of ordinary African 'readers' of the Bible, and what role do they play in African biblical scholarship?

*Ordinary African Modes of 'Reading'*

There is no precision in African biblical scholarship as to the interpretative interests of ordinary African 'readers' of the Bible, though recent work is beginning to take up the task of characterizing their modes of reading (Mijoga 2000; Ukpong 2000b). My own work in this area so far also makes an attempt, but succeeds only in sketching the domain of interpretative interests in rather broad strokes (West 1999: 79-107). I play with and explore a range of metaphors in an attempt to grasp some of the dimensions of ordinary Africans' engagement with the biblical text, arguing that ordinary African 'readers' of the Bible 're-member' a 'dis-membered' Bible, by means of 'guerilla exegesis' (Hendricks 1995), by reading with the nose (de Oliveria 1995), by a process of 'engraf(ph)ting' (Fulkerson 1994: 152), by 'a looseness, even a playfulness' towards text (Wimbush 1991: 88-89) and, I would add, by 'conjuring' with text (T.H. Smith 1994) and a hermeneutic of 'strangeness' (Camp 1993: 166-69). All of this is wonderfully suggestive and provides a host of impulses for digging deeper and becoming more precise. And, as I have said, African biblical scholarship is not averse to these textual resources of ordinary African 'readers' of the Bible, particularly on the countless occasions when African biblical scholars and ordinary African 'readers' of the Bible read together in the churches and communities.

But, I want to ask, what explicit place do such interpretative interests and reading strategies have in the other locations of African biblical scholarship, the biblical studies classroom of the seminary and university? Is there a place for the interpretative interests of ordinary African 'readers' of the Bible in our pedagogy? As Ukpong's analysis indicates (see also LeMarquand 2000b) and as Knut Holter would concur from the perspective of African Old Testament scholarship (Holter 2000a, b), our classrooms tend to bracket (at best) the textual interpretative 'reading' resources of ordinary Africans.

A large part of placing these reading resources in parenthesis in our scholarship and pedagogy is that we do not know how to characterize or categorize them. We have no trouble at all in documenting and displaying the varied interpretative interests and methods of Western biblical scholarship; our libraries are full of such secondary accounts of biblical studies method—even if in many of our African libraries the books are rather outdated—and we ourselves are fairly familiar with these methods, having been trained in them, whether in African institutions or elsewhere away from the continent. We, then, perpetuate the cycle, training the next generation to do as we have done. Fortunately, such is the powerful presence of our African realities that we cannot but help being retrained by ordinary African 'readers' of the Bible and their lived experience as soon as we venture outside. But is this lurch in terms of reading practice as we move in and out of the academy necessary or desirable?

A negative answer is offered further support by the contention in the work of Vincent Wimbush that early African American (African slaves in America) encounters with the Bible have functioned 'as phenomenological, socio-political and cultural foundation' for subsequent periods (Wimbush 1993: 131). If Wimbush is right in asserting that the array of interpretative strategies forged in the earliest encounters of African Americans with the Bible are foundational, in the sense that all other African American readings are in some sense built upon and judged by them, then such analysis has tremendous hermeneutical significance for our current contexts. What Wimbush's work suggests, and its contribution lies in its heuristic capacity rather than in its detail, is that ordinary African American readers of the Bible embody a long history of biblical hermeneutical strategies that can be traced back to their formative encounters with the Bible—then in the hands of their masters and mistresses, but which they began to appropriate, both by watching how whites used this book and by forging their own interpretative resources so that they could wrest control of this potentially powerful book (Wimbush 1991; 1993). Further, his work emphasizes the layered nature of ordinary African American biblical interpretation, reminding us that whatever we might do in the academy is just one more layer. Not only do ordinary African American readers (and African 'readers') of the Bible not come to seminary and university empty handed—without interpretative strategies—but what they do bring has been foundationally shaped by the very earliest encounters of their ancestors with the Bible—by the Bible as *bola*.

I am persuaded by Wimbush's work and, given some remarkable resonances with our African contexts, believe that his work is worth drawing from for our own reflection and research. Implicit in Wimbush's analysis is that we cannot take up the task of identifying and documenting the reading resources of ordinary African 'readers' of the Bible unless we introduce an historical dimension to our hermeneutical concerns. We must go back to the Bible as *bola* before we can move forward, following the traces of the Bible as *bola* into the present. But when we do move forward, what do we find? In the remainder of this essay I attempt a tentative answer.

## *Biblical Interpretation as* Marabi

In the present the Bible is central to the lived faith of ordinary African Christians. While some Black and African theologians may wish this was not the case, even those who raise real questions about the Bible in Africa —Takatso Mofokeng (Mofokeng 1988), Itumeleng Mosala (Mosala 1989), Mercy Amba Oduyoye (Oduyoye 1995), Musa Dube (Dube 2000) and Tinyiko Maluleke (Maluleke 2000)—acknowledge that the Bible is a significant resource for African Christians. Maluleke, probably the most nuanced of African theologians on this matter, acknowledges this quite specifically, pointing to the many ways in which the Bible is a resource in Africa: as the most widely translated book it makes a contribution to the construction of indigenous grammars and texts; it is a basic textbook in primary and higher education; literacy has been closely tied to Bible reading and memorization; it is the:

> most accessible basic vernacular literature text, a storybook, a compilation of novels and short stories, a book of prose and poetry, a book of spiritual devotion (i.e. the 'Word of God') as well as a 'science' book that 'explains' the origins of all creatures. In some parts of Africa, the dead are buried with the Bible on their chests, and the Bible is buried into the concrete foundations on which new houses are to be built. In many African Independent Churches it is the physical contact between the sick and the Bible that is believed to hasten healing (Maluleke 2000: 91-92).

Clearly African Christians relate to the Bible in various ways, and this is Maluleke's point (and mine), *that we recognize the diverse ways in which ordinary Africans actually engage with the Bible*. This, I would argue, is a task for *African* biblical scholarship. And, as Maluleke has suggested, there are two related components to the task: to analyse how ordinary Africans actually *read* and *view* the Bible. Put somewhat differently, and introducing the historical dimension our analysis requires, from the perspective of the Tlhaping, the Bible as *bola* is both worn and read!

My own work mentioned above on indigenous interpretative techniques, painted in broad strokes, is an attempt to tackle the first of these components.[22] Bewitched as I am by tools of the West and intrigued as I am by the fine texture of texts, my emphasis has been on how ordinary African Bible users interpret the Bible as written text. Ordinary Africans do engage with the Bible as an opened text. The Bible is read. Even those who cannot read have it read to them by those who can. Every ordinary reader, then, whether literate or not, interprets the read text, the Bible as text. But I need to hone my analysis more carefully than I have so far if I am going to do justice to the reading resources of my students and the local communities of the poor and marginalized with whom we in the Institute for the Study of the Bible read the Bible (West 2000a).

Emerging work in the interface between orality and literacy and my own preliminary analysis of the most indigenous forms of biblical interpretation I can find (in the present) have yielded a finer, though still tentative, account of what might be called a 'neo-traditional' hermeneutic. This phrase, which I have borrowed, together with a whole series of yet-to-be-developed associations, from Christopher Ballantine's fine study of early South African jazz (Ballantine 1993: 26), denotes the derivation of early forms of South African jazz, *marabi*, from traditional African musics. Fundamental to indigenous African musics is 'a cyclic harmonic pattern'. This rhythmic repetition of harmonic patterns, provided traditionally by a drum or, in an urban situation, 'a player shaking a tin filled with small stones', formed the 'root progression' on top of which melodies (and sometimes lyrics) were superimposed. These melodies too followed a cyclical form, with:

> cyclical repetitions of one melody or melodic fragment yielding eventually, perhaps, to a similar treatment of another melody or fragment, and perhaps

---

22. For an account of the former, and the inseparability of these two dimensions among ordinary African users of the Bible, see Adamo (1999; 2000).

then still others, each melody possibly from a different source. And in this manner 'you played with no stop—you could play for an hour-and-a-half without stopping' (Ballantine 1993: 26-27).

The cited quotation within my quotation, from an interview conducted by Ballantine with *marabi* musician Edward Sililo, captures another aspect of this neo-traditional form of interpretation: its duration. That *marabi* goes on and on is an element of its form. But duration is not an end in itself, which becomes clear when we listen to Wilson Silgee's recollection of what it was like to attend a *marabi* party:

> Marabi: that was the environment! It was either organ but mostly piano. You get there, you pay your ten cents. You get your scale [drinking vessel] of whatever concoction there is, then you dance. It used to start Friday night right through Sunday evening. You get tired, you go home, go and sleep, come back again: bob a time, each time you get in. The piano and with the audience making a lot of noise. Trying to make some theme out of what is playing (cited in Ballantine 1993: 28-29).

There is almost an element of contestation in this description; *marabi* is a communal attempt to make some common sense or theme 'out of what is playing'. *Marabi* is a communal and cyclical (and, perhaps, contested) act of interpretation.

While *marabi* was the interpretative form (of music) of secular social occasions (Ballantine 1993: 26), particularly in black urban areas, its form mirrors the interpretation of the Bible in countless African churches of all and every denomination and in both rural and urban contexts. *Marabi* as music and *marabi* as a metaphor for biblical interpretation are examples of those 'purposive act[s] of reconstruction' in which indigenous peoples have 'created a middle ground between a displaced 'traditional' order and a modern world whose vitality was both elusive and estranging', by 'the repositioning of signs in sequences of practice', a *bricolage*, that promises 'to subvert the divisive structures of colonial society, returning to the displaced a tangible identity and the power to impose coherence upon a disarticulated world' (Comaroff 1985: 253-54).[23]

---

23. The work of Jean Comaroff cited here is profoundly relevant to my study, particularly as the subjects of her study are near neighbours of the Thlaping, the Tshidi. Her study provides a remarkable analysis of how this people appropriate aspects of Protestant orthodoxy and European colonialism which are then 'resituated within practices that promise to redirect their flow back to the impoverished, thus healing their afflictions' (Comaroff 1985: 253).

But my use of *marabi* to designate forms of indigenous African biblical interpretation is more than a metaphor; the hermeneutic moves which characterize *marabi* are found in other neo-indigenous forms. In his attempt at 'developing a new critical methodology for oral texts', Duncan Brown tracks, historically and hermeneutically, the traces of a 'cyclical construction' that, in his words, 'appears to be bound up with African ontology which (in contrast to the linear, progressive, and teleological colonial-Christian model) emphasizes the circularity of religious, social and historical life' (Brown 1998: 107). Brown finds this cyclical patterning in a diverse range of African oral forms: in the songs and stories of the /Xam 'Bushmen' (66), in the formal public praise-poems (*izibongi*) of the Zulu praise poets (*izimbongi*) (107), in the hymns of Christian prophet Isaiah Shembe and the Church of the Nazarites (150), in the Black Consciousness poetry of Soweto poet Ingoapele Madingoane (184) and in the political resistance poetry of Mzwakhe Mbuli and Alfred Qabula (229).

Brown's description of the hymns of Isaiah Shembe is remarkable for its resonance with my discussion of *marabi* above. Brown reminds us of the work of Bengt Sundkler in which Sundkler stresses that 'The hymn is not first of all a versified statement about certain religious facts. The hymn is sacred rhythm. And the rhythm is naturally accentuated by the swinging to and fro of their bodies, by loud hand-clapping and by beating the drum' (Sundkler 1948: 196, cited in Brown 1998: 150).

> The start of the dance is signalled by the beating of the ughubu drum [the Nazarite drum which has a central place in their worship], and the hymn leader then begins to sing. She or he may begin at any point in the hymn, offering a lead which is taken up by the group of singers. Rhythm takes precedence over textual fidelity to linear structure (beginning-middle-end), and the singing of a four-verse hymn may last for up to an hour, with the leader taking the group through the hymn many times, not always in the same verse order, and ending at any point in the hymn (Brown 1998: 150).

Moving from description into analysis, via the work of Carol Muller (Muller 1994: 136), Brown underlines Muller's argument that:

> Shembe's 'reinsertion of the traditional concept of cyclicity into the articulation of ritual time and space' has political implications in the colonial context of the hymns' generation and performance: 'Isaiah's insistence on this trope most powerfully reflected the symbolic contest between colonized and colonizer, whose organization of time and space was symbolized in the principle of linearity (Brown 1998: 150, citing Muller 1994: 136).

The particular usefulness of Brown's study is that it does have an historical dimension. Both the songs and stories of the \Xam and the praise-poems of indigenous southern African peoples predate the missionaries and colonizers. Though not always as detailed as I would like, Brown's hermeneutic analysis is suggestive for my own project, identifying as he does a communal cyclical interpretative process, founded on a rhythmic form (whether of drumming, dancing, singing or praying). The emerging 'text' is constructed on cycles of repetition which participants may contribute to by making ' "cuts" back to a prior series through an explicit repetition of elements which have gone before' (Brown 1998: 107-108).

We find just such a communal and cyclical process of interpretation of the Bible in almost every southern African church. To date the only analysis of this interpretative phenomenon is found in the work of Musa Dube (Dube 1996: 119-21; 2000: 190-92).[24] She characterizes this form of interpretation, what she calls a *Semoya* (of the Spirit) reading, as a communal and participatory mode of interpretation through the use of songs, dramatized narration and repetition (Dube 2000: 190). The text, decided on for the occasion by an individual, once read, becomes the property of the group. All, both young and old, women and men, clergy and laity 'are free to stand up and expound on the text in their own understanding'. While they are doing this, listeners may 'contribute to the interpretation by occasionally interrupting with a song that expounds on the theme of the passage', or the 'interpreter herself/himself can pause and begin a song that expresses the meaning of the passage' (190). Listeners, through song, participate in the interpretation of the passage. Such interruption-interpretations are particularly significant, suggests Dube, because of the form that exposition tends to take.

The predominant form of exposition is 'largely grounded on the assumption that "a story well told is a story well interpreted"' (Dube 2000: 190; Mijoga 2000: 49-60):

> This indigenous method of interpretation capitalizes on recalling, narrating, and dramatizing the story without explicitly defining what it means. Instead, the meaning is articulated by graphically bringing the story to life through a dramatic narration.

---

24. Hilary Mijoga's recent study of preaching in African Instituted Churches in southern Malawi does not deal explicitly with this cyclical form of preaching, but his book is invaluable in providing a full and detailed account of the many facets of AIC preaching (Mijoga 2000).

Even those who lack a particular gift for dramatic representation recall and retell the story, 'almost verbatim'. In every case, whether the performance is dramatic or pedantic, the nuances of interpretation are 'to be read in the interjected songs and the repeated phrases' (190). Particular songs, interjected in particular places, and particular repetitions constitute and contribute to the communal interpretation, contending for meaning for as long as it takes around the cyclical axis of preaching.

Wilson Silgee's account of *marabi* above could be an account of an African Christian revival service or an all-night vigil, with a few modifications. Exchange the Spirit for the alcoholic concoction and the Bible for the piano, and you have ordinary Africans 'trying to make some theme out of what is playing/preaching'. My own unfinished fieldwork among the Tlhaping, made possible by the respectful and resourceful fieldwork of Gopolang Moloabi (himself a member of the BaTlhaping), resonates strongly with the interpretative patterns discerned by others. Moloabi's transcripts of four revival/vigil-type services, amply demonstrate the interpretative devices detected in the work of those discussed above. Again, more detailed analysis is required, but that awaits another article. Yet enough has been done to indicate that there are interdisciplinary resources for taking up Maluleke's task of analysing how ordinary Africans actually *read* (and *view)* the Bible.

## Conclusion

While much more detailed work needs to be done, and while more careful connections need to be established between the Bible as *bola* and the emergence of *marabi*-like interpretative moves, there is clear evidence of indigenous African hermeneutic forms, forged by a host of factors and constituted by many others. The task of further analysis is to probe more deeply in order to understand 'the order of things' that we find here. If we laugh at these indigenous forms, then it must be with the laughter of Foucault as he encounters the passage in Borges from a certain Chinese encyclopaedia—we must laugh with wonderment (Foucault 1973: xv). For though as strange and wonderful as the taxonomy of animals in the Chinese encyclopaedia,[25] there is an order here (and in the encyclopaedia—and this is Foucault's point). We may have yet to understand it, but that

---

25. For those who are unfamiliar with this passage, here it is: 'This passage', writes Foucault, 'quotes "a certain Chinese encyclopaedia" in which it is written that "animals are divided into: (a) belonging to the Emperor, (b) embalmed, (c) tame, (d) suckling

does not detract from its reality as an interpretative resource coursing through the veins of black theological students and the countless 'readers' of the Bible in local churches and communities. And *this form of discourse belongs in our formal African biblical studies scholarship and pedagogy*. It is inappropriate to say as Elizabeth Moore does, supportive though she is of hearing the voices of ordinary African interpreters of the Bible, of the interpretative strategies of ordinary African 'readers' of the Bible that we (presumably Western biblical scholars and theologians) should 'recognize "ordinary" believers' ability and authority as creative theologians, without requiring them to prove that their insights are somehow "biblical"' (E. Moore 2000). We may throw our bones differently, but that does not mean the interpretations of some are more 'biblical' than those of (African) others![26]

pigs, (e) sirens, (f) fabulous, (g) stray dogs, (h) included in the present classification, (i) frenzied, (j) innumerable, (k) drawn with a very fine camelhair brush, (l) *et cetera*, (m) having just broken the water pitcher; (n) that from a long way off look like flies"' (Foucault 1973: xv).

26. This formulation is more insightful than I had imagined, for, as Mark Brett pointed out to me, Jonathan Z. Smith has argued that 'the relationship between canon and hermeneute is perhaps best illustrated by practices of divination: the genius of the diviner lies in matching the relatively fixed "canon" of divinatory objects to the client's particular situation' (Brett 2000a: 64; J.Z. Smith 1982).

# BIBLIOGRAPHY

Abrams, M.H.
    1989    'The Deconstructive Angel', in Michael Fischer (ed.), *Doing Things with Texts: Essays in Criticism and Critical Theory* (New York and London: W.W. Norton & Co.): 237-52, nn. 409-11.

Adamo, D.T.
    1999    'African Cultural Hermeneutics', R.S. Sugirtharajah (ed.), *Vernacular Hermeneutics* (Sheffield: Sheffield Academic Press): 66-90.
    2000    'The Use of Psalms in African Indigenous Churches in Nigeria', in G.O. West and M. Dube (eds.), *The Bible in Africa: Transactions, Trajectories and Trends* (Leiden: E.J. Brill): 336-49.

Ahlström, G.W.
    1993    *The History of Ancient Palestine from the Palaeolithic Period to Alexander's Conquest* (JSOTSup, 146; Sheffield: Sheffield Academic Press).

Aichele, G.
    2001    *The Control of Biblical Meaning: Canon as Semiotic Mechanism* (Harrisburg, PA: Trinity Press International).

Aichele, G (ed.)
    2000    *Culture, Entertainment, and the Bible* (Sheffield: Sheffield Academic Press).

Aichele, G., and R. Walsh (eds.)
    2002    *Screening Scripture: Intertextual Connections Between Scripture and Film* (Harrisburg, PA: Trinity Press International).

Albertz, R.
    1994    *A History of Israelite Religion in the Old Testament Period. II. From the Exile to the Maccabees* (trans. J. Bowden; London: SCM Press).

Alexander, L.
    1994    'Paul and the Hellenistic Schools: The Evidence of Galen', in Troels Engberg-Pedersen (ed.), *Paul in His Hellenistic Context* (Edinburgh: T. & T. Clark): 60-83.

Alter, R.
    1981    *The Art of Biblical Narrative* (New York: Basic Books).

Amit, Y.
    1994    '"Am I Not More Devoted to You Than Ten Sons?" (1 Samuel 1.8): Male and Female Interpretations', in Athalya Brenner (ed.), *A Feminist Companion to Samuel and Kings* (The Feminist Companion to the Bible, 5; Sheffield: Sheffield Academic Press): 68-76.
    1999    *History and Ideology: An Introduction to Historiography in the Hebrew Bible* (The Biblical Seminar, 60; trans. Yael Lotan; Sheffield: Sheffield Academic Press).

Andersen, T. David
1994 'Genealogical Prominence and the Structure of Genesis', in Robert D. Bergen (ed.), *Biblical Hebrew and Discourse Linguistics* (Winona Lake, MI: Eisenbrauns): 242-66.

Anderson, J.
1992 'The Dancing Daughter', in J. Anderson and S. Moore (eds.), *Mark and Method: New Perspectives on Biblical Studies* (Minneapolis: Fortress Press): 103-34.

Appadurai, A.
1990 'Disjuncture and Difference in the Global Cultural Economy', *Public Culture* 2:1-24.

Armour, E.T.
1999 *Deconstruction, Feminist Theology, and the Problem of Difference: Subverting the Race/Gender Divide* (Chicago and London: Chicago University Press).

Bach, A.
1993 'Signs of the Flesh: Observations on Characterization in the Bible', *Semeia* 63: 61-79.

Bachofen, J.J.
1967 *Myth, Religion and Mother Right* (trans. R. Manheim; Princeton, NJ: Princeton University Press).

Bakhtin, M.M.
1986 'Discourse in the Novel', in Michael Holquist (ed.), *The Dialogic Imagination* (trans. Caryl Emerson and Michael Holquist; Austin: University of Texas Press): 259-422.
1988 'From the Prehistory of Novelistic Discourse', in David Lodge (ed.), *Modern Criticism and Theory: A Reader* (London: Longman): 125-56.

Bal, M.
1988 *Death and Dissymmetry: The Politics of Coherence in the Book of Judges* (Chicago: University of Chicago Press).
1999 *Narratology* (Toronto: University of Toronto Press, 2nd edn).

Ballantine, C.
1993 *Marabi Nights. Early South African Jazz and Vaudeville* (Johannesburg: Ravan).

Barr, J.
1968 'The Image of God in the Book of Genesis. A Study of Terminology', *BJRL* 51: 11-26.

Barthes, R.
1986 *The Rustle of Language* (trans. Richard Howard; Berkeley and Los Angeles: University of California Press).
1988 *The Semiotic Challenge* (trans. Richard Howard; New York: Hill & Wang).

Barton, J.
1986 *Oracles of God: Perceptions of Ancient Prophecy in Israel After the Exile* (London: Darton, Longman & Todd).
1997 *Holy Writings, Sacred Text: the Canon in Early Christianity* (Louisville, KY: Westminster/John Knox Press).

Baudrillard, J.
1992 'Rise of the Void Towards the Periphery', in Charles Dudas (trans.), *Critical*

|  |  |
|---|---|
|  | *Theory* (Internet discussion group http://english-www.hss.cmu.edu/ctheory/), article 16, excerpt from *L'illusion de la fin*. |
| 1994 | *Simulacra and Simulation* (trans. Sheila Faria Glaser; Ann Arbor: University of Michigan Press). |

Bauer, W.
- 1971    *Orthodoxy and Heresy in Earliest Christianity* (trans. Robert A. Kraft, Gerhard Kroedel *et al.*; Philadelphia, PA: Fortress Press). Electronic edn, Robert A. Kraft (ed.), 1991–93 (German original, Tübingen: J.C.B. Mohr, 1934).

Baur, F.C.
- 1866–67    *Paulus der Apostel Jesu Christi: sein Leben und Wirken seine Briefe und seine Lehre. Ein Beitrag zu einer Geschichte des Urchristenthums* (Leipzig: Fues's Verlag).
- 1875    *Paul, the Apostle of Jesus Christ: His Life and Work, His Epistles and His Doctrine. A Contribution to the Critical History of Primitive Christianity* (2 vols.; trans. A. Menzies; London: Williams & Norgate, 2nd edn).

Bechtel, L.
- 1994    'What if Dinah is Not Raped? (Genesis 34)', *JSOT* 62: 19-36.

Belich, J.
- 1986    *The New Zealand Wars and the Victorian Interpretation of Racial Conflict* (Auckland: Auckland University Press).

Benjamin, W.
- 1968    *Illuminations* (trans. Harry Zohn; New York: Schocken Books).

Berger, K.
- 1984    'Hellenistische Gattungen im Neuen Testament', *ANRW* 25.2: 1031-43.

Berkovitch, S.
- 1996    'A Literary Approach to Cultural Studies', in Marjorie Garber *et al.* (eds.), *Field Work: Sites in Literary and Cultural Studies* (New York: Routledge): 247-55.

Bible and Culture Collective, The
- 1992    *The Postmodern Bible* (New Haven/London: Yale University Press).

Bird, P.
- 1997    Preface, *Missing Persons and Mistaken Identities: Women and Gender in Ancient Israel* (Minneapolis: Fortress Press): 1-10.

Bloom, H.
- 1986    'From J to K, or the Uncanniness of the Yahwist', in Frank McConnel (ed.), *The Bible and the Narrative Tradition* (New York: Oxford University Press): 19-35.

Blum, V., and H. Nast
- 1996    'Where's the Difference? The Heterosexualization of Alterity in Henri Lefebvre and Jacques Lacan', *Environment and Planning D: Society and Space* 14/4: 559-80.

Boer, R.
- 1997    *Novel Histories: The Fiction of Biblical Criticism* (Sheffield: Sheffield Academic Press).
- 2001a    *Last Stop Before Antarctica: The Bible and Postcolonialism in Australia* (Sheffield: Sheffield Academic Press).

# Bibliography 229

| | |
|---|---|
| 2002 | 'Marx, Method and Gottwald', in R. Boer (ed.), *Tracking the Tribes of Yahweh: On the Trail of a Classic* (Sheffield: Sheffield Academic Press). |
| 2003 | *Marxist Criticism of the Bible* (London: Continuum). |

Boer, R. (ed.)
 2001b    *A Vanishing Mediator? The Presence/Absence of the Bible in Postcolonialism* (*Semeia* 88; Atlanta, GA: Society of Biblical Literature).

Bornkamm, G.
 1971    *Paul* (trans. M.G. Stalker; New York: Harper & Row).
 1995    'The Letter to the Romans as Paul's Last Will and Testament', in Karl P. Donfried (ed.), *The Romans Debate* (Peabody, MA: Hendrickson, rev. edn): 16-28.

Boulous Walker, M.
 1998    *Philosophy and the Maternal Body: Reading Silence* (London: Routledge).

Brett, M.G.
 2000a    'Canonical Criticism and Old Testament Theology', in A.D.H. Mayes (ed.), *Text in Context: Essays by Members of the Society for Old Testament Study* (Oxford: Oxford University Press): 63-85.
 2000b    *Genesis: Procreation and the Politics of Identity* (London: Routledge).

Brewer, D.S.
 1974    *Cleanness: An Alliterative Poem on the Deluge, the Destruction of Sodom and the Death of Belshazzar* (ed. I. Gollancz; Cambridge: D.S. Brewer).

Bright, J.
 1972    *A History of Israel* (London: SCM Press, 2nd edn).

Bronner, L.L.
 1999    'The Invisible Relationship Made Visible: Biblical Mothers and Daughters', in A. Brenner (ed.), *Ruth and Esther* (A Feminist Companion to the Bible, 2nd series; Sheffield: Sheffield Academic Press): 172-91.

Brooten, B.
 1982    *Women Leaders in the Ancient Synagogue: Inscriptional Evidence and Background Issues* (Brown Judaic Studies, 36; Chico, CA: Scholars Press).

Brown, D.
 1998    *Voicing the Text: South African Oral Poetry and Performance* (Cape Town: Oxford University Press).

Brueggemann, W.
 1982    *Genesis* (Atlanta, GA: John Knox Press).

Bruner, F.D.
 1990    'The Why and How of Commentary', *Theology Today* 46: 399-404.

Burchell, W.J.
 1824    *Travels in the Interior of Southern Africa* (London: Longman, Hurst, Rees, Orme, Brown & Green; repr. Cape Town: C. Struik, 1967).

Burnett, F.
 1993    'Characterization and Reader Construction of Characters in the Gospels', *Semeia* 63: 1-28.

Butler, J.
 1993    *Bodies that Matter: On the Discursive Limits of Sex* (London: Routledge).

Bynum, C.W.
 1991    *Fragmentation and Redemption: Essays on Gender and the Human Body in Medieval Religion* (New York: Zone Books).

Camp, C.V.
1993 'Feminist Theological Hermeneutics: Canon and Christian Identity', in E. Schüssler Fiorenza (ed.), *Searching the Scriptures: A Feminist Introduction* (New York: The Crossroad Publishing Company): 154-71.
2000 *Wise, Strange and Holy: The Strange Woman and the Making of the Bible* (JSOTSup, 320; Sheffield: Sheffield Academic Press).

Campbell, J.
1815 *Travels in South Africa: Undertaken at the Request of the Missionary Society* (London: Black, Parry, & Co; repr. Cape Town: C. Struik, 1974).

Cardman, F.
1999 'Women, Ministry and Church Order in Early Christianity', in R. Kraemer and M. D'Angelo (eds.), *Women and Christian Origins* (New York: Oxford University Press): 300-29.

Chaplin, J.P.
1985 *Dictionary of Psychology* (New York: Laurel, 2nd edn).

Chung, H.K.
1993 'Introduction', *Struggle to be the Sun Again: Introducing Asian Women's Theology* (Maryknoll, NY: Orbis Books): 1-9.

Clark, J., and B. Whitelaw
1974 *Cleanness: An Alliterative Tripartite Poem on the Deluge, the Destruction of Sodom, and the Death of Belshazzar*, by the poet of Pearl (ed. Israel Gollancz; trans. D.S. Brewer; Cambridge: D.S. Brewer).
1985 *Golden Summers: Heidelberg and Beyond* (International Cultural Corporation of Australia).

Clines, D.J.A.
1994 'Themes in Genesis 1 to 11', in Hess and Tsumura 1994: 285-309.

Collins, T.
1993 *The Mantle of Elijah: The Redaction Criticism of the Prophetical Books* (The Biblical Seminar, 20; Sheffield: JSOT Press).

Comaroff, J.
1985 *Body of Power, Spirit of Resistance: The Culture and History of a South African People* (Chicago: University of Chicago Press).

Comaroff, J., and J.L. Comaroff
1991 *Of Revelation and Revolution: Christianity, Colonialism and Consciousness in South Africa* (Chicago: University of Chicago Press).

Comaroff, J.L., and J. Comaroff
1997 *Of Revelation and Revolution: The Dialectics of Modernity on a South African Frontier* (Chicago: University of Chicago Press).

Crüsemann, F.
1996 'Human Solidarity and Ethnic Identity: Israel's Self-definition in the Genealogical System of Genesis', in M.G. Brett (ed.), *Ethnicity and the Bible* (Leiden: E.J. Brill): 57-76.

Culler, J.
1982 *On Deconstruction: Theory and Criticism after Structuralism* (London: Routledge).

Damian, P.
1982 *Book of Gomorrah: an Eleventh-Century Treatise against Clerical Homosexual Practices* (trans. with an introduction and notes by Pierre J. Payer; Waterloo, Ont.: Wilfrid Laurier University Press).

Darwin, C.
1963 *The Origin of Species: By Means of Natural Selection of the Preservation of Favoured Races in the Struggle for Life* (New York: Washington Square Press).

Davies, P.R.
1998 *Scribes and Schools: The Canonizatrion of the Hebrew Scriptures* (Louisville, KY: Westminster/John Knox Press).

Davison, G.
2000 *The Use and Abuse of Australian History* (St Leonards, NSW: Allen & Unwin).

Debray, R.
1996 'The Book as Symbolic Object', in G. Nunberg (ed.), *The Future of the Book* (Berkeley: University of California Press).

Debrunner, A.
1965 'λεγω', *Theological Dictionary of the New Testament* (ed. G. Kittel; Grand Rapids, MI: Eerdmans, 1965), IV: 69-172.

Deleuze, G., and F. Guattari
1987 *A Thousand Plateaus* (trans. Brian Massumi; Minneapolis: University of Minnesota Press).

de Oliveria, R.S.
1995 'Feminist Theology in Brazil', in O. Ofelia (ed.), *Women's Vision: Theological Reflection, Celebration, Action* (Geneva: World Council of Churches): 65-76.

Derrida, J.
1976 *Of Grammatology* (trans. Gayatri Chakravorty Spivak; Baltimore, MD: The Johns Hopkins University Press).
1994 *Given Time. Counterfeit Money* (trans P. Kamuf; Chicago: University of Chicago Press).

Dewey, J.
1994 'The Gospel of Mark', in E. Schüssler Fiorenza (ed.), *Searching the Scriptures*, vol. 2 (New York: Crossroad, 1994): 470-509

Diski, J.
2000 *Only Human: A Comedy* (London: Virago Press).

Docker, J.
2001 *1492: A Poetics of Diaspora* (London: Continuum).

Dollimore, J.
1991 *Sexual Dissidence: Augustine to Wilde, Freud to Foucault* (Oxford: Clarendon Press).

Dube, M.W.
1996 'Readings of *Semoya*: Batswana Women's Interpretations of Matt. 15.21-28', *Semeia* 73: 111-29.
1998 'Savior of the World but not of This World: A Postcolonial Reading of Spatial Construction on John', in R.S. Sugirtharajah (ed.), *The Postcolonial Bible* (Sheffield: Sheffield Academic Press). 118-35.
2000 *Postcolonial Feminist Interpretation of the Bible* (St Louis, MO: Chalice).

Dunn, J.D.G.
1998 *The Theology of Paul the Apostle* (Grand Rapids, MI: Eerdmans).

Eco, U.
- 1981 *The Role of the Reader: Explorations in the Semiotics of Texts* (London: Hutchinson)
- 1986 *Travels in Hyperreality* (trans. William Weaver; Orlando, FL: HBJ).
- 1990 *The Limits of Interpretation* (Bloomington: Indiana University Press).
- 1992 *Interpretation and Overinterpretation* (ed. S. Collini; Cambridge: Cambridge University Press).

Ehrman, B.D.
- 1993 *The Orthodox Corruption of Scripture* (Oxford: Oxford University Press).

Eisen, U.
- 2000 *Women Officeholders in Early Christianity. Epigraphical and Literary Studies* (Minnesota: The Liturgical Press).

Eisenstein, E.L.
- 1979 *The Printing Press as an Agent of Change* (2 vols.; Cambridge: Cambridge University Press).

Elam, H.R.
- 1996 'Textuality', in Alex Preminger *et al.* (eds.), *New Princeton Encyclopedia of Poetry and Poetics* (Princeton: Princeton University Press): 1276-77.

Elvey, A.
- unpub. 'Gestations of the Sacred: Ecological Feminist Readings from the Gospel of Luke' (PhD thesis, Centre for Women's Studies and Gender Research, Monash University, 1999).
- 2002 'Connecting and Reconnecting: Tracing Some Intersections between Senses of Genealogy and Senses of Place', *Coming into Country: PAN (Philosophy Activism Nature)* 2: 109-117.

Faur, J.
- 1986 *Golden Doves with Silver Dots* (Bloomington, IN: Indiana University Press).

Fewell, D.N., and D.M. Gunn
- 1991 'Tipping the Balance: Sternberg's Reader and the Rape of Dinah', *Journal of Biblical Literature* 110: 193-211.

Fishbane, M.
- 1985 *Biblical Interpretation in Ancient Israel* (Oxford: Oxford University Press).

Flanagan, J.
- 1996 'Construction of Ancient Space' (http.//www.cwru.edu/affil/GAIR/papers/96papers/Constructs/flanagan/jfoutline.htm [accessed 23 May 2002]).
- 1999 'Mapping the Biblical World: Perceptions of Space in Ancient Southwestern Asia' (http://www.cwru.edu/affil/GAIR/canada/Windsor/Windsor.htm [accessed 23 May 2002]).
- 2001 'Ancient Perceptions of Space/Perceptions of Ancient Space', *Semeia* 87: 15-43.

Fokkelman, J.P.
- 1993 *Narrative Art and Poetry in the Books of Samuel: A Full Interpretation Based on Stylistic and Structural Analysis.* IV. *Toward Desire (1 Sam. 1-12)* (Minneapolis: University of Minnesota Press).

Foucault, M.
- 1973 *The Order of Things: An Archaeology of the Human Sciences* (New York: Random House).
- 1980 *Power/Knowledge: Selected Writings and Other Interviews 1972–1977* (New York: Pantheon).

Fowl, S.E.
1990 'The Ethics of Interpretation; or, What's Left over after the Elimination of Meaning', in. D.J.A. Clines, S.E. Fowl, and S.E. Porter (eds.), *The Bible in Three Dimensions: Essays in Celebration of the Fortieth Anniversary of the Department of Biblical Studies, University of Sheffield* (Sheffield: JSOT Press): 379-98.

Fox, R.
1996 'Women in the Bible and the Lectionary', *Liturgy* 90, reprinted with permission by Call To Action on Internet website http.//www.cta-usa.org/reprint6-96/fox.htm.

Freud, S.
1937 'Wenn Moses ein Ägypter war…', *Imago: Zeitschrift für Psychoanalytische Psychologie, Ihre Grenzgebiete und Anwendungen* 23: 387-419.
1951 *Moses and Monotheism* (trans. Katherine Jones; The International Psycho-Analytical Library, 33; London: Hogarth, and the Institute of Psycho-Analysis).

Friedman, S.S.
1991 'Weavings: Intertextuality and the (Re)Birth of the Author', in J. Clayton and E. Rothstein (eds.), *Influence and Intertextuality in Literary History* (Madison: The University of Wisconsin Press): 146-80.

Friedrich, G.
1965 'κηρυσσω', in G. Kittel (ed.), *Theological Dictionary of the New Testament* (3 vols.; Grand Rapids, MI: Eerdmans, 1965): 683-717.

Frostin, P.
1988 *Liberation Theology in Tanzania and South Africa: A First World Interpretation* (Lund: Lund University Press).

Fulkerson, M.M.
1994 *Changing the Subject: Women's Discourses and Feminist Theology* (Minneapolis: Fortress Press).

Gadamer, H.-G.
1975 *Truth and Method* (trans. G. Barden and J. Cumming; New York: Seabury).

Gamble, H.Y.
1995 *Books and Readers in the Early Church* (New Haven, CT: Yale University Press).
1997 'The Codex', *ABD* (CD-ROM edn).

Garbini, G.
1988 *History and Ideology in Ancient Israel* (London: SCM Press).

Gardner, A.
2000 'Ecojustice: A Study of Genesis 6.11-13', in Habel and Wurst 2000: 117-29.

Geertz, C.
1973 *The Interpretation of Cultures: Selected Essays* (New York: Basic Books).

Geia, J. (ed.)
2001 *?Lost and Found: A Shared Search for Belonging* (two exhibitions that provided an opportunity to reflect on the potential for new relationships between indigenous and culturally diverse Australians, 17 May to 11 November 2001, Immigration Museum; 1 May to 30 June 2001, Koorie Heritage Trust).

Gelder, K., and J.M. Jacobs
    1998    *Uncanny Australia: Sacredness and Identity in a Postcolonial Nation* (Melbourne: Melbourne University Press).

Genette, G.
    1997    'Introduction', in J.E. Lewin (trans.), *Paratexts: Thresholds of Interpretation* (Cambridge: Cambridge University Press): 1-15.

Gevirtz, S.
    1994    'Lamech's Song to His Wives (Genesis 4.23-24)', in Hess and Tsumura 1994: 405-15.

Goldenson, R.M. (ed.)
    1984    *Longman Dictionary of Psychology and Psychiatry* (New York: Longman).

Goodall, H.
    1999    'Telling Country: Memory, Modernity and Narratives in Rural Australia', *History Workshop Journal* 47: 160-90.

Gottwald, N.
    1999    *The Tribes of Yahweh: A Sociology of the Religion of Liberated Israel, 1250–1050 BCE* (The Biblical Seminar; Sheffield: Sheffield Academic Press).

Green, B.
    1999    'Great Trek and Long Walk: Readings of a Biblical Symbol', *Biblical Interpretation* 7: 272-300.

Greenspan, S.L.
    1963    'English Versions of the Bible AD 1525–1611', *Cambridge History of the Bible: The West from the Reformation to the Present Day* (Cambridge: The University Press): 141-74.

Grosz, E.
    1989    *Sexual Subversions: Three French Feminists* (St Leonards, NSW: Allen & Unwin).
    1995    *Space, Time and Perversion: Essays on the Politics of Bodies* (London: Routledge).

Gunkel, H.
    1987    'The Prophets as Writers and Poets', in D.L. Petersen (ed.), *Prophecy in Israel: Search for Identity* (trans. J.L. Schaaf; Philadelphia, PA: Fortress Press; London: SPCK): 22-73.

Habel, N.C.
    1995    *This Land is Mine: Six Biblical Land Ideologies* (Minneapolis: Fortress Press).
    2000    'Geophany: The Earth Story in Genesis 1', in Habel and Wurst 2000: 34-48.

Habel, N.C., and S. Wurst (eds.)
    2000    *The Earth Story in Genesis. The Earth Bible Volume Two* (Sheffield: Sheffield Academic Press).

Hallam, P.
    1993    *The Book of Sodom* (London: Verso).

Harrison, R.P.
    1992    *Forests: The Shadow of Civilization* (Chicago: Chicago University Press).

Hartman, G.H., and S. Budick (eds.)
    1986    *Midrash and Literature* (New Haven, CT: Yale University Press).

Hawk, L.D.
    1991    *Every Promise Fulfilled: Contesting Plots in Joshua* (Louisville, KY: Westminster/John Knox Press).

Heard, R.C.
   2001        *Dynamics of Diselection: Ambiguity in Genesis 12–36 and Ethnic Boundaries in Post-Exilic Judah* (Atlanta, GA: Society of Biblical Literature).

Hendricks, O.O.
   1995        'Guerrilla Exegesis: "Struggle" as a Scholarly Vocation: A Postmodern Approach to African-American Interpretation', *Semeia* 72: 73-90.

Hengel, M.
   1989        *The 'Hellenization' of Judaea in the First Century* (Harrisburg, PA: Trinity Press International).
   1991        *The Pre-Christian Paul* (trans. J. Bowden; London: SCM Press).

Hess, R.S.
   1994        'The Genealogies of Genesis 1-11 and Comparative Literature', in Hess and Tsumura 1994: 58-72.

Hess, R.S., and D.T. Tsumura (eds.)
   1994        *'I studied inscriptions from before the Flood': Ancient Near Eastern, Literary, and Linguistic Approaches to Genesis 1-11* (Winona Lake: Eisenbrauns).

Hesse, C.
   1996        'Books in Time', G. Nunberg (ed.), *The Future of the Book* (Berkeley: University of California Press).

Hester, J.D.
   1995        'Dramatic Inconclusion: Irony and the Narrative Rhetoric of the Ending of Mark', *JSNT* 57: 61-86.

Holquist, M., and C. Emerson
   1981        'Glossary', in M. Holquist (ed.), *The Dialogic Imagination* (Austin: University of Texas Press): 423-34.

Holter, K.
   1998        'It's Not Only a Question of Money! African Old Testament Scholarship between the Myths and Meanings of the South and the Money and Methods of the North', *Old Testament Essays* 11: 240-54.
   2000a       'Old Testament Scholarship in Sub-Saharan African North of the Limpopo River', in West and Dube, 2000: 54-71.
   2000b       *Yahweh in Africa: Essays on Africa and the Old Testament* (New York: Peter Lang).

Homer
   1964        *The Odyssey* (trans. E.V. Rieu; Harmondsworth: Penguin Books).
   1984        *Odyssey* (trans. A.T. Murray; Loeb Classical Library; Cambridge: Harvard University Press), I.

Hooker, M.
   1991        *The Gospel According to St Mark* (Black's New Testament Commentaries; London: A. & C. Black).

Irigaray, L.
   1985a       *This Sex Which is Not One* (trans. Catherine Porter; Ithaca, NY: Cornell University Press).
   1985b       *Speculum of the Other Woman* (trans. Gillian C. Gill; Ithaca, NY: Cornell University Press).
   1991        'Women-Mothers, the Silent Substratum of the Social Order', in M. Whitford (ed.), *The Irigaray Reader* (trans. D. Macey; Oxford: Basil Blackwell): 47-52.

1993     *Sexes and Genealogies* (trans. Gillian C. Gill; New York: Columbia University Press).

1994     'The Forgotten Mystery of Female Ancestry', *Thinking the Difference: For a Peaceful Revolution* (trans. Karin Mouton; London: Athlone Press): 89-113.

Isaacs, J.

1940     'The Sixteenth-Century English Versions', in H.W. Robinson (ed.), *The Bible in its Ancient and English Versions* (Oxford: The Clarendon Press): 146-95.

Jabès, E.

1963     *Le Livre des Questions* (Paris: Gallimard).

Jakobson, R.

1987     *Language and Literature* (eds. K. Pomorska and S. Rudy; Cambridge, MA: Belknap Press of Harvard University).

Jameson, F.

1988     'Metacommentary', in *Situations of Theory*. Vol. 1 of *The Ideologies of Theory: Essays 1971–1986* (Minneapolis: University of Minnesota Press): 3-16.

1991     *Postmodernism, or the Cultural Logic of Late Capitalism* (Durham, NC: Duke University Press).

Jantzen, J.G.

1993     *Genesis 12-50: Abraham and All the Families of the Earth* (Grand Rapids, MI: Eerdmans).

Jay, N.

1992     *Throughout Your Generations Forever: Sacrifice, Religion, and Paternity* (Chicago: University of Chicago Press).

Jobling, D.

1998     *1 Samuel* (Berit Olam: Studies in Hebrew Narrative and Poetry; Collegeville, MN: Liturgical Press).

1999     'A Bettered Woman: Elisha and the Shunammite in the Deuteronomic Work', in Fiona C. Black, Roland Boer and Erin Runions (eds.), *The Labour of Reading: Desire, Alienation, and Biblical Interpretation* (Festschrift for Robert C. Culley; Semeia Studies, 36; Atlanta: Society of Biblical Literature): 177-92.

Johnson, L.

1993     'Preface', *The Word and Eucharist Handbook* (San Jose, CA: Resource Publications, rev. edn): vii-ix.

Jordan, M.

1997     *The Invention of Sodomy in Christian Theology* (Chicago: University of Chicago Press).

Juel, D.

1994     *Master of Surprise: Mark Interpreted* (Minneapolis: Fortress Press).

Keefe, A.A.

1993     'Rapes of Women/Wars of Men', *Semeia* 61: 79-97.

Keiser, E.B.

1997     *Courtly Desire and Medieval Homophobia: The Legitimation of Sexual Pleasure in Cleanness and its Contexts* (New Haven, CT: Yale University Press).

Kelber, W.

1985     'The Apostolic Tradition and the Form of the Gospel', in F. Segovia (ed.), *Discipleship in the New Testament* (Philadelphia, PA: Fortress Press): 24-46.

Kermode, F.
1957        *Romantic Image* (New York: Random House).
1967        *The Sense of an Ending: Studies in the Theory of Fiction* (New York: Oxford University Press).
1975        *The Classic* (New York: The Viking Press).
Kinukawa, H.
1994        *Women and Jesus in Mark: A Japanese Feminist Perspective* (Maryknoll, NY: Orbis Books).
Klein, L.R.
1994        'Hannah: Marginalized Victim and Social Redeemer', in Athalya Brenner (ed.), *A Feminist Companion to Samuel and Kings* (The Feminist Companion to the Bible, 5; Sheffield: Sheffield Academic Press): 77-92.
Koskenniemi, H.
1956        *Studien zur Idee und Phraseologie des griechischen Briefes bis 400 n. Chr* (Annales Academiae scientiarum fennicae: Series B, vol. 102.2; Helsinki: Suomalaisen Kirjallisuuden Kirjapaino).
Kraemer, R.
1992        *Her Share of the Blessings: Women's Religions among Pagans, Jews and Christians in the Greco-Roman World* (New York: Oxford University Press).
Kraemer, R. (ed.)
1988        *Maenads, Martyrs, Matrons, Monastics: A Sourcebook on Women's Religions in the Greco-Roman World* (Philadelphia, PA: Fortress Press).
Kristeva, J.
1969        'Pour une semiologie des paragrammes', *Σημειωτική: Recherches pour une sémananalyse* (Paris: Seuil): 174-207.
1980        'The Bounded Text', in L.S. Roudiez (ed.), *Desire in Language: A Semiotic Approach to Literature and Art* (trans T. Gora *et al.*; New York: Columbia University): 36-63.
1986a       'Word, Dialogue and Novel', in T. Moi (ed.), *The Kristeva Reader* (trans. A. Jardine *et al.*; Oxford: Basil Blackwell): 34-61.
1986b       'Revolution in Poetic Language', *The Kristeva Reader* (trans. M. Waller; ed. T. Moi; Oxford: Basil Blackwell): 89-136.
1996        'Intertextuality and Literary Interpretation' (1985 interview conducted by Margaret Waller), in R. Mitchell Guberman (ed.), *Julia Kristeva Interviews* (New York: Columbia University Press): 188-203.
1997        'My Memory's Hyperbole', in K. Oliver (ed.), *The Portable Kristeva* (trans. Athena Viscusi; New York: Columbia University Press): 1-21.
Kuhn, T.S.
1970        *The Structure of Scientific Revolutions* (Chicago: University of Chicago Press).
Kümmel, W.G.
1975        *Introduction to the New Testament* (trans. H.C. Kee; Nashville, TN: Abingdon Press, rev. edn).
Landau, P.S.
1995        *The Realm of the Word: Language, Gender, and Christianity in a Southern African Kingdom* (Portsmouth: Heinemann).
Landow, G.P.
1996        'Twenty Minutes into the Future, or How Are We Moving Beyond the

Book?', in G. Nunberg (ed.), *The Future of the Book* (Berkeley: University of California Press).

Lefebvre, H.
1970    *Du rural á l'urbain* (Paris: Anthropos).
1974    'La production de l'espace', *L'Homme et la société* 31-32 (January–June): 15-32.
1986    *Le retour de la dialectique. 12 mots clés* (Paris: Messidor Éditions Sociales).
1991a    *The Production of Space* (trans. Donald Nicolson-Smith; Oxford; Basil Blackwell [French 1974, 1984]).
1991b    *Critique of Everyday Life* (trans. John Moore; London: Verso).
1996    *Writings on Cities* (trans. and intro. by Eleonore Kofman and Elizabeth Lebas; Oxford; Basil Blackwell).

LeMarquand, G.
2000a    'A Bibliography of the Bible in Africa', in West and Dube, 2000: 633-800.
2000b    'New Testament Exegesis in (Modern) Africa', in West and Dube, 2000: 72-102.

Linville, J.R.
1998    *Israel in the Book of Kings: The Past as a Project of Social Identity* (JSOTSup, 272; Sheffield: Sheffield Academic Press).

Lionnet, F.
1995    *Postcolonial Representations: Women, Literature, Identity* (Ithaca, NY: Cornell University Press).

Lodge, D. (ed.)
1988    'Introductory Notes to Chapter 7: Mikhail Bakhtin', in D. Lodge (ed.), *Modern Criticism and Theory: A Reader* (London: Longman): 124-25.

Long, T.
1996    'A Real Reader Reading Revelation', *Semeia* 73: 79-107.

Luther, M.
1960    *Lectures on Genesis: Chapters 6-14* (trans. George Schick; St Louis: Concordia Publishing House).
1961    *Lectures on Genesis: Chapters 15-20, Works*, Vol. 3 (trans George Schick; eds. J. Pelikan and H.T. Lehman; St Louis: Concordia Publishing House).

Lutz, H., A. Phoenix and N. Yuval-Davis
1995    'Introduction: Nationalism, Racism and Gender—European Crossfires', in *idems* (eds.), *Crossfires: Nationalism, Racism and Gender in Europe* (London: Pluto Press): 1-25.

Lyotard, J.-F.
1984    *The Postmodern Condition: A Report on Knowledge* (trans. Geoff Bennington and Brian Massumi; Minneapolis: University of Minnesota Press).

Maitland, S.
1987    *A Book of Spells* (London: Michael Joseph).

Malbon, E.
1983    'Fallible Followers: Women and Men in the Gospel of Mark', *Semeia* 28: 29-48.

Malherbe, A.
1989    *Paul and the Popular Philosophers* (Minneapolis: Fortress Press).

Maluleke, T.S.
2000    'The Bible among African Christians: A Missiological Perspective', in

T. Okure (ed.), *To Cast Fire Upon the Earth: Bible and Mission Collaborating in Today's Multicultural Global Context* (Pietermaritzburg: Cluster Publications): 87-112.

Marx, K., and F. Engels
1976 *The German Ideology* (Moscow: Progress Publishers).

Matahaere-Atariki, D.
1998 'At the Gates of the Knowledge Factory: Voice, Authenticity, and the Limits of Representation', in Rosemary Du Plessis (ed.), *Feminist Thought in Aotearoa New Zealand: Connections and Differences* (Auckland: Oxford University Press): 68-75.

Matera, F.
1987 'The Plot of Matthew's Gospel', *CBQ* 49: 233-53.

McCracken, D.
1993 'Character in the Boundary: Bakhtin's Interdividuality in Biblical Narratives', *Semeia* 63: 29-42

McGinn, S.
1994 'The Acts of Thecla', in E. Schüssler Fiorenza (ed.), *Searching the Scriptures*, Vol. 2 (New York: Crossroads): 800-828.

McGuire, A.
1999 'Women, Gender and Gnosis in Gnostic Texts and Traditions', in R. Kraemer and M. D'Angelo (eds.), *Women and Christian Origins* (New York and Oxford: Oxford University Press): 257-99.

McKinlay, J.
1996 *Gendering Wisdom the Host: Biblical Invitations to Eat and Drink* (Gender, Culture, Theory, 4; Sheffield: Sheffield Academic Press).

McKnight, E.V.
1993 'Reader-Response Criticism', in S.L. McKenzie and R. Haynes (eds.), *To Each Its Own Meaning: An Introduction to Biblical Criticisms and Their Application* (Louisville, KY: Westminster/John Knox Press): 197-219.

Meyers, C.
1994 'Hannah and her Sacrifice: Reclaiming Female Agency', in Athalya Brenner (ed.), *A Feminist Companion to Samuel and Kings* (The Feminist Companion to the Bible, 5; Sheffield: Sheffield Academic Press): 93-104.

Mijoga, H.B.P.
2000 *Separate but Same Gospel: Preaching in African Instituted Churches in Southern Malawi* (Blantyre: Kachere).

Miller, A.
1992 *The Ancestor Game* (St Leonards, NSW: Allen & Unwin).

Mitchell, J.
2001 *Beyond Fear and Silence: A Feminist-Literary Reading of Mark* (New York: Continuum).

Moffat, R.
1969 *Missionary Labours and Scenes in Southern Africa* (London: John Snow, 1842; repr. New York: Johnson Reprint Corporation).

Mofokeng, T.
1988 'Black Christians, the Bible and Liberation', *Journal of Black Theology* 2: 34-42.

Moi, T.
1986  Introductory notes to 'Word, Dialogue and Novel', in T. Moi (ed.), *The Kristeva Reader* (Oxford: Basil Blackwell): 34-35.

Moore, E.
2000  'Review of the *Academy of the Poor: Towards a Dialogical Reading of the Bible*, Gerald O. West (Sheffield Academic Press 1999)', *Theology* 125.

Moore, S.D.
1989a  'Doing Gospel Criticism as/with a "Reader"', *BTB* 19: 85-93.
1989b  *Literary Criticism and the Gospels: The Theoretical Challenge* (New Haven and London: Yale University Press).

Moreton-Robinson, A.
2000  *Talkin' Up to the White Woman: Indigenous Women and Feminism* (St Lucia: University of Queensland Press).

Morgan, L.H.
1985  *Ancient Society* (Tucson, AZ: University of Arizona Press).

Morgan, S.
1987  *My Place* (Fremantle: Fremantle Arts Centre Press).

Mosala, I.J.
1989  *Biblical Hermeneutics and Black Theology in South Africa* (Grand Rapids, MI: Eerdmans).

Muller, C.
1994  *Nazarite Song, Dance and Dreams: The Sacralization of Time, Space and the Female Body in South Africa* (PhD thesis, University of New York).

Munro, W.
1982  'Women Disciples in Mark?', *CBQ* 44: 225-41.

Muraro, L.
1994  'Female Genealogies', in C. Burke, N. Schor, and M. Whitford (eds.), *Engaging with Irigaray: Feminist Philosophy and Modern European Thought* (New York: Columbia University Press): 317-33.

Murnaghan, S.
1995  'The Plan of Athena', in B. Cohen (ed.), *The Distaff Side: Representing the Female in Homer's Odyssey* (New York: Oxford University Press): 61-80.

Murphy, R.E.
2000  'Forum: A Note on the Biblical Character of the Lectionary', *Worship* 74/6: 547-50.

Myers, C.
1990  *Binding the Strong Man: A Political Reading of Mark's Story of Jesus* (Maryknoll, NY: Orbis).

Nichol, F.
1970  *Christian Beliefs* (Melbourne: Joint Board of Christian Education of Australia and New Zealand).

Nietzsche, F.
1910  *The Joyful Wisdom* (trans. Thomas Common; X. *The Complete Works of Nietzsche*; Edinburgh: T.N. Foulis).
1911  *Dawn of the Day* (trans. J.M. Kennedy; IX. *The Complete Works of Friedrich Nietzsche*; Edinburgh: T.N. Foulis).
1954  *Werke in drei Bänden* (ed. Karl Schlechta; Munich: Carl Hanser), I.
1960  *Joyful Wisdom* (trans. Thomas Common; NY: Frederick Ungar).

| | |
|---|---|
| 1968 | *The Will to Power* (trans. W. Kaufmann and R.J. Hollingdale; New York: Random House). |
| 1969 | *Thus Spoke Zarathustra* (trans., R.J. Hollingdale; Penguin Classics; Baltimore, NY: Penguin Books). |

Noort, E.
1999 'Gan-Eden in the Context of the Mythology of the Hebrew Bible', in Gerard Luttikhuizen (ed.), *Paradise Interpreted: Representations of Biblical Paradise in Judaism and Christianity* (Leiden: E.J. Brill): 21-36.

Norris, C.
1991 *Deconstruction: Theory and Practice* (London: Routledge, rev. edn).

Norton, D.
2000 *A History of the English Bible as Literature* (Cambridge: Cambridge University Press).

Noth, M.
1991 *The Deuteronomistic History* (trans. J. Douall *et al*.; JSOTSup, 15; Sheffield: Sheffield Academic Press, 2nd edn).

Oduyoye, M.A.
1995 *Daughters of Anowa: African Women and Patriarchy* (Maryknoll, NY: Orbis Books).

Okure, T.
1993 'Feminist Interpretation in Africa', in E. Schüssler Florenza (ed.), *Searching the Scriptures: A Feminist Introduction* (New York: Crossroads): 76-85.

Parmelee, A.
1960 *A Guidebook to the Bible* (London: The English Universities Press).

Pattel-Gray, A.
1995 'Not Yet Tiddas: An Aboriginal Womanist Critique of Australian Church Feminism', in Maryanne Confoy, Dorothy A. Lee, and Joan Nowotny (eds.), *Freedom and Entrapment: Women Thinking Theology* (North Blackburn, Vic.: Dove): 165-92.

Peterson, E.H.
1990 '"Preface": Symposium: On Writing Commentaries', *Theology Today* 46: 386.

Plato
1973 *Phaedrus* (trans. W. Hamilton; Harmondsworth: Penguin Books).
1982 *Euthyphro, Apology, Crito, Phaedo, Phaedrus* (LCL; trans. Harold North Fowler; Cambridge, MA: Harvard University Press).

Plumwood, V.
1993 *Feminism and the Mastery of Nature* (London: Routledge).

Porter, F., and C. Macdonald (eds.)
1996 *'My hand will write what my heart dictates': The Unsettled Lives of Women in Nineteenth-Century New Zealand as Revealed to Sisters, Family and Friends* (Auckland: Auckland University Press with Bridget Williams Books).

Prior, M.C.M.
1997 *The Bible and Colonialism: A Moral Critique* (The Biblical Seminar, 48; Sheffield: Sheffield Academic Press).

Pyper, H.S.
1998 'The Selfish Text: the Bible and Memetics', in J.C. Exum and S. Moore (eds.),

Ramshaw, G.
1999 'The Gift of Three Readings', *Worship* 73/1: 2-12.
Rapaport, H.
1995 'Deconstruction's Other: Trinh T. Minh-ha and Jacques Derrida', *Diacritics* 25/2: 98-108.
Read, P.
2000 *Belonging: Australians, Place and Aboriginal Ownership* (Cambridge: Cambridge University Press).
Roberts, C.H., and T.C. Skeat
1983 *The Birth of the Codex* (London: Oxford University Press).
Roman Missal
1981 *Roman Missal, Lectionary I: Proper of Seasons, Sundays in Ordinary Time*, revised edition, approved for use in the churches of England and Wales, Scotland, Ireland (London: Collins Liturgical Publications/Geoffrey Chapman).
1999 *Paul: The Man and the Myth* (Minneapolis: Fortress Press).
Rose, Deborah Bird
2000 *Dingo Makes Us Human: Life and Land in an Australian Aboriginal Culture* (Cambridge: Cambridge University Press, paperback edn).
Rubin, G.
1976 'The Traffic in Women: Notes on the "Political Economy" of Sex', in R.R. Reiter (ed.), *Towards an Anthology of Women* (New York: Monthly Review Press): 157-210.
Sabin, M.
1998 'Women Transformed: The Ending of Mark is the Beginning of Wisdom', *Crosscurrents*, 48/2 (Summer): 149-68.
Sahlins, M.
1974 *Stone Age Economics* (London: Tavistock).
Schapera, I., and J.L. Comaroff
1991 *The Tswana* (London and New York: Kegan Paul International).
Schech, S., and J. Haggis
2000 'Migrancy, Whiteness and the Settler Self in Contemporary Australia', in John Docker and Gerhard Fischer (eds.), *Race, Colour and Identity in Australia and New Zealand* (Sydney: UNSW Press): 231-39.
Schlier, H.
1965 'ἀλείφω', *TDNT*, 1: 229-232.
Schneiders, S.M.
1993 'The Bible and Feminism', in C.M. LaCugna (ed.), *Freeing Theology: The Essentials of Theology in Feminist Perspective* (New York: HarperSanFrancisco): 31-57.
Schottroff, L.
1993 *Let the Oppressed Go Free: Feminist Perspectives on the New Testament* (Louisville, KY: Westminster/John Knox Press).
Schüssler Fiorenza, E.
1983 *In Memory of Her* (Boston: Beacon).
1992 *But She Said: Feminist Practices of Biblical Interpretation* (Boston: Beacon Press).

Schweizer, E.
- 1981 *The Good News According to Mark* (Sixth Impression; London: SPCK).

Scott, Kim
- 1999 *Benang: From the Heart* (Fremantle: Fremantle Arts Centre Press).
- 2001 'Australia's Continuing Neurosis: Identity, Race and History' (*Alfred Deakin Lectures*; Melbourne Town Hall, Monday, 14 May 2001; transcript and audio at *Radio National* websites: http://www.abc.net.au/rn/deakin/content/session_6.html; http://www.abc.net.au/rn/deakin/stories/s291485.htm

Sedgwick, E.K.
- 1994 *The Epistemology of the Closet* (Harmondsworth: Penguin Books)

Segovia, F.F.
- 1995 'And They Began to Speak in Other Tongues: Competing Modes of Discourse in Contemporary Biblical Criticism', in F.F. Segovia and M.A. Tolbert (eds.), *Reading from This Place: Social Location and Biblical Interpretation in the United States* (Minneapolis: Fortress Press): 1-32.

Shields, R.
- 1999 *Lefebvre, Love and Struggle: Spatial Dialectics* (London: Routledge),

Simone, R.
- 1996 'The Body of the Text', in G. Nunberg (ed.), *The Future of the Book* (Berkeley: University of California Press).

Simons, J.
- 1994 'The "Table of Nations" (Genesis 10). Its General Structure and Meaning', in Hess and Tsumura 1994: 234-53.

Smelik, K.A.D.
- 1991 'Introduction' and 'This is the document about Balaam, the son of Beor', *Writings From Ancient Israel* (trans. G.I. Davies; Edinburgh: T. & T. Clark): 1-17; 79-92.

Smith, C.
- 2001 'Biblical Perspectives on Power', *JSOT* 93: 93-110.

Smith, J.A.
- 2000 *Marks of an Apostle: Context, Deconstruction, (Re)citation and Proclamation in Philippians* (PhD Thesis, University of Sheffield).

Smith, J.Z.
- 1982 *Imagining Religion* (Chicago: Chicago University Press).

Smith, T.H.
- 1994 *Conjuring Culture: Biblical Formations of Black America* (Oxford and New York: Oxford University Press).

Smith-Christopher, D.L. (ed.)
- 1995 *Text and Experience: Towards a Cultural Exegesis of the Bible* (Sheffield: Sheffield Academic Press).

Soja, E.
- 1996 *Thirdspace: Journeys to Los Angeles and Other Real-And-Imagined Places* (Cambridge, MA: Basil Blackwell).

Sontag, S.
- 1997 'Against Interpretation', in Susan L. Feagin and Patrick Maynard (eds.), *Aesthetics* (New York: Oxford University Press): 244-55.

Spivak, G.C.
- 1988 'French Feminism in an International Frame', in *In Other Worlds: Essays in Cultural Politics* (New York: Methuen): 134-53, 288-92.

    1993          'French Feminism Revisited', in *Outside in the Teaching Machine* (London and New York: Routledge): 141-71, 309-12.

Stasiulis, D., and N. Yuval-Davis
    1995          'Introduction: Beyond Dichotomies—Gender, Race, Ethnicity and Class in Settler Societies', in Stasiulis and Yuval-Davis (eds.), *Unsettling Settler Societies: Articulations of Gender, Race, Ethnicity and Class* (London: Sage Publications): 1-38.

Steinberg, N.
    1993          *Kinship and Marriage in Genesis: A Household Economics Perspective* (Minneapolis: Fortress Press).

Sternberg, M.
    1985          *The Poetics of Biblical Narrative: Ideological Literature and the Drama of Reading* (Bloomington: Indiana University Press).
    1990          'Time and Space in Biblical (Hi)story: The Grand Chronology', in R. Schwartz (ed.), *The Book and the Text: The Bible and Literary Theory* (Cambridge, MA: Basil Blackwell): 81-145.

Still, J., and M. Worton
    1993          *Intertextuality: Theories and practices* (Manchester: Manchester University Press).

Stowers, S.K.
    1986          *Letter Writing in Greco-Roman Antiquity* (Philadelphia, PA: Fortress Press).
    1988          'Social Typification and the Classification of Ancient Letters', in Jacob Neusner *et al.* (eds.), *The Social World of Formative Christianity and Judaism* (Philadelphia: Fortress Press): 78-90.
    1994          *A Rereading of Romans: Justice, Jews, Gentiles* (New Haven, CT: Yale University Press).

Sugirtharajah, R.S.
    1998          'A Postcolonial Exploration of Collusion and Construction in Biblical Interpretation', in Sugirtharajah (ed.), *The Postcolonial Bible* (Sheffield: Sheffield Academic Press): 91-116.

Sundkler, B.
    1948          *Bantu Prophets in South Africa* (London: Lutterworth Press).

Telford, W.R.
    1999          *The Theology of the Gospel of Mark* (Cambridge: Cambridge University Press).

Thornton, A.
    1970          *People and Themes in Homer's Odyssey* (Dunedin: University of Otago Press).

Thraede, K.
    1970          *Grundzüge griechisch-römischer Brieftopik* (ZETEMATA: Monographien zur klassischen Alterumswissenschaft 48; Munich: C.H. Beck).

Tolbert, M.
    1997          'How the Gospel of Mark Builds Character', in J.D. Kingbury (ed.), *Gospel Interpretation: Narrative-Critical and Social-Scientific Approaches* (Hyarrisburg, PA: Trinity Press International): 72-85.

Tombs, D.
    1999          'Crucifixion, State Terror, and Sexual Abuse', *Union Seminary Quarterly Review* 53: 89-109.

Tompkins, J.P.
1980 'The Reader in History: The Changing Shape of Literary Response', in Jane P. Tompkins (ed.), *Reader Response Criticism: From Formalism to Post-Structuralism* (Baltimore, MY: The Johns Hopkins University Press): 201-32.

Torgovnick, M.
1981 *Closure in the Novel* (Princeton: Princeton University Press).

Trible, P.
1978 'Clues in a Text', *God and the Rhetoric of Sexuality* (Philadelphia, GA: Fortress Press): 1-30.

Tull, P.
2000 'Intertextuality and the Hebrew Scriptures', *Currents in Research: Biblical Studies* 8: 59-90.

Ukpong, J.S.
1995 'Rereading the Bible with African Eyes', *Journal of Theology for Southern Africa* 91: 3-14.
1996 'The Parables of the Shrewd Manager (Lk. 16.1-13): An Essay in the Inculturation of Biblical Hermeneutics', *Semeia* 73: 189-210.
2000a 'Popular Readings of the Bible in Africa and Implications for Academic Readings: Report on the Field Research Carried out on Oral Interpretations of the Bible in Port Harcourt Metropolis, Nigeria under the Auspices of the Bible in Africa Project, 1991-94', in West and Dube 2000: 582-94.
2000b 'Developments in Biblical Interpretation in Africa: Historical and Hermeneutical Directions', *Journal of Theology for Southern Africa* 108: 3-18.

Ukpong, J.S. (ed.)
2002 *Reading the Bible in the Global Village: Cape Town* (Atlanta, GA: Society of Biblical Literature).

Vagaggini, C.
1976 'How the Liturgy Makes Use of Scripture', *Theological Dimensions of the Liturgy* (trans. L.J. Doyle and W.A. Jurgens from the 4th Italian edn; Collegeville, MN: Liturgical Press): 455-86.

van Iersel, B.
1998 *Mark: A Reader-Response Commentary* (JSNTSup, 164; Sheffield: Sheffield Academic Press).

van Wolde, E.
1996 'Intertextuality: Ruth in Dialogue with Tamar', in A. Brenner and C. Fontaine (eds.), *A Feminist Companion to Reading the Bible: Approaches, Methods and Strategies* (Sheffield: Sheffield Academic Press): 426-51.

Vatican II
1966 'Dogmatic Constitution on Divine Revelation', in W.M. Abbott (ed.), *The Documents of Vatican II* (London: Geoffrey Chapman): 111-28.

Vice, S.
1997 *Introducing Bakhtin* (Manchester and New York: Manchester University Press).

Walbank, F.W.
1993 *The Hellenistic World* (Cambridge, MA: Harvard University Press, rev. edn).

West, G.O.
1995 *Biblical Hermeneutics of Liberation: Modes of Reading the Bible in the*

|  |  |
|---|---|
|  | *South African Context* (Maryknoll, NY: Orbis; Pietermaritzburg: Cluster Publications). |
| 1999 | *The Academy of the Poor: Towards a Dialogical Reading of the Bible* (Sheffield: Sheffield Academic Press). |
| 2000a | 'Contextual Bible Study in South Africa: A Resource for Reclaiming and Regaining Land, Dignity and Identity', in West and Dube 2000: 595-610. |
| 2000b | 'Mapping African Biblical Interpretation: A Tentative Sketch', in West and Dube, 2000: 29-53. |
| 2001 | 'On the Eve of an African Biblical Studies: Trajectories and Trends', *Journal of Theology for Southern Africa* 99: 99-115. |

West, G.O., and M.W. Dube
  2000  *The Bible in Africa: Transactions, Trajectories and Trends* (Leiden: E.J. Brill).

Westermann, C.
  1984  *Genesis 1-11: A Commentary* (trans. John J. Scullion; London: SPCK).

White, P.
  1956  *The Tree of Man* (Middlesex: Penguin Books).

Whitford, M.
  1991  *Luce Irigaray: Philosophy in the Feminine* (London: Routledge).

Wilken, R.L.
  1971  *The Myth of Christian Beginnings* (Garden City, NY: Doubleday).

Wilson, R.R.
  1980  *Prophecy and Society in Ancient Israel* (Philadelphia, PA: Fortress Press).
  1994  'The Old Testament Genealogies in Recent Research', in Hess and Tsumura 1994: 200-23.

Wimbush, V.L.
  1991  'The Bible and African Americans: An Outline of an Interpretative History', in F.C. Felder (ed.), *Stony the Road We Trod: African American Biblical Interpretation* (Minneapolis: Fortress Press): 81-97.
  1993  'Reading Texts through Worlds, Worlds through Texts', *Semeia* 62: 129-40.

Witherington, B.
  1984  *Women in the Ministry of Jesus* (Cambridge: Cambridge University Press).

Wittenberg, G.
  2000  'Alienation and "Emancipation" from the Earth: The Earth Story in Genesis 4', in Habel and Wurst 2000: 105-16.

Wittfogel, K.
  1963  *Oriental Despotism* (New Haven, CT: Yale University Press).

Wright, J.
  1981  *The Cry for the Dead* (Melbourne: Oxford University Press).
  1995  *The Generations of Men* (Sydney: HarperCollins, rev. edn [1959]).

# INDEXES

## INDEX OF REFERENCES

### OLD TESTAMENT

| *Genesis* | | 3.20 | 97 | 6.9-10 | 155, 159 |
|---|---|---|---|---|---|
| 1–11 | 145-47, 149-55, 157, 159 | 3.24–4.1 | 153 | 6.9 | 150, 159 |
| | | 4–11 | 158 | 6.11–9.27 | 154, 159 |
| | | 4 | 154, 155 | 6.11-13 | 155 |
| 1–3 | 158 | 4.1-2 | 153, 159 | 9.28 | 155, 159 |
| 1 | 112, 150 | 4.3-16 | 159 | 10 | 152, 154-56 |
| 1.1–2.4 | 112 | 4.12 | 155 | | |
| 1.1–2.3 | 151, 159 | 4.14-19 | 152 | 10.1-32 | 154, 159 |
| 1.1 | 150, 159 | 4.16-17 | 153 | 10.1 | 150, 155, 156, 159 |
| 1.2 | 151 | 4.17-22 | 159 | | |
| 1.21 | 150 | 4.17 | 152, 153, 159 | 10.2 | 156 |
| 1.24-25 | 150 | | | 10.3 | 156 |
| 1.24 | 151 | 4.18-19 | 154 | 10.4 | 156 |
| 1.25 | 151 | 4.20-25 | 153 | 10.5 | 155, 156 |
| 1.26-27 | 150, 153 | 4.20 | 153, 159 | 10.6 | 156 |
| 1.27 | 150, 153, 192 | 4.22 | 153, 159 | 10.7 | 156 |
| | | 4.23-24 | 154, 159 | 10.8 | 156 |
| 1.28 | 126 | 4.25 | 153, 159 | 10.13 | 156 |
| 2 | 151 | 4.26 | 154, 159 | 10.15 | 156 |
| 2.4 | 150, 151, 159 | 5–11 | 160 | 10.18 | 156 |
| | | 5 | 152, 154-56 | 10.20 | 155, 156 |
| 2.5-25 | 159 | | | 10.21 | 155, 156 |
| 2.7-8 | 151 | 5.1-2 | 153, 159 | 10.22 | 156 |
| 2.8 | 145 | 5.1 | 150 | 10.23 | 156 |
| 2.10-14 | 151 | 5.3-32 | 159 | 10.24 | 156 |
| 2.10 | 156 | 5.3 | 153, 155 | 10.25 | 155, 156 |
| 2.11 | 151 | 5.18-24 | 154 | 10.26 | 156 |
| 2.13 | 151 | 5.24 | 155 | 10.29 | 156 |
| 2.21-23 | 151 | 5.29 | 155 | 10.31 | 155, 156 |
| 2.24 | 97 | 6.1–9.27 | 155 | 10.32 | 150, 155, 156, 159 |
| 3 | 158 | 6.1-8 | 159 | | |
| 3.1-24 | 159 | 6.4 | 153, 155, 160 | 11 | 146, 154-56, 161 |
| 3.17 | 155 | | | | |

| Genesis (cont.) | | 13.1 | 142 | 34.1 | 5, 6, 86, |
|---|---|---|---|---|---|
| 11.1-9 | 154, 156, | 13.7 | 142 | | 88, 95, |
| | 159 | 13.9 | 142, 156 | | 97-100, |
| 11.1 | 156 | 13.11-12 | 190 | | 105, 106, |
| 11.2 | 156 | 13.11 | 156 | | 108 |
| 11.3-9 | 156 | 13.14 | 156 | 34.2-31 | 88 |
| 11.4 | 156 | 14 | 189 | 34.2 | 88, 93, 98, |
| 11.8 | 156 | 17.8 | 134 | | 100, 108 |
| 11.9 | 156 | 18–19 | 7 | 34.3 | 88, 93, 94, |
| 11.10-32 | 154 | 18 | 185 | | 99, 100 |
| 11.10-26 | 159 | 18.1-15 | 187, 190 | 34.4 | 86, 93, 95 |
| 11.10-25 | 156 | 18.9 | 191 | 34.5 | 88 |
| 11.10 | 146, 156, | 19 | 185, 187, | 34.7 | 88, 99 |
| | 159 | | 191 | 34.8 | 88, 99, |
| 11.20 | 150 | 19.4-11 | 187, 193 | | 100 |
| 11.26-32 | 156 | 19.12-14 | 187, 198 | 34.9-10 | 102 |
| 11.26 | 146 | 20.12 | 97 | 34.12 | 100 |
| 11.27-30 | 159 | 21.21 | 97 | 34.17 | 88, 100 |
| 11.27 | 150, 156, | 23 | 146 | 34.18 | 88 |
| | 159 | 24.4 | 147 | 34.19 | 99 |
| 11.28 | 157, 159 | 24.7 | 147, 158 | 34.31 | 106 |
| 11.29 | 146, 157 | 24.28 | 97 | 35.5 | 87 |
| 11.30 | 138, 141, | 24.55 | 97 | 43.29 | 97 |
| | 157, 159 | 24.67 | 97 | 44.20 | 97 |
| 11.31–12.9 | 134 | 25.23 | 156 | | |
| 11.31 | 136, 156, | 27.11 | 97 | Exodus | |
| | 157, 159 | 27.13 | 97 | 1.15-21 | 122 |
| 11.32 | 157, 159 | 27.14 | 97 | 3 | 124 |
| 12–19 | 185, 187 | 27.29 | 97 | 3.15 | 124 |
| 12–17 | 187, 188 | 28.2 | 97 | 25–30 | 183 |
| 12–14 | 6 | 28.5 | 97 | 35–40 | 183 |
| 12 | 6, 131, | 28.7 | 97 | | |
| | 132, 136, | 29 | 146 | Numbers | |
| | 142, 146, | 29.10 | 97 | 12 | 141 |
| | 156, 187, | 30 | 146 | 22–24 | 119 |
| | 189 | 30.14 | 97 | 25 | 6, 125, |
| 12.1-3 | 132 | 30.21 | 86, 97, | | 126 |
| 12.1 | 132, 133, | | 100, 106 | 25.1-5 | 141 |
| | 147, 157 | 30.40 | 156 | 31 | 6, 125, |
| 12.2 | 132 | 31.3 | 147 | | 127 |
| 12.5-6 | 131 | 31.13 | 147, 158 | | |
| 12.5 | 132, 136 | 32.11 | 97 | Deuteronomy | |
| 12.6-9 | 139 | 34 | 5, 86-89, | 3.29 | 125 |
| 12.6 | 136 | | 92-98, | 4 | 5 |
| 12.7 | 136 | | 100, 102, | 4.1-8 | 124, 125, |
| 12.8 | 136 | | 105, 106, | | 127 |
| 12.10 | 139 | | 108 | 4.1-2 | 5, 6, 123, |
| 12.11-13 | 139 | 34.1-4 | 93 | | 128 |

## Index of References

| | | | | | |
|---|---|---|---|---|---|
| 4.1 | 126 | 16.13 | 176 | 14.16 | 58 |
| 4.3-5 | 125 | 19.18-23 | 176 | 14.25 | 57 |
| 4.3-4 | 126 | 20.1 | 176 | 14.27 | 57, 58 |
| 4.5 | 126 | 25.1 | 176 | 15.8–17.6 | 58 |
| 4.6-8 | 5, 6, 123, 128 | 28.3 | 176 | 15.8 | 58 |
| 4.9 | 125 | *2 Samuel* | | 15.12 | 58 |
| 22.19 | 94 | 2.12-17 | 180 | 15.16 | 160 |
| 22.28-29 | 102 | 2.20-21 | 177 | 17 | 5, 50, 54, 55, 59, 61 |
| | | 2.21 | 180 | | |
| *Joshua* | | 2.22-36 | 180 | 17.1-6 | 52 |
| 12.3-4 | 132 | 2.25 | 180 | 17.6 | 54 |
| 12.12 | 132 | 7 | 50 | 17.7-23 | 59 |
| | | 13 | 98 | 17.7-20 | 55 |
| *Judges* | | | | 17.7-18 | 52 |
| 2.11-19 | 50 | *1 Kings* | | 17.7-17 | 52-55 |
| 3.7-11 | 56 | 3–11 | 183 | 17.7 | 52 |
| 19 | 98 | 3.16-28 | 182 | 17.8 | 53 |
| 21.24-25 | 174 | 5.15–7.38 | 183 | 17.16 | 53-55 |
| | | 6.1 | 181 | 17.19-20 | 52, 53 |
| *1 Samuel* | | 8 | 183 | 17.20 | 52 |
| 1–2 | 6, 173, 174, 182, 184 | 11 | 50 | 17.21-23 | 52, 55 |
| | | 12.25-33 | 181 | 17.23 | 59 |
| | | 12.28 | 55 | 17.24-41 | 52, 59 |
| 1.1 | 174 | 12.32 | 55 | 17.24-34 | 59 |
| 1.2 | 175 | 14 | 55 | 17.34-40 | 59 |
| 1.3 | 176 | 14.7-14 | 54, 55 | 17.34 | 59, 60 |
| 1.4 | 179 | 14.15-16 | 55 | 17.35 | 60 |
| 1.6 | 177 | 14.15 | 54, 55 | 17.40 | 60 |
| 1.7 | 179 | 14.16 | 58 | 17.41 | 59 |
| 1.8 | 176 | 15.27-30 | 55 | 22 | 9 |
| 1.9 | 176 | 16.33 | 54 | 23.15-20 | 60, 181 |
| 1.11 | 180 | 18.21 | 54 | 23.17 | 60 |
| 1.15 | 178 | 21.20-24 | 54 | | |
| 1.16 | 178 | 21.29 | 54 | *2 Chronicles* | |
| 1.19-20 | 177 | | | 1.18–4.22 | 183 |
| 1.19 | 175, 180 | *2 Kings* | | 3.3 | 9 |
| 1.20 | 180 | 8.12 | 160 | 3.6 | 9 |
| 1.21 | 175 | 9–10 | 54 | 5–7 | 183 |
| 1.22 | 180 | 10.29 | 55 | | |
| 1.24 | 176, 177 | 10.30 | 58 | *Nehemiah* | |
| 2.1-10 | 178 | 10.32-33 | 57 | 9.7 | 132 |
| 2.11 | 176 | 13 | 57 | | |
| 2.19 | 176 | 13.2-5 | 56, 57 | *Psalms* | |
| 3 | 48 | 13.3 | 57 | 14.2-5 | 129 |
| 7.17 | 176 | 13.6 | 54 | 15 | 6, 124, 127 |
| 8.4 | 176 | 13.7 | 57 | | |
| 12 | 50 | 13.23 | 58 | 106 | 6 |
| 15.34 | 176 | 13.25 | 57 | 106.28-31 | 125 |

| | | | | | |
|---|---|---|---|---|---|
| *Isaiah* | | *Ezekiel* | | 7.4 | 46 |
| 1.1 | 48 | 1.2-3 | 42 | 7.7 | 46 |
| 1.2 | 48 | 1.3 | 47 | 7.10 | 46 |
| 6 | 48 | 7.26-28 | 47 | 8.1 | 46 |
| 8.16 | 48 | 33.24 | 132 | | |
| 51.2 | 132 | 40–48 | 183 | *Micah* | |
| | | 43.10-12 | 47 | 1.2 | 48 |
| *Jeremiah* | | *Joel* | | *Habakkuk* | |
| 1.11 | 46 | 1.2 | 48 | 2.2-3 | 48 |
| 1.13 | 46 | 3.1 | 47 | | |
| 2.8 | 47 | | | *Zechariah* | |
| 7 | 46 | *Amos* | | 13.3-4 | 47 |
| 18.2 | 46 | 1.2 | 46 | | |
| 18.18 | 47 | 1.13 | 160 | Apocrypha | |
| 19.1 | 46 | 3.3 | 46 | *2 Esdras* | |
| 24.2 | 46 | 3.4 | 46 | 14 | 9 |
| 25.30 | 46 | 3.5 | 46 | | |
| 26 | 46 | 3.6 | 46 | *Baruch* | |
| 36.2-3 | 46 | 7.1 | 46 | 36.5 | 46 |

NEW TESTAMENT

| | | | | | |
|---|---|---|---|---|---|
| | | 4.20 | 77 | 8.34 | 72 |
| *Matthew* | | 4.33 | 77 | 8.38 | 77 |
| 1.1-17 | 64 | 4.40 | 71 | 9.2-10 | 75 |
| 28.16-20 | 64 | 4.41 | 70 | 9.2-9 | 71 |
| | | 5.20 | 77 | 9.6 | 75 |
| *Mark* | | 5.34 | 71 | 9.9 | 71, 75 |
| 1.4 | 77 | 5.37 | 76 | 9.10 | 75, 77 |
| 1.14 | 77 | 5.42 | 76 | 9.30-37 | 71 |
| 1.17-20 | 70 | 6.1-6 | 70 | 9.32 | 76 |
| 1.17-18 | 69 | 6.6 | 71 | 10.2-12 | 72 |
| 1.29-31 | 70 | 6.12-13 | 74 | 10.19 | 72 |
| 1.38 | 77 | 6.17-29 | 71 | 10.22 | 77 |
| 1.45 | 77 | 6.52 | 70 | 10.24 | 77 |
| 2.1-12 | 70 | 7 | 6, 127 | 10.32-40 | 71 |
| 2.2 | 77 | 7.1-8 | 130 | 10.33 | 72 |
| 3.13-15 | 70 | 7.13 | 77 | 10.34 | 72 |
| 3.14 | 77 | 7.14-15 | 130 | 10.37 | 76 |
| 3.21 | 70, 71 | 7.21-23 | 130 | 10.41-45 | 69 |
| 3.31 | 71 | 7.24-30 | 71 | 11.29 | 77 |
| 3.34-35 | 71 | 7.29 | 77 | 12.13 | 77 |
| 4.14 | 77 | 7.36 | 77 | 13.10 | 77 |
| 4.15 | 77 | 8.21–10.52 | 71, 76 | 13.31 | 77 |
| 4.16 | 77 | 8.27-33 | 71 | 14.1 | 68 |
| 4.17 | 77 | 8.32 | 77 | 14.3-9 | 72, 74 |
| 4.18 | 77 | 8.33 | 76 | 14.8 | 74 |
| 4.19 | 77 | | | | |

| | | | | | |
|---|---|---|---|---|---|
| 14.9 | 77 | 16.5 | 75 | 1.21-22 | 129 |
| 14.28 | 70 | 16.7 | 70, 77, 78 | 1.27 | 129 |
| 14.31 | 72 | 16.8 | 63, 75, 76, | | |
| 14.32-42 | 76 | | 78, 79 | Apocrypha | |
| 14.34 | 76 | | | *Gospel of Thomas* | |
| 14.39 | 77 | *Luke* | | 61 | 83 |
| 14.50 | 70 | 3.23-38 | 152 | 114 | 83 |
| 14.51-52 | 75 | | | | |
| 14.66-72 | 72 | *John* | | Classical | |
| 15.40–16.8 | 74 | 1 | 127 | Eusebius | |
| 15.40–16.1 | 78 | 6.63 | 129 | *Ecclesiastical History* | |
| 15.40-47 | 69 | 6.68 | 129 | 3.39.4 | 9 |
| 15.40-41 | 69, 72-74, | | | | |
| | 78 | *Romans* | | Homer | |
| 15.40 | 69 | 12.17-24 | 59 | *Odyssey* | |
| 15.42 | 68 | 16.7 | 82 | 10.561 | 40 |
| 15.46 | 73 | | | | |
| 15.47 | 69, 72 | *1 Corinthians* | | Plato | |
| 16.1-8 | 63, 65, 66, | 15.21 | 58 | *Phaedrus* | |
| | 68, 83 | | | 275E-267A | 32 |
| 16.1 | 69, 73, 74, | *James* | | 275 | 9 |
| | 78 | 1 | 6, 127 | 275E | 32 |
| 16.3 | 74 | 1.17-18 | 129 | 276A | 32 |

INDEX OF AUTHORS

Abrams, M.H.  119
Adamo, D.T.  220
Ahlström, G.W.  132, 133
Aichele, G.  1, 3, 4, 8, 10, 17, 18
Albertz, R.  132
Alexander, L.  37
Alter, R.  133
Amit, Y.  133, 179
Andersen, T.D.  150
Anderson, J.  71
Appadurai, A.  131
Armour, E.T.  140

Bach, A.  67, 68, 73
Bachofen, J.J.  175
Bakhtin, M.M.  113-16
Bal, M.  102, 113
Ballantine, C.  220, 221
Barr, J.  112
Barthes, R.  17, 20
Barton, J.  10, 11
Baudrillard, J.  15, 19
Bauer, W.  10
Baur, F.C.  29
Bechtel, L.  86, 101, 103
Belich, J.  134, 142
Benjamin, W.  12, 13, 19, 22
Berger, K.  35
Berkovitch, S.  113
Bible and Culture Collective, The  111-13
Bloom, H.  32
Blum, V.  178
Boer, R.  2, 6, 7, 126, 127, 145, 181, 210
Bornkamm, G.  29
Boulous Walker, M.  87, 92, 96, 106
Brett, M.G.  2, 86, 100-103, 133, 138, 146, 147, 149-51, 154, 155, 225
Brewer, D.S.  185

Bright, J.  132
Bronner, L.L.  85
Brown, D.  222, 223
Brueggemann, W.  146, 151
Bruner, F.D.  34
Budick, S.  11
Bultmann, R.  29
Burchell, W.J.  204, 207
Burnett, F.  67
Butler, J.  178
Bynum, C.W.  111

Camp, C.V.  86, 92, 101, 103, 105, 217
Campbell, J.  202-208
Carden, M.  6, 7
Cardman, F.  81, 82
Chaplin, J.P.  31
Chung, H.K.  121
Clark, J.  154
Clines, D.J.A.  154
Collins, T.  43
Comaroff, J.  203-205, 208, 209, 221
Conrad, E.W.  2, 4, 7, 45
Crüsemann, F.  146, 156
Culler, J.  33

Darwin, C.  206
Davies, P.R.  44
Davison, G.  152
Debray, R.  10, 21
Debrunner, A.  77
Deleuze, G.  3, 17, 173
Derrida, J.  36, 37, 116, 148, 201
Dewey, J.  69, 71, 72, 78-80
Dickson, K.  201
Diski, J.  137, 143
Docker, J.  1, 2

## Index of Authors

Dollimore, J. 186
Dube, M.W. 142, 210, 219, 223
Dunn, J.D.G. 28, 30, 31, 33, 34

Eco, U. 19, 43-45
Ehrman, B.D. 9, 11
Eisen, U. 81, 82
Eisenstein, E.L. 13, 14
Elam, H.R. 116
Elvey, A. 6, 7, 144, 148
Emerson, C. 114
Engels, F. 165

Faur, J. 11
Feiner, S. 1
Fewell, D.N. 1, 86, 101, 103
Fishbane, M. 112
Flanagan, J. 162
Fokkelman, J.P. 181
Foucault, M. 201, 207, 224, 225
Fowl, S.E. 214, 217
Fox, R. 122
Freud, S. 31, 32, 94, 106, 113
Friedman, S.S. 113
Friedrich, G. 77
Frostin, P. 214
Fulkerson, M.M. 217

Gadamer, H.-G. 14
Gamble, H.Y. 9, 10
Garbini, G. 133
Gardner, A. 155
Geertz, C. 43
Geia, J. 144, 160
Gelder, K. 138
Genette, G. 119
Gevirtz, S. 154
Goldenson, R.M. 31
Goodall, H. 149
Gottwald, N. 175
Green, B. 127
Greenspan, S.L. 122
Grosz, E. 89, 91, 92, 97, 178
Guattari, F. 3, 17, 173
Gunkel, H. 43
Gunn, D.M. 86, 101, 103

Habel, N.C. 132, 134, 136, 150, 151
Haggis, J. 158

Harrison, R.P. 150
Hart, K. 1
Hartman, G.H. 11
Hawk, L.D. 141
Heard, R.C. 133
Hendricks, O.O. 217
Hengel, M. 38
Hess, R.S. 154
Hesse, C. 15, 21
Hester, J.D. 65, 69, 73, 79
Holquist, M. 114
Holter, K. 212, 218
Hooker, M. 69, 78

Irigaray, L. 5, 85, 88-92, 94, 96, 101-108, 148
Isaacs, J. 122

Jabès, E. 34
Jacobs, J.M. 138
Jakobson, R. 19
Jameson, F. 16, 17, 33, 38, 181
Jay, N. 105
Jobling, D. 1, 4, 50, 51, 56, 60, 174, 175, 178, 179
Johnson, L. 124
Jordan, M. 185, 192
Juel, D. 76

Kanyoro, M. 201
Keefe, A.A. 98, 103
Keiser, E.B. 185
Kelber, W. 78
Kelso, J. 3, 5-7
Kermode, F. 11, 14, 16, 17, 65, 66, 83
Kiley, B. 5, 7
Kinukawa, H. 69
Klein, L.R. 179
Koskenniemi, H. 35
Kraemer, R. 81
Kristeva, J. 5, 113-17, 119-21, 201
Kuhn, T.S. 206
Kümmel, W.G. 29

Landau, P.S. 204
Landow, G.P. 19
LeMarquand, G. 212, 218
Lefebvre, H. 6, 162, 164-73, 175, 177-79, 181

Lévi-Strauss, C. 89
Linville, J.R. 51, 52
Lionnet, F. 131
Lodge, D. 116
Long, T. 211
Luther, M. 185-99
Lutz, H. 139, 140
Lyotard, J.-F. 16

Macdonald, C. 135, 136, 139
Maitland, S. 137, 143
Malbon, E. 69, 78
Malherbe, A. 37
Maluleke, T.S. 209, 210, 219, 220, 224
Marx, K. 165, 166
Matahaere-Atariki, D. 121
Matera, F. 63, 64, 66
Mbiti, J. 201
McCracken, D. 67
McGinn, S. 82
McGuire, A. 82
McKinlay, J.E. 1, 2, 6, 7, 124
McKnight, E.V. 111
Meyers, C. 176, 177, 179, 180
Mijoga, H.B.P. 217, 223
Miller, A. 152, 160
Mitchell, J. 78
Moffat, R. 208
Mofokeng, T. 219
Moi, T. 113
Moore, E. 225
Moore, S.D. 211
Moreton-Robertson, A. 147
Morgan, L.H. 175
Morgan, S. 149
Mosala, I.J. 203, 219
Muller, C. 222
Munro, W. 69
Muraro, L. 85
Murnaghan, S. 110
Murphy, R.E. 122
Myers, C. 69, 72

Nast, H. 178
Nichol, F. 123
Nietzsche, F. 17, 25, 26, 31, 33, 34
Noort, E. 145

Norton, D. 14
Noth, M. 181

Oduyoye, M.A. 201, 219
Okure, T. 211, 213, 215
Oliveria, R.S. de 217

Parmelee, A. 122
Pattel-Gray, A. 147
Peterson, E.H. 33
Phoenix, A. 139, 140
Plumwood, V. 147
Porter, F. 135, 136, 139
Prior, M.C.M. 132, 133
Pyper, H.S. 8

Ramshaw, G. 123
Rapaport, H. 32
Read, P. 145
Roberts, C.H. 10
Roetzel, C. 29
Roman Missal, The 125
Rose, D.B. 149
Rubin, G. 89

Sabin, M. 78
Sahlins, M. 175
Schapera, I. 208
Schech, S. 158
Schlier, H. 74
Schneiders, S.M. 120, 123
Schottroff, L. 69, 78
Schüssler Fiorenza, E. 69, 79, 120, 147
Schwartz, R. 1
Schweizer, E. 78
Scott, K. 160
Segovia, F.F. 214
Shields, R. 165, 170, 171
Simone, R. 21
Simons, J. 155
Skeat, T.C. 10
Smelik, K.A.D. 118-20
Smith, C. 142
Smith, J.A. 4, 7, 38
Smith, J.Z. 225
Smith, T.H. 217
Smith-Christopher, D. 213-15

## Index of Authors

Soja, E. 162
Sontag, S. 32
Spivak, G.C. 148
Stasiulis, D. 134, 147
Steinberg, N. 146
Sternberg, M. 70, 101
Still, J. 116
Stowers, S.K. 29, 35, 36
Sugirtharajah, R.S. 142
Sundkler, B. 222

Taylor, A. 5, 7
Telford, W.R. 78
Thornton, A. 110
Thraede, K. 35
Tolbert, M.A. 67
Tombs, D. 215
Tompkins, J.P. 35, 36
Torgovnick, M. 62
Trible, P. 112
Tull, P. 116, 119

Ukpong, J.S. 210, 212, 215-18

Vagaggini, C. 123
van Iersel, B. 78
van Wolde, E. 113
Vatican II 123
Vice, S. 115, 116

Walbank, F.W. 38
West, G.O. 3, 7, 209-12, 217, 220
Westermann, C. 146
White, P. 147
Whitelaw, B. 154
Whitford, M. 107, 108
Wilken, R.L. 10
Wilson, R.R. 154, 215
Wimbush, V.L. 217, 218
Wittenberg, G. 153
Wittfogel, K. 175
Worton, M. 116
Wright, J. 145, 156, 158

Yuval-Davis, N. 134, 139, 140, 147